Boston'

From Callbox to Courthouse

By

Captain Jack Daley

CONTENTS

The front door of the bank was locked. I kept banging on it until the security guard, who had been shot in the leg, limped to the door and let me in. I asked him what was going on. He answered feebly, "downstairs."

I found the stairs and headed down. On the lower level I entered a large room. I could see one door leading toward the rear of the bank and another door that led to a corridor about 30 feet long which extended from the front to the back of the bank. Three police officers were near the front, with me. The gunman was at the rear and shooting towards us. Other officers were behind the door on the right, at the end of the corridor nearest to the gunman. They had entered the bank through a broken window, the same one the gunman had broken and used to get into the bank. They were trapped. They could not see the gunman nor could they open the door without being exposed to him at very close range.

I looked down the corridor but didn't see anyone. I looked again and saw a gun pointed in my direction. I couldn't get a shot off fast enough. The long corridor with bare walls was no cover for anyone who might try to rush the suspect. It was a standoff and it stayed that way for about 30 minutes.

Bullets flew back and forth. When it was over one officer was dead.

***

This is the story of my career as a police officer. An officer sees and experiences things that the average person does not. He or she engages with bad people and good. I was fortunate to have been involved in interesting and compelling investigations. And the years that I served in the Boston Police Department were tumultuous, bringing social, economic and cultural changes. I had a front row seat.

I was born in Boston in 1927 and I grew up in St. Brendan's Parish. It was an Irish Catholic area. My family didn't suffer during the Great Depression because my father had reliable employment as a refrigerator repairman. I had one brother, George and he and I grew up in relative comfort. Our family was stable and happy.

World War II started when I was 13 years old and two years later I was working in defense plants in the summer and after school. When I turned 17 I enlisted in the Navy. All of my friends had done so. I was inducted in February, 1945. The war ended soon after that.

Less than two years later I was out and needed to think about a career. I thought I might be an electrical engineer and spent more than two years in engineering school. But I never really liked it. I heard that the Boston Police were hiring. I took the exam, did well and was appointed on November 14, 1951.

I was 23 years old. I didn't realize it at the time but I had found my life's work.

The Rookie

I was one of 100 recruits. We reported to headquarters, had a brief interview with Tom Sullivan, the police commissioner and the superintendent of police Edward Fallon. The only question of substance they asked was why we wanted to become police officers; the almost universal answer was job security.

Our recruit class was broken into two sections, mornings and afternoons. Half of the day was spent at stations to which we were assigned and the other half in the academy on Milk Street. I was assigned to District Nine in Roxbury. We received instruction in first aid, general laws, rules and regulations and proper use of a gun. Some of my fellow recruits were obsessed with guns and I got the sense that they might not be good prospects. There was no psychiatric screening in those days.

The training period lasted one month. When we reported to the station houses we were each assigned to a seasoned beat officer. These officers were not happy to have a trainee with them. We either walked with our beat officer or spent time in the back of a police car. The beat officers would tell us to disappear and meet them two hours later at a designated location. They clearly did not want us to know what they were doing.

Throughout the academy training targets were set out on the walls of the classroom and recruits were encouraged to aim at them and dry squeeze the triggers. In the middle of December we were issued bullets for our guns, which nearly caused a tragedy a few days later. A recruit forgot that he had put bullets in his gun and narrowly missed a lieutenant instructor during practice. After that, there was no more dry firing in the classroom.

The academy training came to an end shortly before Christmas and we were ready to receive our first permanent assignment. The Traffic Division was looking for new officers to cover the increased traffic during the holidays so my entire class was assigned to Traffic. It was a disaster for me. On my first day I was sent to the exit of the Sumner Tunnel in the North End. It was a cold December day and I had my overcoat on. The work was boring, tedious and unchallenging.

My idea of being a policeman was not standing in as a human traffic light. At least I was assigned to the day shift, which was better as I was planning to get married in the near future.

It didn't take long for us to realize that the police department had many weaknesses, including drinking on the job, bookie operations and chiseling (demanding free services).

There were several reasons for this sorry state of the department. For one thing, the pay was low. We were making $51 a week in 1951. Officers who had stayed on in the department during the war saw defense workers making two or three times their pay and were frustrated they weren't making more. So they did something about it. Many senior officers were corrupt--up to and including those in the highest ranks. The money poured in for these officers, mainly from vice operations. Gaming was the major source of these 'look the other way' payments. Alcohol and prostitution operations also contributed.

Much of this practice went back to the days of prohibition when everybody violated the drinking law. Now everybody was breaking the gambling laws. Officers were paid to look the other way or provide protection. Of course, there were some officers who were not corrupt and everyone knew who they were. Overall though, there was an attitude of acceptance. Corruption was the norm. The payoffs seemed to be extensive and well organized. We recruits observed some of this in action as we made the rounds with and without our beat officer.

Some of my fellow recruits seemed to become seasoned veterans as soon as the school ended. I was confident and young but still unsure of how I would conduct myself when I got out on the street. I noticed that many of these seasoned veterans left the force after a few years or sought jobs out of the public eye. Thirty years later, almost none of these hotshots were still on the job.

We were issued long blue woolen overcoats for the winter. They were very heavy, especially in the rain after they got wet. The collars would rub against our necks and irritate the skin. It took many months before our necks hardened to this abuse. They were warm though and we spent a lot of time wearing them in the winter.

When you first appear in uniform in public it can be awkward. You get a sense that everyone is looking at you. You are expected to have the right answers to everyone's questions. You are expected to take action if something occurs in your immediate vicinity that violates a citizens' peace and tranquillity. There is no question that you are conspicuous and you feel it. People expect a lot of a uniformed officer. This was brought home to me one night when I was riding home on the bus. I had spent most of that day on my feet directing traffic. I saw an empty seat and sat down. The bus filled up later and a woman standing near me made the remark, "Aren't you people supposed to stand?" I got the message, but was beyond exhausted, so I remained seated. I didn't ride the bus in uniform after that even though uniformed officers could ride for free on the bus and subway.

**

The day shift was ten hours: 7:45 am to 5:45 pm. The night shift was divided into two parts, known as the "first half", or evening shift and "last half", the midnight shift.

First half went from 5:45 pm to 12:30 am. The last half was 12:30 am until 7:45 am. We worked six days followed by two days off. Every fifth and sixth week we got an extra day off.

I soon learned that everyone was chiseling, including the Deputy Commissioner. If you were stationed in the Haymarket area merchants gave you groceries to take home. Every officer had a place to eat for nothing. Parking tickets were used as leverage against the merchants so to be a traffic officer or "tagger" was be one of the elite. Merchants and others paid the traffic officers on a regular basis to not have their cars tagged. In those days no visible tags were put on the illegally parked cars, so officers could skip some cars with impunity. Motorcycle officers did most of the tagging but there were some walking officers who tagged. Although the areas the officers covered were changed monthly, the system was so well organized that these officers just exchanged lists of the paying customers.

One day I was assigned to the Haymarket area and at the end of the day a merchant gave me a box of vegetables to take home. It contained six parsnips, a couple of turnips and some lettuce and tomatoes, all barely edible. I came to the conclusion that it was ridiculous to owe someone because he gave you free vegetables and I never took anything again. As a rookie I reserved judgement on the other officers who were supplementing their income in this way (and getting a lot more than parsnips) because at that time it was so widespread and accepted that it was considered part of your salary.

I made my first arrest about this time. I was stationed on the Boston side of the East Boston ferry at Fleet and Commercial Streets, where the boat would come in every 40 minutes. I grabbed two old drunk men staggering along the street and dragged them to the police callbox nearby. I opened the box with my box key and called for the police wagon to pick them up. Two officers from District One showed up and took my prisoners. They were not very impressed. I, on the other hand, was as proud as could be and felt that I had just locked up Public Enemy Number One.

***

I was assigned to direct traffic in District One, which was located in the North End. It seemed to me that the officers in the district were almost all corrupt, including the captain. The bookies and liquor establishments had a direct pipeline into the station and woe to any officer who attempted to take independent action. The captain used to appear at roll call and state that if anyone knew of any illegal gaming, after-hours operations or any other vice operation, that officer was to make out a report and give it to him immediately. The purpose of this speech was twofold; to cover him in case of an outside investigation and to discover if anyone was operating without his authorization and not paying.

It was a practice of the police department to have every sergeant assigned to a district station complete a monthly vice report. These reports always said the same thing: that the sergeant had no knowledge of any vice conditions in his district. I did not realize how organized this scheme was until I was assigned as a sergeant to the North End station a decade later.

We traffic officers participated very little in the actual workings of the police department. We were actually looked down upon. I discovered this one day when I answered a call on the police callbox. Before walkie-talkies, the callbox was the way beat officers communicated with the station. If a light flashed on the callbox, there was an emergency and someone from the station was trying to contact an officer in the area. That day I noticed the light flashing on

9

a Back Bay callbox and answered the call. The man on the signal desk told me that they were looking for a real policeman to answer the call, not a traffic officer. This angered me so much that I went charging into the station and confronted him before accepting his apology.

Occasionally traffic officers would become involved in violent crimes simply because they were out on the street and visible. If a bank or a store was held up, the victim's first thought was to find the traffic officer. So it was the traffic officer who often arrived at the scene first, usually alone. Some traffic officers were killed in these confrontations.

Most officers assigned to traffic posts were very conscientious. They stayed put on the street in bitterly cold weather. As a result, many had rough red faces like lobsters and skin like leather. The most I could take was about thirty minutes under the worst conditions. One had to admire the older officers. And as Christmas approached, those permanent traffic officers rarely left their post, no matter what the weather, because that's when the gifts from merchants and the public arrived.

The gifts were mostly because the merchants knew and liked the officer and appreciated the hard work that he had done through the year. It was a good policy to be friends with the local traffic officer because you never knew when you might need him.

Traffic was almost always stalled in the Haymarket area as trucks tried to back into loading docks on the narrow streets lined with beef and produce wholesalers. At times a truck would just stop in the middle of the street waiting for a space to open up. Once I came across a truck driver doing just that and I ordered him to move on. He refused. He said he had been trying for an hour to back in and was not going around again. I was affronted by this challenge to my authority and marched him to the station with every intention of arresting him, although I wasn't quite sure on what charge. An old lieutenant on the desk nullified my arrest. He gave a stern lecture to the driver and sent him back with orders to move his truck. I took it as a lesson that a police officer had to take into consideration the difficulties of others before taking action and issuing ultimatums.

**

During my stay in Traffic I volunteered to direct traffic near the Opera House on Huntington Avenue when the Metropolitan Opera came to town. The Opera House was a grand building located across from Northeastern University. The opera company stayed for ten days and I worked straight through, day and night. It was wonderful if you were an opera fan, as I was. It was great fun to be able to go backstage and see and hear the inner workings of the Met. One day I got my wife and her girlfriend in, but their seats were so high in the theatre that they could barely see the show. Years later the Opera House was torn down to make room for Northeastern University dormitories. Not a good trade.

The Department had a total of about 2800 sworn officers, 300 of whom were in the Traffic Division. Traffic was commanded by Deputy Superintendent Hinchey, plus two captains, O'Brien and Petite. They were assisted by a few lieutenants and a large group of sergeants. Many officers were content to stay in Traffic, with the exception of the captains who were anxious to command their own stations.

We new officers did not get permanent assignments. We covered for officers at various locations when they were on vacation, out sick, or had a day off, so a new officer could be assigned to almost any place in the city. I remember being assigned to a traffic crossing near the emergency entrance of Boston City Hospital. A police wagon roared in and I went to assist the operators in taking two men out of the wagon and into the hospital. I was shocked to see that the injured were police officers. They were unconscious, lying on the stretchers on their stomachs with their toes pointed down. They looked dead to me. It seems that they had been assigned to a patrol car during their last half tour and had backed into a snow bank, which blocked the car's exhaust pipe. Carbon monoxide fumes filled the car and rendered them unconscious. When they failed to check off after their tour ended, a search was made and they were found in that state. Incredibly, they both survived with no apparent ill effects.

I grew to dislike the traffic duties so much that I was willing to do anything to get out of them. The motorcycle and tagging jobs were sewn up and never became vacant. When I was offered the job of driving one of the captains around, I took it. The captain had very little to do, so I too had little else to do but sit in the car and wait for him. On one occasion, I heard a report of a holdup and that the suspect was coming our way. I saw the suspect approaching us in the described vehicle and called it to the captain's attention. He dismissed my observations and I lost my big chance. The holdup man got away. Later this captain did get his own station command and did a good job. He had some weaknesses, though; he was a heavy gambler and too close to the bookies. Maybe that helped his career.

I was with the captain a little over one year. During this time, I kept in touch with real police work by taking overtime work in bars and nightclubs, usually sleazy joints. These paid details were given to the traffic division because no one at the district wanted them. The assignments were generally on Friday and Saturday nights and the pay was two dollars an hour. They were difficult assignments because you didn't know the patrons and they didn't know you. Once you became known, though, the jobs became much easier.

***

We were a large crop of younger officers, fresh from the service and schools and rather undisciplined. The older officers were very conservative and were shocked at the chances we took, such as leaving our posts without permission and being far away from our sectors without authorization. One day I was in Park Square with an older officer named Bob. Eastern Airlines was offering promotional flights over Boston from their office in the Statler Hotel (now the Park Plaza) and I went to the office and signed up for a flight. I was gone for almost three hours. Bob was shocked. I know he would love to have gone with me but it was not part of his makeup to violate the rules.

In keeping with my intent to avoid traffic duties, I volunteered for any assignment that allowed me to escape. In June of 1953, a freak tornado struck Worcester, 50 miles west of Boston. A contingent of Boston officers was sent to help for a week. We were there to prevent looting though I never saw any evidence of looting nor did I hear of any other officer who saw any. The damage was incredible. I spoke with some people who were there when the tornado hit and they described the sound as being like a train bearing down on them. One man told me that he was inside his house, heard a very loud noise, looked out his window and saw that the three-family house across the street from him had been blown away.

I finally got out of the Traffic Division when I met an officer, Frank Haugh, who was working nights in the Back Bay station. Because of issues at home he needed to switch to a day job. It was difficult to change shifts in those days and it was even more difficult to get assigned to District 16, a much sought after assignment. But a swap was easier. Frank and I agreed to swap and the change was made. I was now a real police officer, in a district, working nights. I had spent about three years in the Traffic Division. I was glad when I got out.

District 16, Back Bay

Patrolman

It was now 1954. Even though I had been on the force for about three years I was still relatively inexperienced. The Back Bay district was not a high crime area but was undergoing changes and some parts were becoming seedy. There were decaying apartment buildings alongside elegant residences but the general picture was one of decline. The station house was over 100 years old and really not suited for police operations. The captain was a decent guy but did not take much of a role in running the station. He had to be picked up at his house every morning and driven home every night. We took turns driving him and we all noticed that he spent the whole ride coughing and spitting. Perhaps he drank and smoked too much.

Police procedures change very slowly and I am sure that the station functioned pretty much the same in 1954 as it did in 1854. We worked rotating shifts, starting with an evening shift from 4 to midnight. We returned the next night at midnight and worked a last half until about 8 am. Then we had to be back to work later that afternoon for another evening shift, or first half. Often that short break was taken up by a required appearance in court, so that we were lucky to get an hour or two of sleep in a twenty four hour period.

We did this six days a week. Our routine was always the same. It was a bizarre way to live. We were sleep deprived, constantly adjusting to the erratic working hours. But when you are young, you can adjust to anything. I did and loved it.

Roll calls were formal. A typical roll call at District 16 consisted of 16 to 24 patrolmen, a lieutenant and one or two sergeants. At the sound of the roll call bell we lined up into two or three rows according to height. The sergeants would inspect us, checking to see if every officer had the required equipment: a street directory, revolver, ammunition, police baton and callbox key. Also required was your pocket notebook called a filler, in which you wrote of incidents that came to your attention during your tour of duty. One important entry to include was the time and place you met the sergeant during your tour. The lieutenant occasionally collected these pocket fillers and read them. At roll call we waited at attention for the lieutenant to enter, take his place on the rostrum and read off the assignments for the tour of duty. At the time, there were only men in our station. A typical distribution of the platoon consisted of four men in two cars, two men in the wagon, two men held in the station for clerical duties and the rest on walking routes. There was a priority in filling these assignments: the vehicles were filled first, clerks next, business routes and residential routes last.

After roll call came the commands, "Right face, forward march." We marched out the front door of the station to our assignments. There could not be much stalling because the officers still on duty from the previous shift could not leave until we took their places. After our group left the station the officers on duty came in to be checked off by the sergeant before they could go. If an officer failed to check off after his tour it was considered a very serious matter and a search immediately was made.

We had no communication with the station after we walked out the door, except through the callboxes located around the district. If the station wanted us, lights would flash on top of the callboxes and we were expected to respond within 20 minutes.

There were three lieutenants on nights, McElhenny, Murphy and Collins. McElhenny worked my platoon and he was a steady and consistent boss. He later made captain. The sergeants on nights were a mixed group, some competent, some not. The older sergeants were poor supervisors who were promoted because there was little competition during the war. There were some tyrants among this group.

About three quarters of the men in my platoon were young men and all veterans of World War II. The rest were patrolmen who had stayed with the department through the war. We were two separate groups. There may have been some resentment of the officers who didn't join the war effort but it wasn't a serious matter and we worked together with little conflict.

The station was actually run by the day lieutenant who was a real tyrant. He had a close circle of friends and if you were not part of his circle you could count on getting every rotten job that came along. It was the custom that when you reported for duty and passed the front desk, you saluted in deference to the officer in charge. It was said that if he noticed and spoke to you, you could be sure of getting a shafting very soon. In my case he never said anything but I got the shafting anyhow.

***

The wagon we used was called a Black Maria, no one was sure why, though it was black. We all took our turn at being the rear-end men on the wagon. The rear-end man sat in the back of the wagon with the prisoners up near the front, sometimes handcuffed and sometimes not. This job was one of the least desirable because you would have to go to court with those arrested for drunkenness during your tour. This was before alcoholism was recognized as a medical issue. For this duty there was a $3 stipend.

The police had a strange ritual for those arrested for drunkenness. Each morning about 4:00 am (except Sundays when court was not in session) the 'drunks' would be dragged from their cells, lined up against a wall opposite the front desk and the lieutenant on duty would ask them a series of questions, for example, "Are you married? Do you have a job? If so, where? Is anyone depending on you for support?" etc. It was an unvarying routine. It was done to enable the lieutenant to fill out a form to be presented to the probation officer when he came to the station. This form helped the officer determine who he should release without going to court. After the interrogation the prisoners were taken back to their cells. It was like waking a patient to give him a sleeping pill. This practice continued for many years and was stopped only when drunkenness was decriminalized. Even if the probation officer released all of the drunks, as was generally the case, the rear-end man still had to go to court, sometimes more than one court.

The wagon served as an ambulance as well. We carried a filthy blanket and a canvas stretcher between two wooden poles along with a couple of crude splints. It also did duty as a truck carrying police barriers and oil lanterns to mark a hazard or street defect.

One night when serving as rear-end man, I violated the rule and sat up front with the driver after we took an accident victim to the hospital. When we backed into the station garage, the stretcher was missing. It had slid out onto the street as we were driving. There was some panic on my part as this was a serious matter. We retraced our

—

16

route and found it and no one was the wiser. The stretcher could not have been worth more than $5 but if we had not found it I would have been in big trouble.

Accident scenes were horrible for us as we were not very good at emergency medical treatment. I recall taking a man with a broken leg to the hospital. His leg had been broken several times and he was waving it around like a piece of cooked spaghetti. I was scared that the bone would come through before we got to the hospital. I was trying to get him to lie still but he was drunk and it was hopeless. We had no practical immobilization devices; the splints in the wagon were of little use.

Sometime we had to physically force victims into the wagon in order to get them treated. I recall one such incident when a man with an ice-pick wound in the abdomen gave me a hard time about getting in the wagon to go get treated. Perhaps others were more skillful than I in giving first aid, but the fact remained that our first thought was to get accident victims to the hospital as quickly as possible.

We had no facilities for women in any station so after women were arrested and booked, they had to be taken to the 'tombs'. This was the city prison located in the basement of the courthouse. It had a male and female section and when station lockups became full, the overflow was sent there. If prisoners became irrational or out of control, they would be sent there as well and put into "the pads"—a padded cell. Both male and female sections of the tombs had padded cells. The prisoner was stripped naked before being locked up in the pads, including females. A matron was present but often she needed assistance and we officers had to help out.

***

There was a stable in the basement of the station and a small exercise yard for the horses. Twelve to 15 horses were stabled there and the holsters, civilian employees of the department, were kept busy with them. Weather permitting the day men, the ones who could ride, took their horses out on their routes. They made a splendid appearance and it was great for public relations. They were also used for parades and other ceremonial duties. The original purpose of the horses in District 16 was to allow officers to ride down the numerous public alleys in Back Bay and to see over the fences. The plus side of having horses in the station was bringing your kids in to see them when you came in to pick up your pay. We got paid in cash at that time and you had to pick up your pay envelope and sign for it. The down side was that the station always smelled of horse shit.

It was forbidden to take your personal car to your route, so we would sometimes get a ride in a patrol car or the wagon, but most of the time we walked. Good routes were highly sought after. Some officers stayed on the same route for their whole careers. Mine was Route 5, running from Clarendon to Exeter Streets and from Boylston to Beacon Street. It was a mix of commercial and residential and I enjoyed working there. It had several restaurants, the Darbury Room and the Algonquin Club, among others. These restaurants fed the police. I sometimes joined the officer on an adjoining route and we had dinner together at the Ritz Carlton. In some restaurants we ate in the dining room, but most of the time we ate in the kitchen. Walking routes, particularly in the summer were very social. This was an early version of what came to be known as community policing.

***

There was a sense of pride in keeping your route or sector crime-free. A middle-aged woman was once the victim of an attempted rape on Beacon Street, just off my route. The description of the suspect was read at a couple of roll calls. A day later, I was at the corner of Newbury and Clarendon when I spotted a man fitting the description. It was about 2 am on a mild evening. I questioned him and was not satisfied with his answers so I elected to arrest him as a suspect in the attempted rape. I grabbed him and brought him to a callbox that was a few yards away. He offered no resistance and wasn't handcuffed. I opened the box and called for the wagon, holding on to the prisoner at the same time. The next thing I knew, I was down on the sidewalk and my prisoner was running up Newbury Street towards the Public Garden. I chased him up the street, drew my gun and fired over his head, ordering him to stop. He kept right on going. Other officers nearby heard the shots and joined in and we were able to grab the man down one of the alleys. The victim identified him as her attacker but later had a change of heart. The suspect had just gotten out of prison and she felt that he was so desperate for sex after being locked up that she actually felt sorry for him. In the end, she refused to testify.

—

The police at that time had a great deal of discretionary power. An arrest could be made if the officer believed that an individual may have committed a felony. It did not take much to reach that threshold of belief, so a citizen could be arrested and charged with being a suspicious person who may have committed a felony. If after a day or two it turned out that he did not commit the felony, he was released. No harm, no foul. The release was at the officers' discretion, so it was no fun being locked up on suspicion. It was not unknown for the arresting officer to take his days off with his prisoner still in a cell. This power was not abused but it was available and used as a last resort. It did have the effect of deterring a lot of housebreaks and street crime. We had other arrest weapons in our arsenal as well. Being abroad in the nighttime without being able to give a good account of yourself was an arrestable offense. The officer determined what constituted a good account or reason for being out and about at night. Sauntering and Loitering could also get you arrested.

The beat officers were required to call in from a different callbox every 40 minutes. These calls, or hits, were recorded by the officer on the signal desk. Nobody followed this rule. An officer would make one or two calls during his tour and the signal desk officer would record them as required by regulation. We took turns on the signal desk to cover ourselves.

Each week we had a light test. The lights atop the callboxes were set flashing and the lieutenant sat at the signal desk and awaited the response. Every officer on the street had 20 minutes to answer. Once the first officer answered and found that it was a test, the word was passed and we all answered. Woe to any officer who missed a light.

During the last half shift, things were pretty quiet after the bars closed. We were there to prevent crime, but if a break in occurred on your route during your tour, the least you could do is find it before the owner did. As a result, we checked every business establishment, both front and back doors. It was a mechanical process, but it kept us out there and every so often we did come across a break in. When we did, we had to go in and find out if the burglars were still inside. This of course was a hairy business. We were alone and had no communication, but it had to be done. It was very rare to find thieves still on the premises, but we had to assume that they were there. Once satisfied that the place was empty, we would call the station from a phone on the premises and in turn the owner would be notified. The owner would come in and secure the premises but that might take a considerable amount of time, so occasionally other officers would come by the store and there could be some pilfering. I was not happy with this but I know it happened, as it was impossible to keep your eye on two or three other officers in the store all the time. If you were known as a straight guy it was never done in front of you.

I recall being inside a liquor store with two other officers and a sergeant one night and the sergeant was urging me to take a bottle. I wouldn't do it. This put him in a tough spot because he still wanted to take a bottle and now he couldn't. This did not make me one of his favorites. I think he may have taken a chance and stolen the whiskey anyhow.

***

If you failed to find a break-in on your route or even if the owner inadvertently did not lock his door and you failed to discover it, you were in trouble. You would be called at home, sometimes awakened and told to make out a report as to why you failed to discover the incident. When this happened, officers would ask themselves why this message couldn't have waited and been delivered to them when they came into work. It certainly made it more difficult to go back to sleep.

I was at District 16 for only a short time when there was a large snowstorm, which shut everything down. I was assigned to a last half and went to bed around 8:00 pm to sleep before going to work, as was my custom. When I got up and went out, conditions had gotten worse and I could not get my car out. I walked to the nearest subway, about a half-mile away and started in on the train. The train went about two stops and then stalled between stations. The train remained immobilized for about two hours. I gave up trying to get to work and walked back home, arriving five hours later. I called the station and told them I could not make it in. This turned out to be a big mistake. When I reported for the next tour, Lieutenant Walkins informed me that I was one of only three officers who failed to make it in. After that he made life miserable for me. I never again missed work because of inclement weather.

***

Lieutenant Walkins followed through, assigning me to every dirty job that came along. One of the first ones began the very next week. I was sent to the Boston Common to guard the Christmas display. There were other officers also assigned to this post. I didn't know what they did to deserve it. It can get very cold on the Common in December at 3:00 in the morning.

Another unwelcome assignment came in response to a rash of handbag robberies on St. Botolph Street. I was sent down there alone with specific instructions to allow no handbag snaps, an impossible assignment for a walking officer. St. Botolph Street is almost a mile long. I was just plain lucky that nothing happened on my watch.

Then came the assignment to the traffic box at Brookline Avenue and the Riverway near the old Sears Building. It was like being in Antarctica on a winter's evening. Police officers expect to get their share of lousy jobs but it is difficult when you feel you are singled out for the lion's share. It can certainly get you down.

***

There were many churches in District 16, including the Christian Science Mother Church. The church nearest to the station was St. Cecilia's, a Catholic church. Monsignor Phalen, the pastor, would inspect the officers personally to see that they were on the post assigned to them and would contact the station if they did not perform their duty as he expected. Naturally he was not popular with the officers. Later I learned he was a decent and generous man. Both of these churches were provided with free police services and they efficiently monitored our presence. Some time later they hired police officers for details and earned our respect.

***

Patrol car duties were the most sought after jobs. They are what police work is all about. It was the younger officers who wanted this assignment and I was one. Once you got these jobs you tended to keep them so it could be a long wait before one opened up. When the regular car men were off, my partner, Ed Tobin and I, filled in. We generally enjoyed a great night of fun.

Almost all of us younger officers were ambitious. On a typical night everyone would try to put some time aside to study the manuals and law textbooks. The exam for sergeant came every two years. I would go into the Boston Public Library and study in the law section on first halfs. On last halfs I would go into the lobby of the Vendome Hotel around 3:00 am and study until about 5:00 am. I could see the callbox from both these locations so I could watch the lights. We all knew each other's routine so if something happened and you were needed, your partner knew where to find you. It was my practice to go to the local Waldorf with the desk clerk of the Vendome Hotel for something to eat very early in the morning.

The Back Bay was not a high crime area at the time. On many a night the walking men would get together, play cards and tell stories, always keeping an eye out for the signal lights. Before and after each tour of duty we would play dominoes in the guard room for quarters and sometimes more. After a tour of duty the dominoes games could go on for hours causing occasional problems at home when a husband failed to return. It became so intense at times that the duty supervisor would intervene, stop the game and kick all the players out of the station. When we were not gambling with the dominoes, we could visit any number of local watering holes and stay long after hours drinking. Our favorite was Jimmy O'Keefe's on Commonwealth Avenue, across from Boston University. Jimmy was a grand guy and very patient but I am sure we were a pain in the neck to him.

One night a group of us were in Jimmy O'Keefe's when one of our number, an officer named George, mentioned that he was in the maintenance shed in the Public Garden earlier that evening and noticed a large supply of grass seed. We all had keys to this shed and used it to get warm in the cold weather and sometimes to play cards. George had just bought a new house and needed a lawn. He was planning on going down there to get some seed. But this was a problem because the gardeners might figure out that the police took the grass seed and might change the lock on the shed, depriving us of the shelter. After George left, I went to the phone and called the emergency number and told the operator that someone was trying to break into the shed. About a half hour later George came back without the grass seed.

***

Because the Back Bay was a low crime area, a good arrest was an event. I was sitting in the back seat of the patrol car late one night. Two friends were assigned to the car. Bob was driving and Tom was in the front passenger seat. I saw three men breaking into a car. We had just passed Audubon Circle outside Kenmore Square. The thieves saw us and took off up an alley towards Brookline. I was out of the car quickly chasing them and only a short distance behind one of them. I heard Bob yell "Halt!," then several gunshots. I hoped that he was not shooting at the man I was chasing but I think that he may have been. Fortunately we apprehended all three men and I didn't get shot. We brought our prisoners back to the station. The suspects were all from the North End and denied knowing each other's names, so we started putting some pressure on them. I got my first lesson in third degree interrogation tactics. These were the days before landmark Supreme Court decisions like Miranda so coerced confessions were admissible. It wasn't pretty but it worked. We recovered all the merchandise stolen from the car and obtained confessions.

Bob was a zealous officer, sometimes too zealous. Once, in an effort to catch a burglar, he pulled down a metal fire escape, hitting me on the head and knocking me to the ground. I was lucky to escape with only a pretty good headache. One could get hurt working with Bob.

***

Working rotating nights was very difficult for me at first. By 5:00 am I was exhausted. One night I had been riding around in the same area for four hours, splitting the driving chore with my partner, Bob Bush. One morning I fell asleep at the wheel while driving down Clarendon Street. Bob was already asleep, which was rare for him. The next thing I knew I had hit a traffic pole. Neither of us was hurt but the car was badly damaged.

Usually the car men would stop rolling about 5:00 am. They would pull into a secluded place and doze, not awake and not asleep. If the dispatcher called you would hear it and respond, sometimes belatedly. Walking men would also get inside between 5:00 and 6:00 am. There were plenty of places available. Hotel lobbies, legion posts, private clubs, even movie theatres and private buildings. Everybody would be back on the street before the general public awoke. Still, there was always a hard core group of officers out on the street all the time. In addition, I learned that the longer one worked nights, the less one needed these rests. And there were many nights when all of the officers were so busy that there was just no time to stop.

There were some officers that just loved publicity. They pandered to the press and some whose pictures appeared regularly in the papers were labelled professional models. Reporters who showed up at crime and accident scenes often needed photos so posed pictures were very common. There was always a police officer available to stand next to a car wreck for a photo. It certainly is good for your ego to see your picture in the paper or to read about your exploits in the news columns, especially when everything reported about you is positive.

***

I was learning every day. One very important lesson I learned was never to run on apartment roofs. Around this time an officer fell off a roof and died, so we were cautious. There were many calls for prowlers and peepers and an ideal location for these activities was the roofs of buildings. If you found someone on a roof, there was an almost irresistible temptation to give chase but it was so dangerous it was just not done. At night it was even more dangerous. Roofs are littered with TV antenna wires. And some had courtyards, a deadly drop that's hard to see until it's already too late. There was no room for mistakes on roofs.

***

The wagon drivers were a special lot. When the wagon was not rolling these officers would sleep on cots and stretchers that they set up in the wagon house. They were mostly older officers; some of them real characters. One guy that stands out was the driver on my platoon, a fellow named John. He was a very charming guy with strong ties to Ireland. Every so often he would give me hints of his link to the IRA. John liked to drink and if he had a little too much he would become a wild man. One night, he had a fight in the wagon house with his partner, Eddie. Both John and Eddie had been drinking and John made some remark about a girl Eddie was seeing. Eddie was a bachelor and a very straight-laced guy so the result was a drunken fight. Fortunately there were no calls for the wagon that night.

John took a very casual view of the police job. I learned this one night when we were on our way back to the station and a call came over the radio alerting us to a man with a gun nearby. I wanted to go but John said that he couldn't. When I asked why, he said he did not have his gun with him.

I had many adventures with John in the wagon. One night we took a prisoner to Boston City Hospital. The prisoner had been injured when he fought with officers at the time of his arrest. At some point in the emergency room we lost sight of the prisoner and he attempted to escape. He got out of the treatment room by going through an open window but he didn't realize that there was a fence around the hospital and now he was trapped in the yard. It was a major offense to lose a prisoner. John and I were determined that it was not going to happen to us. We charged through an operating room and out the window. We got our guy but only after a brief and violent struggle during which the prisoner received even more injuries and I was covered with his blood. The hospital people were mad as hell at us as they were working on a patient and did not appreciate our barging into an operating room during surgery. We brought the prisoner back to the station and called a doctor. This time the prisoner was treated in his cell.

John was extremely good to me. When he gave up his second job servicing fire extinguishers he passed it on to me.

***

I learned soon enough that police officers see a lot of death. They see it in accidents, suicides and homicides but most often in homes, rooming houses, hotels and apartments. My first exposure to sudden death came late one Sunday morning. We answered a call at a rooming house on Commonwealth Avenue and found an old man dead in a chair. He had not been dead long but that distinctive smell of death was in the room and he had the usual waxy appearance. A priest was on the scene and he told us that he was with the deceased when he died. The first death scene awed me. I dwelt on the man's life and the circumstances of his death. Later in my career, I was to see a great deal of death and became largely indifferent to it, but I never did get indifferent to the smell of decomposing bodies. If the smell was really bad a dab of Vicks Vaporub in each nostril did the trick.

Eventually we became so indifferent to death that we young officers had to learn not to laugh at our own private jokes or other incidents at death scenes when relatives were present. One night Eddie Tobin, Bob Tierney, John McDonald and I were taking a body out of a second floor apartment near Kenmore Square. The victim was a big guy and had just died from a heart attack. We were using our canvas stretcher from the wagon and each one of us had a handle. As we started down the stairs the pole slipped from my hands and the body fell off the stretcher and down the stairs. The family cried out in horror while we desperately tried to keep from laughing.

On another wagon incident, an officer who was an old timer and who had rear end duty, was called to the scene just before quitting time. My partner and I were assisting a heart attack victim who then died and the old timer was upset. "This bastard is going to keep us late!" he remarked. He was right. It did run late. A pronouncement of death had to be made and then the body had to be delivered to the morgue. There was no extra pay for overtime.

***

The police play a unique and necessary role in the matter of sudden deaths. If an individual dies without a doctor present or under violent, mysterious or suspicious circumstances, the medical examiner and the police have a duty to look into the cause of death and to safeguard the deceased's property. It is the responsibility of the police to search the death scene with a superior officer, sergeant or above. I never saw or heard of anybody doing something inappropriate, though I had heard stories of officers who carried self-addressed stamped envelopes in their pockets so they could send cash they might find to themselves. I never observed any misconduct. In my experience an honest accounting was always done. Later in my career, when I was a sergeant, I searched the apartment of an elderly lady in Brighton who had been found dead. We found thousands of dollars in cash that she had hidden in different locations throughout her apartment. She was a very old lady with few, if any, living relatives. It would have been easy to grab a few thousand but it just wasn't done. Everything of value found was turned over to the medical examiner.

***

Prisoners at that time were treated differently than they are in the present day. If an arrest had been made of a notorious offender, (a child molester or a cop fighter, for example) that individual was brought out to the cell block and displayed to all officers at roll call. "Take a good look at this guy. If you see this guy around, bring him in" was the invariable comment. The prevailing feeling was that this worked because the offender would take pains to stay out of the district once he got back out on the street.

Another practice long since abandoned was the line-up that was held every morning at police headquarters. Each station transported all who were arrested for any significant offense to headquarters for the occasion. The line-up was held in a large room designed for this purpose, complete with a stage where the suspects were paraded against a white backdrop marked with horizontal height lines. Bright lights illuminated the suspects while witnesses and police sat in the darkness. Lt. Crowley generally ran it.

It was just like you would see in the movies. Prisoners were ordered to turn certain ways, say certain words, walk back and forth, smile, frown and perform as ordered. Witnesses in the room would be asked if they recognized their attacker. If the answer was in the affirmative it was very bad news for the suspect. The suspect would have no idea who was fingering him. The prisoners were berated verbally and told that they were liars and crooks. This was before the Supreme Court decision regarding self-incrimination. There were no lawyers in the line-up room. These were the days of arrest on just a suspicion of committing a felony.

The running of the station was not democratic; there were no unions or associations to appeal to in the event of unjust treatment. It was common upon coming to work for a first half Saturday evening to be ordered to work a day tour Sunday. You were never asked if this may be inconvenient for you. The lieutenant may have decided to give some of his day men an extra day off. Good for them... bad for you. If you were ordered to work Sunday, your assignment would be in a car and it was a long quiet day, usually resulting in one or two calls in a ten-hour period. Generally boring, maybe just a call for a peeper or an indecent exposure. A typical indecent exposure involved a male caller who would gain entry to the hallway of a women's dormitory, slip a paper under a door, knock on the door and then run down the hallway. The girl would open the door, see the paper and read it. It would say something like, "If you want to see a real man, look down the hall." He would be down there exposing himself. Thankfully nothing violent, but it still did upset the female students.

Working nights was a totally different story. Some nights were filled with nonstop action and the tour went by in a flash. City police officers experience an incredible variety of situations, some pleasant, some unpleasant, some criminal, some civil and they see a side of people that the average person never sees. One might see a relative, neighbor or clergyman with a woman (or man) in a compromising situation. Laws and rules govern the police conduct in many situations but the police officer often has to fall back on his common sense.

One night Eddie and I were sent to an apartment on Boylston Street on a report of a disturbance. When we arrived we were admitted by a woman around 35, drunk and topless. I suspect that she was the one who called the police and the only reason that I can think of was for the company. She was out of control and we took her into custody.

Another time we responded to a disturbance on Beacon Street and were admitted to the apartment by an intoxicated woman. She may have sensed that we might arrest her, even though that was not our immediate intention. She grabbed her 7-year-old daughter and threatened us with a butcher knife. She held the daughter in front of her and held us off with the knife. We talked for a while and finally persuaded her to let the girl go to the bathroom. When the girl left I picked up a kitchen chair and used it to corner the woman, getting her to drop the knife.

It was wonderful working nights in the summertime. Some nights I enjoyed just sitting on a park bench and listening to someone play a harmonica or once in a while, a sweet potato ocarina. I recall standing in the middle of Boylston and Dartmouth streets at 5:00 am, just at dawn in the summertime, alone, with no cars in sight. It was a wonderful feeling and I felt like Wordsworth standing on Westminster Bridge. "And all that mighty heart is lying still."

***

Strange social dynamics can take place when two officers ride together in police cars over a period of time. Usually an agreement is reached over who is to drive and who is to be the observer but even that small decision could sometimes cause problems. It has to be agreed upon who will make the decisions at incidents and if an arrest follows who will take the case to court. It was generally accepted that the officer not doing the driving would be the major partner, make the decisions, do the paperwork and take any cases to court. When the officers swapped jobs, they would swap roles. Partners have to get along reasonably well. They are together eight hours each night and if they clash it could be a very long tour of duty. It was inevitable that from time to time two patrolmen assigned to the same vehicle would not be compatible. When that happened steps were taken to separate them. I did my best to get along with my partners but occasionally had some difficulties. It was no one's fault.

Some officers had no interest in the job and looked only for the pay check. They never should have become policemen. As the years went on they became unhappy in the job. This was the worst fate of all. There were others whose conduct bordered on cowardice. I was with an officer one night when we were alerted that a man in a restaurant was carrying a gun. I went into the restaurant, approached the man, questioned him and frisked him. When I looked up there was my partner, still outside, watching me through the window. It was embarrassing to me and I assume to him, so we never spoke about it. Fortunately the majority of patrol officers are competent, hardworking and decisive.

***

We still had the same commissioner, Tom Sullivan and superintendent, Edward Fallon, in control of the department. They were exalted and distant figures, often with little sense of labour relations. One year they were faced with a rise in traffic due to folks coming into the city to go Christmas shopping. The commissioner chose to solve the issue by adding two hours on to the night officers' shift. So instead of coming to work at 5:45 pm, we came in at 4:00 pm. Traffic duty was 4-6 pm. That meant that if I finished my last half tour of duty at 8:00 am and had to go to court that morning, there was little chance of getting to bed before noontime. I would be lucky if I got three hours sleep in a 24-hour period. This schedule change was made without any input from the officers involved and with no extra pay. The new hours were met with bitterness by the rank and file and inspired a movement towards unionizing the police.

***

I seemed to be assigned the Public Garden area a lot on morning watch tour, not the worst duty. In the summer one had to keep the Swan Boats safe. The perimeter of the Garden, especially around Arlington and Beacon Streets, was a common area for gay men to meet and I'd see them often. They came from all over greater Boston to make their connections in this area. It was a time when homosexuality was not generally accepted by society and the city may have offered a sense of anonymity. Other meeting places were at the Greyhound Bus Station and in the public toilets in the Arlington Street subway stop. This was a problem because of the heavy traffic. Eventually the Greyhound Bus Company hired a police officer from midnight to 7:00 am, seven days a week to keep order in the terminal.

Occasionally I would see officers from the district who had worked the first half hanging around this area in plain clothes. At first I thought that they were dedicated officers working on a case on their own time. I received a rude awakening. I learned later that these officers operated in pairs to try to rob gay men. One would be the bait and allow himself to be solicited. He and the man would then go by car to a secluded place. It was never very far, just down one of the alleys by the Charles River. The second officer would follow in another car and approach the pair moments later, display his badge and catch them. The officer in plain clothes would suggest to the victim that they give the officer some money so he would let them go. Both would empty their pockets and give the cash to the officer and all would leave in a different direction. The two officers would meet later and cut up the profits. Pretty bad stuff.

***

Eddie Tobin and I were good friends and often worked together both walking and riding in the patrol cars. At the end of each morning watch tour we would gather about a block from the station and sit around and shoot the breeze before we could go into the station and be relieved. It was a silly time; we were all tired and had many a laugh over the night's events. We were doing just that when one night, one of the cars was sent to Bay State Road on a report of a

—
30

woman needing help. About six of us went, including Eddie and I. Our exhausted state led to a comedy of errors. When we arrived I rang the bell, knocked on the door and received no response. Someone then went back to the car and check on the radio to see if we were at the right location. We were but were informed that the lady in trouble could not make it to the front door. I tried to kick the door open with no luck. The doors in these apartments were massive. One of my partners tried the handle and discovered that the door was not locked. We all entered. The occupant, a woman about 60 years old was standing by a window overlooking the Charles River. It was a very big double hung window and she had one hand on the windowsill under the window. She could not get her hand out and she was crying. One of the panes had come down on her hand, perhaps the result of a broken pulley rope, trapping her. Buster McDonald went to her and eased the window up and released her hand. The woman steadied herself with the other hand. Buster let go of the window and it came crashing down on the woman's other hand. She howled as he got her out a second time. Buster took quite a bit of ribbing for this.

***

The district included exclusive shops that exposed expensive items in the windows, which were not alarmed. It seemed to me that fur shops were the most reckless in that they left expensive furs in windows. At times one of these windows would be broken and a fur stolen. All the thief had to do was make a small hole in the glass and use a coat hanger to drag a piece of fur through the holes. When a fur was stolen in this manner there was an investigation of course, but the focus of the investigation was whether the duty officer at the time of the break was negligent in any way. It was one of our greatest dreams to catch a fur thief. I missed an opportunity for stardom during one morning watch when I saw an individual some distance away from me in front of a fur store. As I approached, the man wandered off and I did not pursue. I should have. In the morning a hole was found in the window and a fur was missing. The man must have had the fur under his coat when I saw him. The fur store was off my route and by now I was in the station long enough to know that I better keep my mouth shut as to what I saw. We all make mistakes but after having made one already when I headed home in the snow storm, I was not going to make another one.

One night I found a suitcase full of all kinds of sexual paraphernalia and I brought it into the station. I was so naive that I did not know what all this junk was and I showed it to the sergeant. He knew what it was and we had a good laugh.

Female victims of sex crimes were generally brought to the station to view photos and give statements but there was one lieutenant who seemed to have an unhealthy interest in these cases. He always wanted to interview the victim privately. We made every effort to deny him these opportunities. I never had a problem interviewing female sex victims but I did hear horror stories of officers berating victims and suggesting that they asked for it. There were no guidelines and little awareness of how to proceed. And we had no female police officers at the time. They would likely have been more understanding and sensitive and probably have been able to obtain more useful information.

***

The year was 1958. As I was now one of the older officers, with about six years on the job, I was gripped by the know-it-all syndrome; no one could tell me anything. I was going to do it my way. I guess it's the arrogance of inexperience and youth. One night I brought a prisoner to the booking desk who I had just arrested for breaking and entering. I was rough with the prisoner and at the booking desk, then when my attention wandered for a moment, the prisoner caught me with a shot to the jaw and it really hurt. I learned something new. Actually two things: 1) don't relax for a second when you have someone in custody and 2) use force only as a last resort after the soft approach has failed.

One old sergeant, Fat Jack, was always giving me a little tickle. It may have been that he thought I was a smart ass. He made a point to keep me busy when I had the rear end of the wagon sending me on all kinds of inconsequential errands. It was true that if you got a reputation as a troublemaker the sergeants would come together and pay extra attention to you.

There was one duty they sometimes gave me that I did not like at all. The officer that had the house route, which is the area in which the police station was located, had to go to the local all-night restaurant, Hayes Bickfords and bring back food for the prisoners and the officers in the station. That officer also took the station coffee pot to the restaurant where it was filled with coffee. Hayes Bickfords had a half price policy for the police, though most of the time the restaurant gave us the coffee and food for free. I grew to resent going over to the restaurant to get the food. The next time I was assigned this task, I charged the stations guys half price for their food even though I paid nothing. They were a very frugal group and did not like having to pay. I was never given this duty again and to make matters worse, I think that they knew I got it for nothing. No wonder Fat Jack considered me a troublemaker.

The personnel in the station were divided into two factions: the uniformed branch and the detectives. Although uniformed officers could conduct limited investigations, it was the detectives' function to do the bulk of the investigative work. The detectives led a much better life. They dressed in plainclothes, worked days, had little supervision and no accountability. They often got their jobs as a result of political influence and some were known to be corrupt. Even so, there were some really good investigators among them. I thought one day I might like to join their ranks, but at that point, I was happy where I was.

***

I had heard that the two detective sergeants in the station collected payments on a regular basis from establishments like the Glass Hat, an after hour's lounge right behind the station. The owners were paying the station and headquarters on a regular basis to look the other way when they stayed open past closing time. But every so often there would be a problem in the lounge, like someone taking a beating and the police would have no choice but to respond. The captain's response was to station a uniformed officer outside the front door from 1:00 am - 3:00 am. I received this assignment more often than my fellow officers thanks to my old friend, Lt. Walkins. I was not happy about it so instead of staying outside the door I would walk right into the lounge at 1:00 am and stay there, forcing them to close down. No one wants to go into a lounge at that hour with a cop standing there. This drove the owners crazy. They would call the station. The Sergeant would come down and send me back to my route.

I didn't like the assignment but other officers seemed to and one night I found out why. That night the owner George Tecce called to me, "Hey Daley, check that parking meter!" I looked and there was a

$10 bill stuck in the meter. That was big money in those days. I didn't take the money and continued on. And I didn't get the assignment much after that.

**

Even on quiet nights crazy things happened. My partner, Bob and I were in the wagon one night. We still used the Black Maria and I was the rear end man. About 3:00 am we were sent to a noisy party on Park Drive in a neighborhood of apartment buildings. It did not take much to disturb the neighbors in this quiet area.

We found a small but loud group there and we told them to quiet down, which they agreed to do. At 4:30 am we were sent back and this time we ordered the guests to leave and made it clear that the party was over. They left, but reluctantly. One of the guests got into his big Lincoln, called out "F*** you, cops" and took off. The wagon was never intended to be a pursuit vehicle but Kelley and I went after him. It was a wild chase with the wagon swinging from side to side, just like in the old Keystone Cops movies. We asked for help on the police radio and with the aid of several other police cars, we finally caught the man and brought him to the station. I had him at the booking desk and was going to charge him with being a disorderly person (another minor offense for which we could arrest without a warrant). He pulled out a big wad of money and offered me a hundred to forget the whole thing. The booking officer, Sergeant Thompson, asked me what the charge was. I replied bribery. Sergeant Thompson was a straight guy and he did not blink an eye and booked him that way. The prisoner turned out to be a made Mafia guy named North End Nick. The case caused quite a stir in the station. They said it was the first arrest for bribery in the history of District 16.

There were many officers involved in this arrest and the case was set for trial in Roxbury Court. As the trial date approached, I noticed a cooling of interest in the case by the other officers involved. The day before the trial a sharp young detective friend came to me and told me why. They all had been given $75 by the defendant and had agreed to back off. Ultimately he was found guilty of a minor offense, a motor vehicle violation and given a mild penalty. I was to have plenty of contact with Nick later in my career. Even though we were on different sides, I came to like him.

34

The crowd who walked the streets around the Public Garden and the Statler Hilton were a crazy mix: predominantly male, some female, a few transvestites and male and female prostitutes. Some cruised on foot and some in cars and it went late into the night. Some officers had a real hatred for this crowd. That seemed pretty harsh to me. One night, a man was brought to the station. There was some doubt as to his sex as he was in drag. The lieutenant on the desk, an old timer, said that he would not be satisfied as to the prisoner's gender until he had proof. A crazy scene followed. The individual ran screaming around the guardroom until he was finally cornered and his underwear pulled down. It struck me as a degrading spectacle but it was an example of the attitude the police had towards homosexuals at the time.

***

We fired our guns a lot in those days, since our regulations permitted firing warning shots to sound the alarm or to summon help. Once I was chasing a thief down an alley near St. Botolph Street. He was getting away from me and I shouted, "Stop or I'll shoot."

He yelled back at me, "Shoot now if you're going to."

I didn't and he got away.

***

Police officers tended to develop a mistrust of lawyers early on for several reasons. A favorite ploy of the defense attorney was to engage an officer in a casual and ostensibly off the record conversation outside the courtroom relative to the case against his client. Then when the officer took the witness stand, the defense lawyer in cross-examination would ask the officer if they had just had a conversation in the hallway. The officer had to answer yes. If the officer had said anything that might have helped the defense, the lawyer then would use it and discredit the officer with his own words. Most officers only get burned this way once.

I recall a time when I clashed with a lawyer during a trial. I was a principal witness in a fatal motor vehicle accident in which an elderly woman pedestrian was killed and the driver was assumed to be at fault. I was the first officer to respond and made out the police report. The victim had no relatives so a public administrator was appointed to represent her estate. A civil action case was made against the driver and his insurance company since the victim was dead with no kin. The only one who stood to gain was the plaintiff's lawyer. The case went to trial and I was summoned. I waited outside of the courtroom for five days. Doctors came in and testified, followed by lawyers, other experts came in and testified, each not having to wait more than five minutes to be called. I complained to the lawyer that I did not like being held so long and his response was, "You're getting paid, aren't you?" I was. $3 a day. I had a growing family to support and had to hustle every day on a second job. He was totally indifferent to my situation. Needless to say, he found me to be a hostile witness with an exhausted memory.

***

I had been a police officer six or seven years and although I thought I was pretty sharp there were things going on right before my eyes that I never saw. A secret government commission had been set up to look into corruption in the Boston Police Department. The commission's main focus was a key shop at 400 Massachusetts Avenue. This shop was the center of a major booking operation in the city and was run by a man named Schwartz. Schwartz's nickname was the "Monkey". The commission set up surveillance cameras in an apartment across the street from the key shop and watched it for a year.

One day the FBI, state police and other outside agencies raided the key shop and broke up the operation. Boston Police were not informed and had no role to play. As luck would have it, on the day of the raid I was doing traffic duty just a hundred yards away at St. Botolph and Massachusetts Avenue. As the raid was winding down a federal officer came up to me and asked for my name. He said that he had to have the name of the nearest uniformed officer. I was stupid enough to give my name, but I really had no choice.

The consequences of the investigation were devastating to the Boston Police Department. The investigators had the names of cops on the take, the amount of money handled by the Monkey and a complete picture of the operation. Payoffs were made on the first of the month and officers were caught on camera pulling up in their police cars and picking up their "monthly." You did not have to be in District 16 to be on the Monkey's payoff. He was very generous. Everybody got a piece of the action.

I wasn't so sharp apparently. I actually thought it was a key shop. In fact I went there once to have a key made and was grateful when they did not charge me. What nice guys, I thought.

Later, the CBS television show 60 Minutes did a major story on the raid, calling it "Biography of a Bookie Joint." The exposure of the bookie operation caused a convulsion in the department. Police Commissioner Leo Sullivan lost his job. Wholesale transfers were made. For me there was a good side to this; Lt. Walkins was transferred and put on nights. Nevertheless, the scandal did not stamp out corruption in the department. In a very short time the money was flowing again. No police officers went to jail. The Monkey refused to testify against the officers, choosing jail instead.

***

By the end of the 1950s, the police department slowly moved into a more modern era. The black Maria, or paddy wagon, was retired, replaced by a small panelled truck. It had doors on the back that could be shut and locked so the rear end man no longer had to sit in the back, a change that was heartily welcomed. It was painted white, not unlike an ice cream truck. The new wagon no longer stayed in the station waiting to be called out, instead it patrolled the streets just like a sector car. It was a hard ride in the wagon for a whole tour of duty but one officer, Jack Gallagher, often volunteered for the assignment. He was a charming fellow, well liked by all. I rode with him in the new wagon many times. A few years later he was shot in a bank holdup.

***

As the calendar page turned to a new decade, some things did stay the same, including our passion for playing dominoes in the guard room. One night in early 1960 a near tragedy occurred during a game. One officer named Fred set off a couple of fireworks, annoying another officer, Ed. Ed told Fred that if he set off any more fireworks he would shoot him. Fred did not take him seriously and set another one off. Ed pulled his gun and fired at Fred, narrowly missing him. A sergeant came running into the guard room at the sound of the gunshot and, unbelievably, took no action. It was a reckless deed and a major felony: assault, with intent to murder. And it was a cowardly response by the sergeant.

***

We worked closely with the Boston Fire Department. We responded to all fire alarms. If the fire department raised ladders, the wagon also responded. If the firehouse was on your route, you went there and closed the doors after the firefighters had gone out on a call. One day Bob Kelley and I responded to a report of an oil spill on Queensberry Street near Fenway Park. An oil delivery of 1,000 gallons had just been made to a building. The problem was, earlier that day the oil tank in that building had already been filled. Bob and I entered the building and found a couple of inches of oil on the basement floor. Oil was burning freely in the oil burner even though the burner was not on. We called the fire department and the chief and his team responded immediately. They went into the basement with us to assess the situation. The chief ordered the building evacuated immediately and the firefighters went to work, dragging hoses into the basement to begin pumping out the oil. Bob and I were still in the basement when suddenly enormous flames shot out of the oil burner and spread to the oil on the floor. In no time the entire basement was in flames. We were scared stiff and hurried for the door. I could see from the looks on the firefighters' faces that they were scared too, but they stood their ground and directed foggy streams of water into the fire, knocking it down. Miraculously, the building was saved and no one was hurt.

The firefighters' actions in this instance were first rate. Unfortunately, there were other fire scenes where the performance of the fire department was not so good. In one instance, John Schofield and I were sent to the Bostonian Hotel on a report of a fire. It was just before Christmas and snowing. John and I went down an alley in the rear of the hotel and looked up. Flames were coming out of a fifth floor window and a man was hanging out the window calling for help. John went around to the front door of the hotel and I stayed in the alley. The fire was getting bigger and hotter. The firehouse was only a couple of blocks away and they had been notified before us, but there was no sign of them. As the snow kept coming down, the man in the window started yelling at me, "You son of a bitch, get me out of here, I'm burning up!"

This was a crowded residential apartment area and amazingly I was the only one in the alley. All I could do was tell him to keep calm and that the fire department was on the way. John did not come back and I learned later that he and a sergeant were trying to get a hose going in the hallway outside the room. That was a lot more than I was doing. After several more precious minutes, the fire department finally arrived, but they could not get their ladder truck down the alley. A ladder was brought into the alley and raised, but it was a floor too short. The fire was very intense now and the man continued to call for help. Eventually a firefighter maneuvered the ladder truck into the alley, raised the stick and another firefighter went up and got the victim out of the window. The victim turned out to be a disabled veteran who had lost his legs. As he came down the ladder he was good humored and thanked the firefighter. He was badly burned, however and later died. I can still remember the steam coming from his body as he came down the ladder. It was not the fire department's finest hour, but no one seemed to notice. If the police had performed like this, we would have been blasted all over the front page.

***

In November 1960, a commercial plane crashed at Logan Airport. Many people were killed. I was working that night and assigned to a walking beat so that made me available. I was sent to the East Boston Relief Station, a kind of local hospital, which was being used as a temporary morgue. The relief station was located directly opposite the exit of the Sumner Tunnel on the East Boston side. There were between 15 and 20 bodies in the station and it was our job to search them for identification and to take and preserve any valuables. The bodies were drenched in aviation fuel and emitted a powerful kerosene odour. Generally they were all in one piece but had lots of broken bones. I didn't have much stomach for this job but there was another officer with me, Bob, who didn't raise an eyebrow. Bob had some experience as a mortician and funeral director before coming on the police force. He was sent to the main mortuary about a week after the crash to help the staff. He was perfect for it.

On December 21, 1961 I worked an overtime detail at the Greyhound Bus Terminal in Park Square. This night was to trouble me for years.

A short time after I started the detail, a little after 1 am, the route officer came by and we talked for a while. He worked the opposite platoon from me and we knew each other, but not very well. He went on his way and I remained at the terminal. About an hour later a local guy, whose face was familiar, but whose name I did not know, came into the terminal and said to me, "In case you're interested, there's someone breaking into the lounge." He was referring to was Leonardi's Lounge, located in one corner of the terminal on St. James Avenue. It had closed at 1:00 am. I told the guy that I was certainly interested. There had been a number of breaks in the area and I was eager to make an arrest.

I exited the terminal on the St. James Avenue side and walked the outside perimeter of the lounge. When I got to the bus driveway side, I saw an open window and two or three cases of liquor piled up under it.

I looked into the window and saw a figure in the darkness. When he saw me he slammed the window shut. Because the window glass was opaque, I couldn't see in. There was a set of stairs coming up from the basement of the lounge and I backed up to where I could view the stairs, thinking the thief would come out that way. He didn't. So I went back to the window and pushed it open. I looked in and I saw a shape moving. He appeared to be wearing a police uniform! He was headed towards an exit door at the other end of the lounge. In my mind I was dealing with a burglar and yet I also had to consider that the thief might be a cop, or at least impersonating one.

I had a terrible problem deciding what to do. I yelled for him to get away from the door. I wanted desperately for someone else to solve this problem but there was no one else. I ordered him to stop. He kept moving towards the door and I fired a warning shot that hit the wall right over his head, spraying plaster down. He went to the floor and I took cover thinking that he was going to shoot back at me, which fortunately didn't happen. This was a situation not covered in the Rules and Regulations. But my decision had been made. I was not going to let the thief escape.

Now I could hear sirens so I knew help was on the way. Two officers arrived and we planned our next moves. Somebody gave us a key and the three of us went in. I did not tell these officers anything other than I thought I had someone trapped in the lounge. We started searching. It was not a big place and a couple of moments later I glanced to my right and there was the route officer that I had seen earlier in the night, coming up from behind to help. He had his flashlight out and was searching right alongside us. I noticed plaster dust on his uniform. If this was the thief, how did he get outside and behind us? Lots of questions. Soon, many other officers were on the scene, including a supervisor. The lounge was searched and no one was found.

The owner of the lounge was notified and came in. The whiskey was returned and the building was locked up. I went into the station to write my report. I told a sergeant, one that I trusted, what had happened and that I thought a police officer might have been involved. Although I had a suspicion, I couldn't be certain who the officer was. To accuse a fellow officer of being a criminal, I would have had to been one hundred per cent sure. There were too many questions here. The sergeant was a sharp guy and offered some advice. My report would indicate, truthfully, that I could not identify the burglar. The report was so written.

There was a further investigation but the identity of the burglar was never determined. The breaks in area mysteriously stopped.

***

The worst fight I ever got into while on duty happened in the winter of 1962 at the Sherry Biltmore Hotel on the corner of Massachusetts Avenue and Belvedere Street. I was on a walking beat that night, but about a half hour before the shift change I agreed to fill in for an officer in the wagon who had a detail and had to leave at midnight. Just after midnight we were sent to the Sherry Biltmore on a report of an officer in trouble. The officer, Paul Power, was indeed in big trouble. An iron workers' Christmas banquet and dance was going on there and quickly getting out of control after a night of heavy eating and drinking. When we arrived Power was battling one guy and as we went to his assistance another guy at the party joined in. Eddie McManus, the wagon driver, was tough but we were having difficulty getting things under control. All of a sudden fights broke out all over the place and we were definitely losing. More officers arrived, including Bill Joyce, Bob Tierney, Bob Kelley, Tony Cesero, Tom Ralph, Don Foley and Bob Lawrence. With this number of officers we were finally able to clear the lobby and restore some order.

We had three people in custody. We put one of them in the wagon and locked the door. When we opened the door a few minutes later to put a second prisoner in, the first prisoner came flying out. He set himself up at the rear of the wagon, kicking and punching anyone who came near and the battle started all over again. I charged the prisoner and pushed him all the way to the other end of the wagon, into the panel behind the driver. He grabbed for my eyes and was trying to gouge them. He was doing a pretty good job on my face too but my main concern was that he not get to my eyes. There was not much room in the wagon but other officers got in and it was heavy going before we finally managed to handcuff him. Emotions were running high and officers who had a chance to use their police clubs were doing so. I saw one officer take a least three good shots at the other prisoner but it did not slow him down.

The weight of our numbers eventually wore the prisoners down and we got them back to the station. We were banged up quite a bit. My face looked like a jigsaw puzzle. Bob Tierney and Bob Lawrence had been kicked in the jaw. Cesero had been hit on the head and his fancy Longines watch was broken. We looked bad but the prisoners looked worse. They appeared to have been in a cement mixer. They were three brothers, all ironworkers, tough and strong as hell and drunk besides. They all went to Roxbury Court and were found guilty. They received fines, no jail time. They were all banged up so the judge must have felt that they had already been punished. It was the worst fight I ever saw as a police officer and there has been nothing like it since. The Iron Workers Ball fight turned out to be a legend.

After fights like this, it is easy to see how police officers tend to develop an "us against them" mentality and turn inward. In my case we saw each other in work as well as socially. We went to each other's homes, our wives became friendly and in short, we stayed pretty much within our own group. It was probably an unhealthy association as we did not get much input from outside the police organization. This tendency seemed to diminish with more years on the job as we came to realize that outside contact was essential.

***

Police pay had increased considerably in the past nine years but all of us patrolmen were constantly scratching for extra money. We took every extra detail that came our way and many of us worked second jobs. I had a fire extinguisher recharging business passed on to me by the old wagon man, John. When that business was slow I drove a taxi in Brookline with my former partner from District 16, Ed Tobin. In addition we both worked in a liquor warehouse near Fenway Park during the Christmas season. There were times that we were pretty burned out when we reported for duty. It was against department rules and regulations to have outside jobs but this rule was only enforced when there was a complaint.

It was my experience that the lazy guys made poor policemen and those who worked the hardest off the job worked just as hard as policemen. There were some officers who took short cuts to the extra money, especially around Christmas time. I was doing a detail in Kenmore Square one day near Christmas when I saw two of my comrades in uniform walking through the square. They had their overcoats on which I thought strange because they patrolled this area at night so I knew they were not on duty. They were dropping in on the local merchants expecting gratuities and getting them. A bottle of whiskey could be easily concealed in the long overcoat. A clerk at our station house supplied the merchants with a list of the day and night officers who patrolled the area. If your name was on the list, you got a present. Of course the clerk who provided this information had his name on all the lists.

This practice could be carried to ridiculous extremes. I know of one officer who was looking for the owner of a lounge on Kilmarnock Street. He went to the lounge three times looking for him. On his fourth try the officer finally found the owner in the basement of the lounge in his locked office. The officer said, "I heard that you were looking for me." I do not know how the officer made out but I had to give him credit for perseverance if nothing else.

***

On May 25, 1962, Patrolmen Jack Gallagher and Tony Cesero received a routine call to Shawmut Bank in Kenmore Square after a report of an ADT burglar alarm going off. The ADT security guard, Harold Gillette, also responded. The three men entered the bank together as the guard had the keys. These alarms were common, so we all knew Harold. It was very rare to find a robber on the premises. The alarm was almost always the result of faulty wiring, rain, wind, an accident or human error. Nevertheless the place had to be searched. Their search led them down to the basement. They searched an L-shaped corridor and came to a dead end. They found nothing suspicious and turned to leave this area. Jack Gallagher was the last of the group.

A burglar, Charles Tracy, had broken a back window and was down in the basement. He apparently heard footsteps and climbed into a cabinet against the wall of the corridor and shut the door. He stayed there as Cesero and Gillette passed by. He had armed himself with a loaded gun belonging to the day security guard, which he found stored in the cabinet.

As Jack Gallagher walked by the cabinets he may have spotted the burglar. Tracy fired at Gallagher, hitting him in the chest and knocking him against the wall where he slid to the floor. Tracy now had Gallagher behind him at the end of the corridor and Cesero and Gillette in front of him. Tracy had no place to flee.

Tracy fired again and this time hit Gillette in the leg. Jack was still conscious. He managed to get his gun out and fired at Tracy, hitting him several times. Tracy fired back at Gallagher and hit him a few more times. They were not 20 feet apart when they exchanged shots.

Cesero and Gillette made it to the end of the corridor. Gillette must have run upstairs and called for help because the police had no portable radios at that time. John Vance and Ted Madden in a mobile unit responded. When they arrived they took positions at the end of the corridor with Cesero.

I had been doing a morning watch and was assigned to the Public Garden. It was a mild and rainy Friday night and there was little police activity. I was talking to two fellow officers, Bush and Jandzunski, near their patrol car on Charles Street about 2:50 am. A call came over the police car radio sending the car to the bank. I jumped into the back seat of the police car and we headed to Kenmore Square. En route we got a message that an officer had been shot.

When we arrived there were several officers standing around but not doing much. I went to the front door of the bank. I lost sight of Officer Bush but I later learned that he went to the rear of the bank.

The front door of the bank was locked. I kept banging on it until the ADT security guard, Harold Gillette, who by that time had been shot in the leg, limped to the door and let me in. I asked him what was going on. He answered feebly, "downstairs." I found the stairs and headed down. Once on the lower level I entered a large room. I saw one door leading toward the rear of the bank and another door that led to a corridor about 30 feet long which extended from the front to the back of the bank. I walked over to it and looked out. At the rear end of this corridor there was a blank wall with doors to the right and left. Three police officers were at the front end of the corridor near me: Patrolmen Madden, Vance and Cesero. The gunman was at the rear of the corridor on the left and shooting towards the four of us at the front of the bank. Sergeant Barry and Patrolman Bush were behind the door on the right at the end of the corridor, nearest to the gunman. They had entered the bank through a broken window, the same one the gunman had broken and used to get into the bank. They could not see the gunman nor could they open the door without being exposed to him at very close range.

I looked down the corridor but did not to see anyone. I looked again and saw a gun pointed in my direction. I couldn't get a shot off fast enough. The long corridor with bare walls was no cover for anyone who might try to rush the suspect. It was a standoff and it stayed that way for about 30 minutes. Bullets flew back and forth.

The officers nearby told me that Jack Gallagher had been shot and was lying behind the gunman. There was no safe way to reach him. None of us was familiar with the layout of the bank basement. There was no effective communication between us and Sergeant Barry and Patrolman Bush. We could hear Sergeant Barry through the closed door urging the gunman to give up.

During the standoff I thought there must be some other way to get to Jack Gallagher and thought of the door I had first observed in the large room. Maybe it led to the rear of the bank. I thought that perhaps Gallagher was behind that door. I had many regrets later that I did not act on this thought. But there was much confusion and I didn't want to get myself shot charging into an unknown situation.

Finally Patrolman Joe Griffin came into the basement with a tear gas gun and gave it to me. I fired one shell down the corridor and it hit the wall behind the suspect, generating tear gas immediately. Because no one had a gas mask on we retreated to the large room in the basement. Soon the shooting stopped as the gas overcame us all.

Detective Bob Cunningham was standing near the door in the rear of the large room and he heard Jack Gallagher call, "Please, come in." The door was locked but Cunningham pushed it through. This was the door that I first noticed when I entered the basement. Cunningham opened it and found Jack Gallagher lying on the ground to his left and the suspected robber lying on the floor to his right.

Both Gallagher and Tracy were still conscious, but just barely. Jack had a bloodstain in the middle of his chest staining his white uniform shirt. Many policemen were now present and helped bring Gallagher and Tracy from the bank to the street. Jack Gallagher said to his partner, Officer Cesero, as he was being taken away, "I don't think I am going to make it." Cesero, an older Marine Corps veteran, assured him that he would and that he had seen men with worse wounds survive and that Jack would be OK.

After seeing Jack off to the hospital, I went back into the bank. We still had no report or communication about the robbery. I did not know if Tracy was the only suspect involved and neither did anyone else. I could tolerate the gas much better now and I went down to the corridor where we had exchanged gunfire. There was still plenty of smoke and gas in the area so it was hard to see. As I started down the corridor a figure came at me out of the smoke. He had a gun in his hand. I had my gun out and was feeling a bit dizzy from the gas. I hesitated a second and in that moment I recognized the man coming towards me. It was a detective, Bob Chennette, in plain clothes. I never did talk to him about this encounter but it was by the slimmest of margins that he escaped being shot. I suppose that he could have shot me just as easily, but the difference was that I was in uniform.

Every incident teaches a little about human nature. There are police officers who project a real macho image but when real danger presents itself are not up to the task. Other officers rise to the occasion. I say this because John Vance and Ted Madden were two low-key guys with little bluster who showed their true colors and held their ground in the bank gun battle.

When it was all over we went back to the station to write our reports. I was in the guardroom a couple of hours later when someone told me that Jack Gallagher had died. I left the guardroom and went off by myself and broke down. Jack was a good friend. I knew his wife Rita and their family very well. I had mixed feelings about Jack's death. In a strange way I envied him. We all have to die sometime and he died like a champion.

Once I regained control of my emotions I felt a great surge of resentment toward the day officers, detectives and specialists who came from headquarters to investigate crimes that occurred at night. They came to work well-rested, clean shaven, well dressed and much superior to us donkeys who worked nights and did the dirty and dangerous jobs. I am sure that my reactions were completely unfair, but that was the way I felt that night. The night officers, at least in my station, were treated as second-class citizens. Later, when I became a supervisor, I took great pride and pleasure working nights with night officers.

Jack's funeral was impressive. Cardinal Cushing said the mass. Afterward we marched in uniform from Jack's local church in Mattapan to the cemetery off Cummings Highway in Roslindale. There was many a joke among us marchers as we plodded along, the shock of Jack's death having long since passed. It was a sharp reminder that you are soon forgotten after you die.

***

Some officers were known for their outrageous scams and we heard about them in station house conversations. Once an officer left his area on a personal errand and crashed his police car while way out of his sector. His radio still worked so he decided to cover his tracks by setting up a fake car chase. He had police cars all over the city chasing a phantom. Of course the chase ended up with his police car wrecked. When he got back to the station, the lieutenant on the desk said to him, "Too bad these cars just don't hold up."

Another scam occurred before Red Sox night games. There were several business parking lots around Fenway Park that were not used at night. When the Red Sox had a night game, which was

47

relatively rare in the 1950s and 1960s, some officers would put on a jacket over their uniform and charge patrons for parking in these lots. This went on until night games became more popular and the lot owners realized their profit potential.

***

One night my partner Bob and I were sent to an apartment in the Fenway area following a report of a sudden death. Seated in a chair was a young man, about 20 years old with a revolver still in his hand and a bullet hole in the middle of his forehead. He was with his girlfriend and was playing Russian roulette when the game went against him. It was an incredibly stupid act. Later in my career when I worked in homicide, I became involved in a case where three people were playing Russian roulette. Two of the players encouraged the third to take his chance and he was unlucky. The two surviving players were convicted of manslaughter.

In the 1950s and 1960s we earnestly made attempts to catch the operators of stolen cars. One night Bob and I were sitting in our patrol car outside a small club on Beacon Street called the Band Box. The registration numbers of stolen cars were posted every tour of duty and it was possible to carry a lot of numbers in your head for at least that tour of duty. Some officers were remarkable in their ability to remember registrations and these officers made a lot of arrests and recovered many stolen vehicles. This particular night Bob was driving. I spotted a stolen vehicle and we took off after it. It was a brief chase. The operator of the stolen car left us in the dust. You can't win them all.

The personnel in each station house was divided into three platoons: one day platoon and two night platoons. Each night platoon was known as one side of the house. A few nights later in the same nightclub, the Band Box, a drunken police officer from the other side of the house took his gun out and threatened to shoot someone. It was after-hours and there were no patrons in the club. The employees were terrified. Jack Sullivan from our side of the house went up there and disarmed the officer. The incident was smothered. No reports submitted.

Soon after that we ran into another problem with a fellow officer. I was just finishing a first half tour in a marked car when my partner Tom and I were sent to a car dealer's lot on Boylston Street near

Fenway Park. It was 12:05 am. Luby Chevrolet owned the lot. We were told that someone was in the lot stripping a car. We checked the lot and didn't find anyone, though we did find a Chevy station wagon with a rear door taken off and lying on the pavement. Two other officers arrived to see if we needed any help. I noticed a fifth officer on the scene whom I did not know. I found out his name, that he was assigned to the City Prison and that he also owned an auto-body repair shop. I spoke privately to one of the officers who came to assist us and asked him to follow this officer when he left the scene. He did and came back to tell me that this officer got into a Chevy station wagon similar to the one being stripped. His car's door was damaged. It appeared that this mystery officer was on his way to work in a customer's car and decided to steal a rear door from one of Luby's cars instead of buying one from a dealer. I went over and told him to get into the police car. He told me, "I have a wife and four kids." I told him, "So do I." He did come to the station but he was not happy. The sergeant on the desk was just as unhappy as the officer I had brought in. This was something he didn't want to have to deal with.

A row of apartment houses overlooked the used car lot. Obviously someone was watching the whole thing, as evidenced by the call to the police. I made out my report, noting what I had seen. An investigation was conducted but nothing ever came from it and no action was taken against the officer.

A couple of days after this incident the captain called me into his office and asked me if I would be happier in another station. I told him no, that I was very happy in District 16 and that I had no desire to change. I think that he was giving me a message that he didn't like controversy. He was a decent and honorable guy but everyone has their limits. He allowed me to stay.

***

For a typical early morning watch, two officers in plain clothes would be sent out in an unmarked car. On December 3, 1962, my partner Bob Harvey and I got this assignment. I was driving the unmarked car about 2:00 am on Newbury Street when I spotted a young man lurking suspiciously near a parking meter with his hands in his pockets. This was a time when there was a rash of people breaking into meters to steal the change, usually with a screwdriver.

I stopped the car, got out and approached him. I asked him his name and what he was doing. He did not respond to my questions and became hostile. Despite my plainclothes I made it clear I was policeman and he certainly seemed to understand that this was the case. He had one hand in his pocket and I told him to take it out. I thought that he may have a weapon or a screwdriver. He absolutely refused, arousing my suspicions that he had something on him that he did not want me to see. I went for him and his pants were torn as I pulled his hand from his pocket. We struggled as I attempted to get him under control.

Bob got out of the police car and as he did so the suspect aimed a kick at him and got him just below the crotch. Bob Harvey responded by hitting the suspect across the nose. It was a punch for a kick, nothing more. Unfortunately the punch broke the suspect's nose and there was blood all over the place. To make things worse, there was no weapon in the suspect's pocket. It was difficult to understand the suspect's behaviour given that he had no weapon. All he had to do was cooperate with us and offer an explanation. It seemed that he was looking for a confrontation.

Now that he was injured we couldn't let him go. The suspect was arrested and charged with being abroad in the nighttime and suspected of unlawful design. It was an old statute but still in force and it fit the circumstances of our encounter. When we brought him to the station, a very experienced desk sergeant, Sergeant Rowan, sensed trouble and suggested that the suspect be also charged with assault and battery on a police officer. Sergeant Rowan was a role model for many of the younger officers, including me. When he gave advice, we took it.

Sergeant Rowan was right about the trouble. The case exploded. The man we arrested was Jackie Washington, a local folk singer. Washington, who was black, soon became the focus of every civil rights lawyer in the city. Cross complaints were filed against Bob and I, charging us with assault and battery. For some reason I became the focal point for the case and took all the heat. Bob, who did the damage, stayed in the shadows. The newspapers were giving the case a lot of ink--not a good sign for Bob and me. This was not the positive kind of publicity.

The case went to trial in the Boston Municipal Court before Judge Lewiton, the chief justice. He was a force on the bench, a man with a good legal mind. He made no effort to duck the case. The civil rights drive for minorities was just getting started and this case appeared to be the perfect vehicle to advance that cause. A civil rights lawyer named Barshack represented Washington pro bono. ADA Jim Foley was the lawyer for the government. I had the sense that Foley was not entirely on my side. His prosecution was lukewarm.

The judge found Washington guilty of the first charge, General Law Ch 41-98, being abroad in the nighttime. He was found not guilty of assault and battery. There were only three witnesses of any import, Washington, Bob Harvey and me. A doctor from the hospital testified about Washington's injuries and Sergeant Rowan as to Washington's conduct at the booking desk. The defense maintained that Jackie Washington took a vicious beating from Harvey and I. That was not the case. It was simply a punch in reaction to a kick.

The judge offered Washington the option of pleading nolo contendere (no contest) and paying a fine of $10 but he and his team refused. The verdict was appealed to the Superior Court and complaints were sought in the federal system alleging that we had violated Washington's civil rights. The case was getting out of control and the newspapers were becoming anti-police.

At this time the city had a new police commissioner, Ed McNamara, a former FBI agent and a new mayor, John Collins. McNamara arranged for the Boston Police Relief Association to hire a lawyer to represent Harvey and me. Larry O'Donnell was flamboyant and expensive but had a good track record. The case went to trial in Superior Court and once again Washington was found guilty.

I remembered distinctly a phrase from our rules and regulations that said that if you act in good faith the department will always stand behind you. At this point however trouble came from a completely unexpected direction. The police department, bowing to newspaper pressure, brought charges against Bob and me. We were charged with using unreasonable force in making the arrest and conduct unbecoming to an officer. We had just gone through two trials and had been vindicated. There had been strong internal support for us, so I was shocked to learn that we now had to face a departmental hearing.

The police commissioner appointed a trial board. We were found not guilty of the charges.

Larry O'Donnell submitted his bill to the Police Relief Association for $5,000, an extraordinary sum for a lawyer's fee in 1962. It was the first time the Association had ever hired a lawyer to represent a police officer. They never did it again. The police formed unions shortly afterwards and the unions took over this responsibility.

**

Some of the older, less competent, sergeants were leaving the police job as they aged out and were being replaced by brighter and more principled individuals. The promotional system, by exam, was working well and seemed to be honestly run. Time in rank was a huge part of your final mark so there was little chance of being promoted if you had less than ten years on the police force. The new bosses were all veterans of World War II. They had different styles and, for the most part, were honest and hard working. One of the new sergeants in District 16 was Jim McDonald, whom I had known for 15 years. We worked together in a meatpacking house for several years in the North End and played on the same football team after World War II. Jim was the one who had encouraged me to take the police exam and I was appointed a couple of years after he was. Now, happily, he was my boss. He stayed in District 16 for about a year.

**

Because we night officers worked rotating shifts it was quite common to suffer a physical and mental letdown about 4:30 am on the last half shift. One night about 5:00 am a fire alarm was sounded at a building on Norway Street. Apparently someone smelled gas. My partner Bob Tierney and I responded as well as another unit, Jack Sullivan and Bob Kelley, with Sergeant Jim McDonald arriving a few minutes later. The fire department arrived about the same time that we did. The firemen checked the building and found that the gas main valve had been taken apart in the basement and raw natural gas was flowing into the building. This was an incredible hazard. Any tenant lighting a cigarette or turning on the stove would have blown the building and us, sky-high. The building was quickly cleared. The gate valve was reinstalled and the building vented. Outside, the fire chief told us that some tools and a cigarette lighter were found near the removed valve. The chief gave the lighter to Bob Tierney.

It was now well after 5:00 am and we were operating at a low energy level. Sergeant McDonald was not, however and he started talking to residents of the building, now gathered out on the street. One couple mentioned a strange young man who lived on the third floor. Sergeant McDonald and I sneaked back into the building and got into this tenant's apartment before the tenants were allowed back into the building. We found more tools and enough other evidence sufficient to arouse our suspicions. The occupant came back to the apartment while we were still in there and we began to talk to him. Sergeant McDonald whispered in my ear, "Go down and get the cigarette lighter from Tierney and slip it to me without the young man seeing it."

I did so, then left the room while the Sergeant talked to the suspect alone for a few minutes. At one point the man went to the bathroom and Sergeant McDonald placed the cigarette lighter on a table. When the occupant of the apartment returned, they continued talking. The suspect took a cigarette from his pocket and reached for the lighter. The Sergeant asked if that was his lighter and the suspect answered yes. The trap closed. Sergeant McDonald informed the young man that the lighter had been found in the basement near the gas valve and he demanded an explanation. The suspect folded and made an admission. This was before the Miranda decision.

The man was promptly arrested, brought to the station and charged with an attempt to commit arson. We went back to his apartment and gave it a good search. There was no time for a search warrant. Warrantless searches were lawful under emergency conditions then as now. We discovered that he was a very disturbed guy.

We did not know just how disturbed he was until the next morning. While in the cell he somehow cut into a vein and was trying to bleed himself to death. It turned out that he was hopelessly suicidal. He had taken the gas main apart and then returned to his room and waited for the building to blow up. Perhaps he was going to use the cigarette lighter to ignite the gas in the basement. We will never know. He never did stand trial. While waiting for his trial he killed himself. He was stopped from killing many others because of Sergeant McDonald's successful effort to stop him.

***

Bostonians were proud when John Kennedy, who had been a senator from our state, was elected president. He truly captured the country. When he held press conferences, which he did often, the country stood still. Television was in its infancy so the sets were tiny, grainy and only transmitted in black and white. Even so, he was its master. He used humor to disarm hecklers. Questions from the press that he did not deem appropriate were smoothly shunted aside.

When the press conferences were held I would leave my post to see and hear him as did everyone else in the country who could.

***

My recollection of his speech at the time of The Cuban Missile Crisis is clear to this day. I was a going out on a first half tour of duty on a walking beat and stopped at the firehouse next to the station where they had a TV set. (We had none in the police station.) There were no jokes this day. Kennedy set out the threat to the nation. It was an incredibly dangerous time for the country and the world. I left the firehouse shaken.

District 14, Brighton

Sergeant

The sergeant's exam was given every two years. I took it regularly as soon as I was eligible, but it was difficult to get promoted if you had less than ten years on the force because the experience factor counted for as much as 30% of your final mark. It insured that inexperienced police officers did not become supervisors. The marking system was changed some years later and the credit for time on the job was reduced quite a bit as a factor. I took the exam under the old rules and did well. I was one of the top 30 candidates. Six months later I was promoted to sergeant. I was 32 years old and, at that time, the youngest sergeant in the police department. I was also the first one in my recruit class to make sergeant. It was February 1963.

Typically new sergeants were moved to a new station. There was a lot of politics involved in being assigned to a good one. I wanted to go to District 4 in the South End or to District 9 in Roxbury, both very active areas. Instead, I was sent to District 14 in Brighton, a relatively quiet area. I learned later that at least part of the reasons that I was not given the assignments I wanted was that I was not one of Chief Superintendent Maloney's favorites.

Prior to being sent to our new assignments we were sent to a promotional school for about a week in an effort to prepare us for our new role. After this brief training, I reported to the Brighton station, District 14 and was assigned night duty. My first tour of duty was a morning watch. It was Friday and I came in around midnight. The only other superior officer scheduled to work that night was late. It was a shaky start but I struggled through. I was nervous but confident. Fortunately for me there were very competent police clerks who knew the desk routine. They were a great help that night and I needed it as it was the first time I worked as the officer in charge. It turned out to be a very busy night.

The transition from patrolman to sergeant is a difficult one. The sergeant has to prove himself before he is accepted. If he gets through this testing period with confidence and grace he will always feel comfortable with his rank. The sergeant is the man, the leader, the boss, the one who makes all the important decisions on the street. He is expected to know the law and have the answers. I found it thrilling to be in this position. I knew the laws but I certainly did not know all the answers. Well, maybe I thought I did. Those first years as a sergeant were the happiest time of my career.

***

There was one lieutenant on nights, Lieutenant Ramsey and four other sergeants: Buckley, Guilfoyle, McMinamin and Deary, all were great guys and easy to work with. There were some very good night detectives, too. Remi Kennedy and Peter O'Malley were fearless workaholics who ground out cases like spaghetti. They were an exceptional team who meshed well together.

The police department still worked a six-day week but I worked as needed. It was not uncommon to work two or three last-halfs in a row. It was a killer schedule and my sleeping habits were thrown completely out of whack. On some of the morning watches it seemed to me that I was the only one awake in the station. The sergeants had a room upstairs in the station with a bed (dirty as hell) and it always was available. I am not sure if I ever used it but there was many a night when I did struggle to stay alert.

Now that I was a sergeant I went to all the sudden deaths, those defined as a death without a doctor present or from an unknown but not criminal cause. I didn't enjoy this duty. I recall a scene in Brighton where a man had put a shotgun in his mouth and pulled the trigger. I wasn't quite ready for this gory scene and asked one of the officers with me if he had a strong stomach. He said yes so I told him to check the body. When I asked him the condition of the body he said, "No face." As time went by I became a lot less squeamish.

I soon settled into the sergeant's job and took my share of the available details. I worked at athletic events at Boston College and at Boston University, as well as carnivals and college dances. One night in June, I was working a detail at a carnival. A fight got out of control and we had to make arrests. In those days we did not have portable radios. Communication with the station was still done by callboxes on the street. To call for the police wagon, we walked the prisoners to the nearest callbox, which was in Oak Square. On the way we passed a group of youths. These kids had always been pains in the neck and this area a trouble spot for years.

As I passed this group one of them got up and jumped me. A wild fight ensued. The officer with me was no tiger and the best he could do was yell loudly at the kids and call for help. I still held my prisoner but he was fighting me too. I slid behind him, got my arm around his neck and he dropped to the ground. Other officers arrived, the prisoner was put in the wagon and the situation was brought under control. It turned out that the youth that jumped me was the brother of my prisoner. Both brothers were taken into custody. They were brought before the court but the penalty was minor. The fix was probably in but I really did not care. These were Brighton boys and it was Brighton court.

***

A very new sergeant is told no more of what is happening in a station house than is absolutely necessary. If he wants to know anything, he has to stick his nose in everywhere. When I came across something that looked a little shady I would push a little and someone would come to me and tell me what was going on. I gradually got a good picture of life in and around the station. Captain Flood was head of the station but I soon learned that the real boss was the sergeant detective. He was a super smooth guy, a very competent policeman who had been around for a long time. He had very powerful connections in the courthouse, in the police department, in city hall and in the State House. Brighton had little violent crime but was a hot bed of gaming activity and the sergeant detective had a firm grip on all of it. He and I had different points of view so it was inevitable that we would clash at some point. As a rookie sergeant though, I had no chance of toppling his kingdom, nor did I desire to. I just had to be careful not to get run over by this speeding train.

The sergeant detective had a uniformed counterpart who firmly controlled all the licensed premises in the district and there were many. He was also a very likable individual and it was impossible to say no to him, but woe to any who crossed him. When he would issue a license for an occasional carnival he would allow the operators to run outright gaming devices in violation of the law.

***

The morality laws had been changed somewhat but many of those old statutes were still on the books. One was a statute concerning

---

obscene material. Eaton's was a popular variety store in Cleveland Circle that sold candy, cigarettes and magazines, including obscene ones. I also suspected that the store was taking gaming action. I dropped in there one evening and grabbed about a dozen of the worst magazines off the shelves. I brought them to Brighton Court at the next sitting with the intention of seeking complaints. It was a pretty good case under the statute and I felt that I would prevail at a trial. The two women clerks in the court were nervous and reluctant to issue complaints. They held the evidence and said they would present the evidence to the judge before issuing any complaints. I never heard another word about the case.

***

I was still getting used to being a sergeant when a newly promoted lieutenant, Mickey McDonald, came to the station and was put on nights. He had fallen from grace and was sent to District 14. He was an extremely competent policeman and turned out to be a great mentor. He liked those who made an effort. He encouraged and advised me and we got along well. He gave me any half-decent case that walked in the door, including the following one.

A girl, about 18 years old, came into the station one night with her boyfriend. After speaking with her, Lieutenant McDonald called me in and told me to investigate. She told me that her father had sexually abused her since she was six years old. She was now serious with her boyfriend and they wanted to get this matter behind them. The facts of the case were so strong that there was no question of the father's guilt.

The question was how to deal with the situation. I went to the father's house and arrested him, charging him with incest. I also spoke with the girl's mother. She seemed surprised by the accusations but not shocked. At one point she said, "Oh my God, I didn't believe Carol."

Carol was the girl's older sister. There was no question that the father had abused the older sister as well. The father was found guilty in Brighton Court but given no jail time. Instead he was ordered to undergo therapy and to stay away from his daughters. The wife took him back. Fortunately he didn't have any younger daughters.

***

Soon after this case I became involved in one that was a classic textbook investigation of a safe break. Very late in a morning watch just before dawn, two uniformed officers, DesRoche and Kennedy, spotted a car in a commercial area of the district. They checked out the car and found three men in it along with a gun and a lot of cash. They arrested the men and charged them with the old standby, Suspicion that they may have committed a felony. We were not yet sure which felony.

When the employees of a local Lincoln car dealership reported to work that morning, they discovered that they were the victims of a safe break. It was a very professional job. The bottom of a large safe had been cut through with torches using a burning bar technique. The torches, which we learned later had been stolen in a previous break, were left at the scene. We were called to the scene and found some solid evidence. It appeared that one of the burglars nicked his head on the ragged edge of the hole cut into the safe, leaving blood and some hairs on the edge of the hole. There was a lot of dust from the concrete and insulation that made up the interior walls of the safe. Footprints were discovered in the dust.

There was little doubt that the three men arrested were the burglars. It just remained to prove it. We were fortunate in that the department had just hired a new chemist, Dana Kuhn. I called him to the scene. The suspects' heads were examined. One of the men was found to have a scratch on his head. Hair samples were taken from him and placed in envelopes. The suspects' shoes were also taken and examined. The suspects' clothes were taken and shaken out to gather the dust on them. Photos were taken of shoe prints at the scene. Everything matched. The hairs found on the safe came from one of the suspects. The dust from the floor matched the dust found on the suspects' shoes and clothing. The footprints on the floor matched the imprints of the suspects' shoes. The evidence was overwhelming.

As the case moved through the courts it drew praise from judges and prosecutors. It was the strongest physical evidence possible. I never saw a case that strong again. The men were convicted. The two officers involved, Kennedy and DesRosche, received a medal at the Policemen's Ball for their efforts. I don't think the chemist did but he certainly deserved one.

Things were going better for me financially. I moved from the third floor of a triple-decker in Dorchester to Hyde Park where I bought a new house. I had one child at the time. My family continued to increase until there were five children. I still had to struggle to support them working details at every opportunity and continuing with the fire extinguisher business.

Nevertheless, I was restless. I didn't find District 14 a very demanding police area and I was anxious to move to a busier one. I looked for a transfer and hoped to be sent to the South End station, District 4. That was not to be. My brother-in-law was a city official and spoke to the police commissioner. Soon afterward I was sent to District 1 in the North End. It was the last time I ever tried to use influence to make a change in the police department.

District 1, Downtown

Sergeant

District 1 was the center of gaming activity in the city and it had the biggest pad. Every sergeant in the city wanted to go there but it was the last place I wanted to be. It did have its attractions of course, the Boston Garden, great restaurants, great bakeries and a big waterfront. It was also a very small geographic area so it could be walked on foot. The neighborhood was relatively safe with little street crime and lot of criminals, including the Mafia living or working in the area.

My education came quickly. The captain was probably the most venal officer I had come across up to that point. He would get his city pay check and have one of his officers cash it. His pay was about 130 dollars. He always wanted one $100 bill and he put that in the bank. He lived off the fat of the land the rest of the week. His routine was well known in the station. He did every detail at the Boston Garden. And when it came to underworld payments he was a serious collector. He was also very careful to share his collections with those higher up in the department.

I was put on nights of course. There were two night lieutenants, Lieutenants Gannon and Devin. Lieutenant Adley worked days. The sergeants, days and nights, were characters. The day sergeants didn't seem very interested in police work. It was their goal to maintain the status quo. Make just enough of an effort so that things did not look too bad. As I remember, their share of the pad was $400 a month and they had no desire to interrupt this cash flow. The night sergeants got half that amount. I assume that there was something for the lieutenants also but I really don't know.

My two uniformed colleagues were ferocious rogues. One of these sergeants and I were walking down North Street one summer evening when a North End resident pulled up in front of the station and parked his car in a no parking area right in front of the station. The man was still in his car when he placed a parking ticket on his windshield. The driver of the car was astounded. He kept saying, "Charlie, Charlie, I know you."

He answered him. "Yeah, I took your money, but now I am giving you a parking ticket."

The sergeant had done a favor for this motorist and been paid for doing it. The motorist believed that because he had taken his money he would always give him a break. The sergeant looked upon it quite differently. The earlier transaction was old business and no obligations remained.

The other night sergeant worked in plain clothes. He was the bag man for the night sergeants and probably the night lieutenants. We got along ok. He was always honest with me, or at least I think he was. The bribe money came from the Angiulo group, the Mafia organization that ran out of the North End. The Angiulos controlled numbers, horse and dog racing, betting and loan sharking. Jerry Angiulo, the head of the family, operated out of a small office on Prince Street nicknamed "The Dog House."

Jerry had a small army of thugs working for him. He not only supplied the pad, he also gave extra cash to the superior officers when they went on vacation and at Christmas time. Sergeant Leone made a pitch to me to take the money. He said that a share of the money was set aside for me and said that if I didn't take it, everybody else would just get a larger share.

I elected not to take the money. I was uncomfortable with that kind of arrangement. I didn't want to restrict my freedom of action. I also didn't believe that Jerry Angiulo did not know to whom his money was going.

***

I became involved in cases right away. I helped search for a gunman who entered the Massachusetts State House and allegedly wounded a Capitol Police officer working security inside the building. I spent hours searching the building with dogs and found nothing. It was later discovered that a Medford police officer, soon to become an MDC police officer, was breaking into the state office building on a regular basis and stealing the answers to the police and other civil service exams. The officer wounded was suspected of being in league with the exam burglars but how he got shot remains a mystery.

***

The North End was and still is, a small and congested area. The population was middle and lower class Italian but young professionals were just beginning to move in. It was an area where a new police sergeant was noticed immediately. On one of my first tours of duty the window of a liquor store on Hanover Street was smashed and several bottles of whiskey that were being displayed were taken. Someone gave us the registration of a car. It was listed to man with an East Boston address. I went to the address and found the car. On the seat of the car were several bottles of whiskey, the same brand that was displayed in the liquor store window. I seized the whiskey bottles and noted the tax stamps on them. I then went back to the store and checked the tax numbers of the bottles that remained in the window; the numbers were consecutive. I arrested the owner of the car, Eugene Testa. He was a big, nasty guy and we took an instant dislike to each other.

I thought it was a clear-cut case, but for some reason, the judge had a problem with the consecutive tax numbers. Nevertheless he found Testa guilty. Testa got no jail time but this was not unusual. Before the trial Testa's brother approached me to see if he could do something to get Eugene off but I would have none of it. It was critical for a new police officer to not back down in any confrontation. If he did, everyone in the North End would know about it. When you were tested you had to shape up. It was the same everywhere, but especially true in the North End. Once you established a reputation, life got a lot easier and there were fewer challenges. I felt that this incident was one of those tests and apparently I passed. Testa later became addicted to drugs and we were to meet many more times, so it was important to have asserted myself early on.

There was a famous story of a new police officer named Ridge. On his first night as a police officer he walked up to a gang standing at a corner in the old West End, an area very similar to the North End. He asked who was the toughest guy among them. One guy raised his hand. Ridge took out his gun and put it to the head of the tough guy and said, "Now I am." This gang never gave Ridge any problems.

***

I worked hard to keep busy in District 1. There was an occasional shooting or robbery but they were tough to solve. It was extremely difficult to get any information. One night while prowling the pushcart market area in Haymarket, I found a basement warehouse open on North Street. I went in and found cases of stylish men's raincoats. This was a butcher shop and I presumed that they were stolen and had them sent to the station. I found the owner and I asked what he was doing with all the raincoats. The owner presented bills of sale for all of them. He owned the coats legitimately but he begged me not to tell anyone. He was selling the coats, pretending that they were hot goods and making a good profit. I gave him back all the coats except one. That missing coat was stolen in the station, I think by one of the lieutenants.

Another night I responded to a man shot on Union Street near the Oyster House resturant. When I got there I saw a man leaning against a building. He had been shot eight times but was still standing. When questioned, he refused to say who shot him. He was taken to the Mass General Hospital where he was operated on to remove the bullets. I stayed and watched the operation from the amphitheatre. It was fascinating. The victim was cut wide open and it seemed to me that he could not possibly survive.

The operation went on for hours. I finally asked one of the doctors what his chances were and he told me that the victim was in no danger at all. I had been listening to the doctors' conversation during the operation and I wondered why they were so casual. Now I knew. The doctor was right, the victim survived, though he still refused to tell us who shot him. He had been hit eight times with .22 caliber bullets.

***

There was a notorious after-hours club in District 1 called the Coliseum Restaurant. I am not sure if it was a Mafia operation or not but there were a lot of Mafia guys in there every night. It was located near Faneuil Hall at the corner of North and Blackstone on the second floor. The restaurant stayed open until 5:00 am. There was no way they could operate legally but they did and quite flagrantly. The operation was so flagrant that the captain wanted to improve appearances since the restaurant was very close to the station house. He issued an order that night sergeants doing a last half must inspect the premises every night and leave a report of his observations. Night sergeants would dutifully go in, stay a few minutes and then go back to the station and write a report saying that no violations of the law were found.

When I was working I would go in as ordered but then I would stay there. This was driving the club owners and the captain crazy. After a few weeks of this, the captain called me into his office and told me that he did not want me harassing the Coliseum. He just wanted me to make a brief appearance and to write a report. I continued to stay anyway. I met a lot of interesting people there including my old adversary, North End Nick, now a made Mafia guy.

***

Around this time I had the opportunity to go to the Dale Carnegie School of Public speaking at the expense of the police department. I was terrified of speaking in public and thought I could only gain by taking this course. I was one of three police officers in the class of about 25 people. The school required that you speak every night; there was no escape. In the beginning I cringed when my turn came but as the course moved on, it came to the point where I could not wait to speak.

Early in the course each student had to speak about an event in his life that moved him or her emotionally. Students were getting up and giving their deepest thoughts and fears and sorrows. It was incredible. There was no way that I was going to expose my innermost feelings to a group of strangers but afterward I did feel comfortable speaking to groups.

It was also a human relations course. At the end of one session we were told to go out and make peace with someone we were having difficulty with and then to report back to the class. In other words we were to turn an enemy into a friend, a pretty tall order.

***

One of my contacts in the Coliseum Restaurant was restaurant owner named Joe Tecce. I was familiar with the Tecce family. Joe had a brother George who was one of the owners of an after-hours place called the Glass Hat on Newbury Street in the Back Bay. Joe had a small restaurant on Salem Street in the North End that was famous for Italian food and for selling wine and liquor in Coke bottles. He did not have a liquor license and no attempt was ever made to stop this practice. Part of the appeal of the restaurant was the illegal sale of the alcohol; his customers liked the idea of illicit booze.

One night I closed down the Coliseum Restaurant. Joe was there and didn't like what I did and we had a confrontation. He told me in front of a lot of people that I would never get into his restaurant. There was no way that I could let that go unanswered. I waited a couple of weeks and then walked into his restaurant on a busy Saturday night with four police officers. I went to every table and seized all the Coke bottles. They all had wine in them. I went into the kitchen and there was a wild scene. I took all the evidence and left the scene with Joe yelling, "You F---- Daley" in front of all his customers.

I sought complaints for the unlawful sale of alcohol and pressed the case. Joe had never been bothered by the police before and had come to believe that he was untouchable. He had friends in court. One of them was his brother-in-law, a heavyweight lawyer, politician and a friend of the presiding justice. He was able to smother the case without anyone's feelings being hurt. After he did so, the brother-in-law approached me in the courthouse to make sure that I was not offended by how the case was settled. He was someone that one could not help but like. I really did not care how the case went and I certainly was not offended. I had made my point.

Joe continued to serve the wine in Coke bottles but he obtained a license for beer and wine sales after my visit. The license was never publicly displayed. As long as the customers thought it was illicit the aura remained.

So for the class assignment, I chose Joe Tecce as the one to improve relations with. I went to his restaurant and told him that I intended to make peace. He was stunned. He said that he was taking a trip to Italy and would bring me back a present. I don't think he was a bad person, just loud. I never did get a present from Italy.

***

Occasionally I made contact with some of the major Mafia operators in the North End. I was having dinner in Giro's restaurant by myself one night when a man sat down at my table and started talking. He said to me, "Do you know who I am?"

I didn't so he said, "I'm Danny." I figured out that this was Danny Angiulo. He came on very smoothly and asked me if I could help him with a problem. His son who was under 25 years old had got into an auto accident with Danny's car. Danny had not paid the extra premium to cover a driver under age 25. I could not believe it. Here was a wealthy guy chiseling on his insurance premiums. I told him that I really could not help him out.

Everybody knew who the made Mafia guys were and that Jerry Angiulo controlled the whole operation from his headquarters on Prince Street known as the Dog House. Some years later the FBI was able to plant bugs in the Dog House using RICO. They destroyed the Angiulo organization and put most of its members in jail. It was an incredible achievement.

***

I saw many results of Mafia activity in the North End. Early one morning I was sent to a crime scene next to the Boston Garden where a young man had been shot to death. He was lying under the overpass. While waiting for homicide to arrive, Detective Eddie Walsh came upon the scene. Eddie and his partner, Tom Connolly, knew all the bad guys in the North End. Eddie quickly identified the victim as a low level gangster named Pallidino. There was some speculation as to who shot Pallidino and why, but there were no clear answers at the time and the murder went unsolved. Many years later a notorious hit-man named John Martorano confessed to killing Pallidino. That was his first victim. Martorano became a serial killer as time went on.

***

About this time armed robbers held up Durgin Park, a famous restaurant in the Faneuil Hall Market area. The robbers tied up the owner and waitresses with the restaurant's famous red and white checked tablecloths and made off with $11,000 from the restaurant safe. I responded and got my picture in the paper. I don't believe that the case was ever solved. I do know that I did not solve it.

It was great to walk the streets of the North End in the summertime. I enjoyed stopping in the Italian pastry shops. Mike's Pastry was my favorite. Both the days and nights were pleasant except it was also the time of the feasts. The feasts had a religious motif but, in reality, they were fundraisers for the local clubs. The first feast was the Fisherman's Feast and their patron saint was Saint Agrippina. This

67

one was followed each week by a different feast honoring a different saint, right up to Labor Day. The last feast was the biggest of them all, the Feast of Saint Anthony.

For each feast it was the custom to parade a statute of the saint through the streets of the North End. Streamers of money would be attached to the statue. Onlookers were encouraged to donate a dollar or two and their donations were pinned to the statue. A band accompanied the statue on its parade. The saint was carried on the shoulders of young men, some of whom were the worst thieves in the North End. They would chant and sing as they marched along. Stands were set up and all kinds of food and mementos. Italian sausages were a big hit and very lucrative for the folks selling them.

The people running the feasts did all kinds of illegal things. They stole electricity from the streetlights. It was difficult tracing the wires backwards to find where they were tapped into the lighting system. They sold beer and wine without a license. When there was trouble it was difficult to take action because of the large crowds. Nevertheless there were times when action had to be taken. I locked up several young men one night during a wild scene. Big crowds ran alongside the police wagon, banging on the side, demanding their release. Even after the prisoners were booked and placed in cells a crowd remained outside the station for a while.

***

Edward Walsh, who would later become Deputy Superintendent and his partner Tom Connolly, spent a lot of time in the North End. They knew all the bad guys and would share their knowledge with other officers. I was riding with Walsh and Connolly when they saw a minor gangland figure walking down Fleet Street carrying a fur coat. It was a warm summer evening and not a night for wearing a fur coat. We stopped, got out, grabbed the suspect and the coat and asked for an explanation. He had none, so he was arrested for receiving stolen goods. It was an easy pinch and in fact was used often to make street arrests, but it was a first for me. They handed the case off to me and I was glad to have the experience. It was a good lesson in practical policing and I never forgot it.

A few years later that guy with the coat and a second individual were shot to death in the Nite Lite Lounge in the North End. A man known as Ralphie owned the lounge. The bodies were gone before the police arrived, but unfortunately for Ralphie, Ed Walsh got word of the murders and arrived just in time to see blood-soaked carpets being removed and new carpets being installed. Ralphie could not explain what happened. He was arrested and charged with accessory after the fact to murder. He was convicted and did his time. He never had anything to say about the two murders.

***

I worked days as the need for sergeants demanded. On one of those days the circus was in town at the Boston Garden. Information came into the station that a man working for the circus was wanted in another state for murder and there were warrants out for his arrest. I was determined to get him. I called a car into the station to take me to the Garden. Angelo Malvone responded. He was big guy and a pretty fair policeman. I told Angelo of my intentions and the two of us headed for the Boston Garden. I picked up the microphone in the car with the intention of having more police officers meet us at the Garden. Angelo said to me, "No need Sarge, we can take care of this ourselves." Against my better judgment, I said OK.

We arrived at the circus and easily found our suspect, the caretaker of the elephants. Arresting him was not so easy. We had a wild fight with all three of us rolling around in the hay at the elephants' feet. The elephants were shrieking all around us. The suspect's head was split when Angelo got in a good shot with his nightstick. We finally got the suspect away from the elephants and back to the station. Another lesson learned. Don't attempt something like this without sufficient manpower.

***

Access to the Boston Garden was one of the advantages of being assigned to District 1. All of the big concerts played there as well as the Celtics and the Bruins. I would see every show either when I was working or doing a detail. I was almost always able to get my family into a show for free. The kids loved to go backstage and so did I.

I had solidified my reputation as a reliable and eager sergeant unafraid to take on entrenched criminal activity. Now if I appeared at a dangerous scene I was automatically expected to be the point man. I didn't mind, despite there being times that other sergeants were present before me. They would quietly duck away when I arrived. I recall one instance on Charter Street where officers had cornered man with a knife. I ended up going into the room to talk him out of it while others, including another sergeant, lent support from the rear. The man gave up the knife and no one was hurt.

**

I started playing handball around this time and played with several great detectives from District 1, including Eddie Butler. He was just as aggressive a handball player as he was a detective. I would also meet my old friend Ed Tobin after my shift and go to Peggy's, a rundown place on State Street. There was always a big crowd there, consisting mostly of cops. We all paid for our drinks. Peggy's husband died leaving her the business and she had to support herself.

The lieutenants did not have much opportunity to get out of the station so their dinners were brought into them. One night Lieutenant Devin opened his dinner and found a dead seagull. We all thought it was a riot but the lieutenant did not see any humor in it. A mischievous sergeant, not me this time, had placed the bird in the box. Lieutenant Devin was forever known afterward as Lieutenant Seagull.

**

As time went on, I realized that the captain was quietly giving me the zing anytime he could. I wanted to work the polls one year on Election Day. It was a pretty good day's pay. At that time, if you wanted to work the polls and you had a day off that day, the detail was always available. On this occasion, the captain changed my day off so that I could not work the polls and gave the assignment to a favored day sergeant. Such was life in the station house.

Suddenly things changed. The captain was transferred out and a new captain, Peter Donovan, took over. He was a quiet guy and he was a friend of Mayor John Collins who was running for re-election. One day the new captain called me into his office and asked me to work a few nights at Collins' headquarters as a volunteer, making calls and addressing envelopes. I refused the captain's request outright. I then went on to tell the captain that I thought his request was inappropriate. I was still under the naive belief that politics had no place in the police department. I was asked to contribute $200 to the Collins campaign and I refused to do that, too.

A Superintendent who owed his job to the mayor was apparently orchestrating the police involvement in Collins' re-election campaign. The day sergeants were asked to contribute $400 each. I heard of no one refusing to give. The rationale was that if you were lucky enough to be working in the North End station and wanted to stay there and continue to collect the monthly from the Mafia, you'd better contribute to the campaign.

I did not really care if I stayed in District 1. I had been there for about two years. I put in a transfer request. I may have been the first sergeant in history to ask for a transfer out of the North End station. The powers that be were glad to oblige and I was gone in two days. This was record time. I was sent to District 11 in Dorchester in November 1966.

District 11, Dorchester

Sergeant

District 11 was probably the least desirable station in the city for a sergeant but I was delighted to go there. The commanding officer was Captain Corbett. When I first reported to him, I am sure that he thought I was crazy. I told him that I was very happy to be in District 11 and that I would work hard and do my very best. Maybe that's why he thought I was crazy.

I was put on nights as I expected and wanted. Only one lieutenant worked nights, Lieutenant Rodday. He was a serious guy, conscientious and wanted to be the boss. We got along fine.

***

There were some disturbing stories circulating about District 11 when I arrived, the most recent one concerning a break into the captain's office the previous Christmas when a quantity of liquor was stolen. The captain could not make a serious investigation without admitting that he had a lot of free Christmas liquor in his office. There was no shortage of suspects but the thieves went undiscovered.

District 11 was located on the corner of Adams Street, a short distance from Dorchester Avenue as it passes through Fields Corner. It was a three-story brick building about 100 years old. The front door was the only door used by the police and the public. To reach it, you had to climb a rather steep set of stairs. The booking desk was behind the front desk so you had to pass the front desk to get to the booking desk and the police guardroom. Prisoners had to be dragged up the front steps, led past the front desk and, after booking, taken down a flight of stairs to the cell block in the basement. The cells still had dirt floors.

I actually had been in that cellblock before. When I was 16 years old I was arrested for drunkenness and put in one of the cells since there were no juvenile facilities at that time. Fortunately I was a juvenile so I escaped having a record. Had I been 17 the arrest would have stayed with me and I would not have been eligible to join the police force.

The District 11 cellblock was a dungeon. Our rules and regulations called for the prisoners to be checked every half hour but it was a long walk down to the cellblock. I suspect that the officers in charge did not see or hear the prisoners in less than one hour intervals. It was truly a hard lockup.

Because there was only one lieutenant working nights, the sergeants had to take the desk and thus be the officer in charge more often than usual. Desk routines are a little different in every station so police clerks who know the drill are a big help to a new sergeant. District 11 had some good ones: Dan Johnson, Joe Smith, Jim Sullivan and Ed Hourihan were some who made life a little easier for me when I had the desk. The boss has his privileges too. He could choose what music to listen to on last halfs midnight shift. I liked classical music so we heard a lot of Beethoven. I am sure that this made the clerks very happy.

***

I had an old childhood friend, Arkie Sutliff, who owned a café in Neponset Circle in Dorchester called the Circle Lounge. When I was working a last half I would stop by about 4:00 am and we would talk for a short time. Sometimes another sergeant would join me. When this sergeant came with me he would not leave as long as a drink was available. Many a morning Arkie had to push him out the door. Not to sound prudish but at no point in my career did I have a drink while working. This sergeant had been a good athlete early in his career but had become frail and did not last too long. He died a few years after I left District 11.

One sergeant in District 11, Al Boyajian, was a physical fitness nut and in great shape. At the time I was a little on the heavy side. He heard that I played handball and challenged me to a match. I beat him and that led to a series of great matches over the years.

***

District 11 was a very big geographical area but at that time not an area of high crime. The restaurants were not in the same league as the North End restaurants. Instead of eating steaks I was eating hamburgers at McDonalds. Gangs were a major problem and took a

---

lot of police time and effort. The captain would give citizens' complaints to the sergeants who then were expected to investigate, solve the problem if possible and submit written reports to the captain.

The detective team working nights consisted of a sergeant and four detectives. The team was really not that busy and did not do much. Their boss was a good man but he liked to take a drink, especially if it was free. His nickname was Two Fingers, because that's how he indicated the level of whiskey to be poured into his glass.

Uniformed officers and detectives could have an uneasy relationship. Many uniformed officers wanted to be detectives because they represented the glamour of police work. On the other hand, detectives were always afraid that a sharp uniformed officer would take a case away from them and put them in a bad light. The detectives had no civil service protection and a good many of them were detectives as a result of political connections.

I got more than my share of cases in District 11 and I became a familiar face in Dorchester Court.

***

I was only in the station a short time when I encountered my first and as it turned out, only mayhem case of my career. Mayhem is described as maliciously injuring an individual with intent to maim or disfigure. Injuries have to be serious or permanent, for example, intentionally cutting off someone's ear. It's a very serious crime, punishable by 20 years in prison. The mayhem incident took place on Washington Street in Dorchester near the intersection of Gallivan Boulevard. A disgruntled former boyfriend attempted to throw sulphuric acid into his former girlfriend's face. He missed and instead the acid landed in the face of the woman's friend. I met the two women at Carney Hospital and got the details. I had no problem finding the assailant and arrested him shortly afterwards. The woman who was hit with acid did not look that bad on the day of the assault, but a few days later her face looked horribly burned.

The case went through the lower courts and the grand jury with no problems. Indictments were returned and the case was set for trial in the Superior Court. The trial judge was well into his 70s. Even in his prime he was a poor judge but now he was just plain incompetent. A well-known criminal lawyer, Joe Sax, who was on the down side of his career, represented the defendant. He came back from some lunch breaks looking a bit glassy eyed. This made him even more confrontational than usual.

The government's case was very strong and started off well. Both women made strong identifications, which was easy because they knew the defendant. Then the defense dropped a bombshell. The defendant was an amateur photographer and had taken photos of himself and his former girlfriend engaged in sexual activity. I saw the photographs and they were truly obscene. Joe Sax demanded that these photos be admitted in evidence and given to the jury. The DA objected, correctly in my opinion. He argued that there were no photos of the victim and the defendant. Even if the photos had been admissible, that did not give the defendant the right to throw acid in someone's face.

Nevertheless, the judge allowed the photos to be admitted. He was completely intimidated by Joe Sax. The jury was offended by the photos and reached an inappropriate conclusion: that the victim, the girlfriend's friend, was also involved in sexual activities with defendant. They returned a not guilty verdict.

The father of the injured girl was not in court when the photos were introduced. After the trial he asked me how the jury could have come back with a not guilty verdict. I made up a story and hoped that he did not make any further inquiries. Justice was not served in this case. The only good that came out of the case was that the woman who had the acid thrown in her face fully recovered.

***

Most nights there was only one sergeant on the street—me. I usually traveled alone in a marked car. I chased everything. Many times I was on the scene before the arrival of the sector car. This was a mistake on my part. I was doing the patrolman's work and making their decisions for them. Had positions been reversed I would have resented this interference by a sergeant.

One night I was first on the scene of a fatal shooting on Rosseter Street. When I entered a second floor apartment I found a man lying on the floor. He had been shot but was still alive. I leaned over him and asked him, "Who shot you?" He was unable to respond. I soon

---

realized I was in a brothel. A few prostitutes appeared in the doorway but no one came up with any good explanation of the shooting. Other police officers soon arrived. I sent all those present to the station. An ambulance arrived and took the victim to the hospital.

While back at the station I received word that the victim died. I learned another lesson than night. Bad news cannot be delivered in bits and pieces. It only prolongs the agony. It is the police officers' responsibility to tell those involved the truth and get it over with. I am not suggesting that one should be cruel and unfeeling but the sooner those affected face the facts, the better they are able to deal with the situation.

When the victim died, homicide took over the investigation. I was now out of the case. The homicide officers never kept me in the loop though they should have because information flows from the bottom up. If they had brought me into the case I would have made a big effort to find out more information. I heard they were unable to build a case against any suspect. Later when I was in vice I saw one of the girls who was in the house that night working the streets. It occurred to me that the shooting on Rosseter Street was probably a dispute between a pimp and prostitute.

***

About 2:00 am one night two uniformed officers were driving through the Savin Hill area near a park when a young woman came running out of the woods and up to a police car. She was stark naked. The officers brought her to the station, got her some clothes, then we listened to her story.

She recounted that she met a man downtown who told her he was a cop. He forced her to get into his car then took her to the park in Savin Hill. He tore her clothes off and tried to rape her. She believed that he really was a cop because she saw his gun. Somehow she was able to get out of his car and ran naked to the passing police car.

We discovered that this young woman was a prostitute. The officers who brought her in backed away because they did not want to get involved with a potentially controversial case concerning a fellow officer. I took the case from there. I took her back out in a marked car to the Savin Hill area in the hopes of finding the individual who attempted to rape her. I was reluctant to involve other officers because of the possibility that a real policeman may have been her assailant. As we drove down Savin Hill Avenue, The young woman spotted a man walking on the sidewalk. She pointed to him and shouted, "That's him!"

He was in plain clothes. I stopped the car, got out, approached him and asked him if he was a police officer. He said that he was. I told him to give me his gun and to get into the car. He did both and we headed back to the station. Once there he admitted being with the young woman but denied trying to rape her. I got his name and identification and told him that if the young woman stuck with her story, I would be forced to seek complaints against him. I allowed him to leave the station.

I told the girl to meet me at the station at 8:00 am and we would go to the courthouse together and set the case in motion. I made out a report to the captain but did not deliver it. As this was not my first experience with police officers on the wrong side of the law, I could not afford to take any chances. I really did not expect her to come to the station in the morning but I wanted to be ready if she did. I told no one else what happened.

There was a new captain at the station, my old mentor from District 14, Mickey McDonald. He saw me hanging around in the morning long after my tour was over and asked me why I was still there. I ducked the question with an evasive answer. Just as I was about to leave, the young woman walked through the door. I had no choice at this point but to tell the captain what was going on. I went into his office and explained the situation. He backed up my plan. Then I went with the victim to Dorchester Court and filed complaints against the officer for attempted rape and kidnapping.

When the trial date came, the only witness, the young woman, was nowhere to be found. A new court date was set. I checked every possible location for her but she had disappeared. I didn't know it at the time but prostitutes often moved from city to city on a regular circuit, usually after they have been arrested a few times. Her pimp must have decided that it was time for her to move on and she was gone.

I was getting criticism about my handling of the case. The department was in a bind. We had an accusation against an officer and we could neither clear nor convict him. A vice officer got some information that the alleged victim was in Hartford so the superintendent decided to send a captain there to find and interview her. He was unable to find her. However, newspapers were now aware of the incident and were asking questions, so we had to keep trying.

The superintendent had no choice but to send me to look for her, but not without supervision. Another sergeant, Jack Everett accompanied me. He was a good guy, but like the captain, did not really want to find anybody. We flew to Hartford and I made a good effort to locate the witness. The best I did was to find out her real name and criminal history. I learned that she was not going to talk to us and that she did not want to come to Boston to testify. The case died and I was not unhappy with the outcome. Nobody gains with this type of case. The victim was unreliable and the defendant was a police officer. And I lost more points with the superintendent.

***

I became interested in learning how to obtain search warrants. At that time, uniformed officers were not encouraged to seek them. Instead, they were encouraged to wait until the next day and ask a detective or sergeant to apply for them. John "Snappy" Holland, the clerk of the court at Dorchester District Court, was willing to help anyone who wanted to learn. His advice was simple: just state why you believe the articles you are searching for are there. It was great practical advice and I never forgot it.

***

About this time a tragedy occurred in District 11. An officer who was a clerk on nights took his own life. He was a smart and conscientious worker, a college graduate, who had a family to support. He had a very sick wife and unknown to any of us, had severe financial problems. Apparently it became too much for him. He shot himself with his own revolver. This was a complete shock to us because none of us had any idea that he was suffering this kind of stress.

There were some good, hard working officers in District 11. Bill Kelley was very good at finding stolen cars. I rode with him one night when he spotted a stolen car and took off after it. It was a wild ride. I don't remember if we caught the stolen car but I do remember that it scared the hell out of me. He was extremely aggressive and so enthusiastic that no one wanted to curb his spirit. He later made sergeant and was with me when I was a lieutenant in the Roxbury station. He always did more than was asked of him.

A new lieutenant, Aldo, came to District 11 working nights. He was in my class at the academy and the first in our class to make lieutenant. One night a prisoner was brought into the station when we were both working. This prisoner turned out to be the brother of a friend of mine who was also a state representative. I got a call from my friend asking me to help his brother. I thought since I was more familiar with this district than the lieutenant he would take my suggestions as how to deal with this problem but he refused outright. I didn't like it but he was the lieutenant and the boss. I thought about it later and realized that he did the right thing in refusing special treatment for my friend's brother.

Lieutenant Aldo was not a bad guy but he could be rigid and sometimes show a lack of common sense. An example of this occurred one very cold and snowy winter night. A young boy about 14 years old came into the station around 9:00 pm. He was freezing and wanted to stay awhile in the station to warm up. Aldo threw him out. I went out and took the kid home in a police car.

***

Police officers are always being tempted. I went to a house on Pleasant Street to take a report because all of the sector cars were busy. It was a relatively minor matter that could be easily handled by one officer. A young lady greeted me and stood very close to me -- a lot closer than she had to -- as I took down the information. It would have been easy to encourage her and it was tempting but the moment passed and she quickly became a citizen reporting a minor crime.

I was a very enthusiastic sergeant. I came to learn that too much enthusiasm can get you into trouble. I was at a fire, a possible arson one night when a citizen came up to me and gave me a can of gasoline that had apparently been used to start the fire. I tried to find out who the arsonist was. I didn't find a suspect at that time but was determined to make further investigation, so I took the gas can into the station. A short time later an irate fire chief came through the door and yelled at me for taking the gas can. It caught me by surprise. I guess I had intruded on the arson squad's jurisdiction. He took the can and marched off. (The arsonist could rest easy. It was very rare for the arson squad to catch an arsonist and in this case, as usual, they did not.)

**

The department had instituted a performance evaluation process for superior officers. My captain did not give me much of a mark. The process was flawed, as there were no real criteria. The evaluations didn't seem to reflect the qualities we thought were important. Police performance was the last thing considered. When I saw that the evaluation given to the worst of the day sergeants was higher than mine I was shocked. The day sergeants all got higher marks than the night sergeants. I was not happy but there was little I could do about it. After a short time the evaluations were recognized as a farce and discontinued.

**

In the mid 1960s there was considerable racial strife in the country and Boston was no exception. In June of 1967, riots broke out in the city, triggered by a demonstration led by mothers at the Grove Hall welfare office. The city was completely unprepared for this kind of unrest. The police just made it worse. A high-ranking police officer ordered the welfare office cleared and forcibly removed the mothers.

There were riots, fires and disorder for several days. The police department eventually got its act together and put every officer out on the street. (Well, almost every officer; there were always some who managed to stay out of trouble and the riots were no exception.)

I was stationed with a squad in the Dudley MBTA station area just outside a barroom. This was at the heart of the black community. The first night of rioting was really intense. We heard gunshots and had some bottles thrown at us, but we managed to maintain order in our small sector. I am embarrassed to say that I saw very few ranking officers on the street during most of the turbulence.

**

During my time in District 11, Mayor Collins left office. It was 1968. When he was mayor I had a small amount of weight in the department as I had a brother-in-law who was close to him. Kevin White was the new mayor. He came to the station one night and appeared to show some real interest in the department. But his legacy in dealing with the police, as I saw it, was to politicize the leadership. It was rumored that high-ranking police jobs not covered by civil service were up for sale. Political contributions in this time were commonly delivered in envelopes filled with cash.

The mayor had come to the station in response to the stabbing of a black man at a football game at Town Field in Dorchester. I was working on the case and got some information that a South Boston guy was responsible. His name was Kevin O'Neil and he had a bad reputation. We had no problems arresting him and had him in custody that night. I was able to get the case as far as Superior Court but at trial the victim would not make a solid identification of O'Neil and the case went down. I can only assume that the victim was either paid or terrorized. Later on I came to know Kevin O'Neil as an intimate of famed mobster Whitey Bulger.

***

I was now taking the lieutenant's exam every two years and getting closer to passing it each time. There was still a problem of short time in rank as sergeant, since time spent in rank was a big part of your score. The truth was that I really enjoyed being a working sergeant. But I could be short on common sense. One night I went to the Fireman Post at Florian Hall in Dorchester responding to a report of a disturbance. As usual I was riding alone in a marked police car and arrived before other officers. Florian Hall is big and was crowded this Friday night. Instead of waiting for other units to arrive, I walked right in. The manager, Charlie O'Rourke of Boston College fame, met me. He told me that a group at one of the tables was causing trouble and he pointed it out to me.

As I approached them the manager turned on the house lights creating a scene that I was not looking for. There were about eight young guys sitting at the table and all had been drinking. I leaned over the table and told them in my best authority voice that they were out of order and would have to leave. There was silence and a moment of indecision and then they got up and left the hall. Had they decided not to leave I would have had a big problem. As they were leaving I heard the sirens of police cars responding and it was a welcome sound.

One night a man came into the station and complained that he had just been robbed in a brothel on Columbia Road. He described the area and the location as well as the prostitute who had robbed him.

I went back and dug up information on the woman who I believed robbed him. The victim was single and willing to appear in Court. He was indifferent to any harm that his reputation might suffer. The woman was brought to the station. I told him, if that was the woman, he was to point at her with his right hand and say, "That's her." If it was not the girl, he was instructed to point with his left hand and say, "That's her." It was my hope and expectation that if she was not the thief, she would object and give up the real robber. The victim made the ID with his right hand. She was arrested and convicted. The victim testified to all the details without embarrassment.

***

About this time, a friend, Henry Berry, started a business selling paper goods and asked me if I would be willing to work for him part time making deliveries. I agreed and it became a two-man business. We set up shop on Thayer Street in the South End. It was rough going at first but business steadily improved and Henry and I made an agreement. If business went well we would take a cruise to Bermuda at the end of the year. The business went very well. My wife and I took the cruise, but Henry could not leave the business. Eventually he asked me if I wanted to work full time. I did not. The police job was my life and I did not want to work for a friend. I stayed a few more years working part time and we parted friends. The business eventually became a multimillion-dollar business. But I had no regrets.

Vice Squad

Sergeant Detective

In spite of my disagreements and arguments over evaluations with the superintendent, I must have been doing something right. I received a call from Lieutenant Detective Jordan, head of the vice squad in November 1968. He asked me if I was interested in transferring to his vice squad. I was indeed interested and on November 11, 1968 I was transferred to vice and narcotics.

The working hours of the vice squad -- from 6:00 pm to 3:00 am -- were very tough on family life. There were no formal role calls but we all pretty much got there on time. We were eager to work and I needed no prompting. I was the head of a new team consisting of two detectives, Jake Bird and Joe Smith, both of whom came to the squad when I did. I had worked with Joe in District 11 and knew that he was a good detective with many informants. I did not know Jake but he turned out to be a good detective. At that point I had been a police officer for about 17 years, the last seven as a sergeant, yet I knew very little about drugs, prostitution or gaming. I would not have recognized heroin if it was placed right in front of me. The officer in charge of the vice squad at night was my old mentor from District 16, Lieutenant Joe Rowan. He and a couple of veteran vice guys, Lynsky and Currier, gave us a one-hour crash course on drugs and sent us out to do battle.

We had a clear mandate. We were to deal with illegal drugs, gaming, alcoholic beverage violations, prostitution, overcrowding in clubs and minors drinking in clubs, all in the Combat Zone, the center of vice activity in Boston. The area boasted XXX movie theaters and peep shows, prostitutes, drugs and gambling.

Information came into the vice unit every day, but as everyone knows, the new guys do not get the best leads so we had to scratch all we got from the street. The three of us were willing and hardworking, so it did not take us long to get into the game. We set up shop on the third floor of the Paramount Hotel located at Boylston and Washington Streets, an area of much drug and other illegal activity in the Combat Zone. From our room we could see drug deals taking place. One member of our team stayed in the hotel room and the other two went out on the street in plain clothes. We communicated by radio. We would pick up the buyers a short distance from the intersection and when we had enough customers we would go back and pick up the dealers.

Most of the sales were of marijuana. It was great to be able to get real close to the customers and dealers when in plain clothes, a stark contrast to being in uniform, which I had been wearing up to this point. Once in a while when we identified ourselves as police officers, a suspect would try to run away, but it was very rare that someone actually got away. The vice squad consisted of about 14 detectives. Some worked undercover and I never saw them. Some were there because of political connections and others worked hard.

About this time the use of drugs began escalating. Marijuana was in general use and there was a small core of heroin users. Cocaine was becoming common and was often found in nightclubs like the Sugar Shack on Boylston Street. Possession of marijuana, even one cigarette, was a felony and even being present where marijuana was illegally kept was an arrestable offense.

My team went everywhere: nightclubs, dance halls, any suspected after-hours establishment, any suspected gaming location and every other place we could think of where violations of the vice laws might occur. When things got quiet we went after the prostitutes who were almost always out on the street. It was incredibly interesting work and we began to make a lot of arrests. No one ever told me to lay off any location or any one.

***

Drug arrests came easier with experience. The street buyer was an easy shot. Once we had the prisoner back in the office we would try to make deals to find the seller or for locations where large quantities of drugs could be found. Many times the prisoner would be willing to give somebody up if he could get a deal. If what was offered was solid, we would make the deal and the prisoner would walk. We could still come back at him or her if what was given up was phony, but that rarely happened. Heroin junkies almost always talked but they never gave up their personal connection. They were really sick cats but I never felt much compassion for them.

With information received from prisoners and confirmed by our own observations, we were able to apply for and get search warrants almost every night. If we were successful, arrests were made and drugs seized. It was not unusual to be still working at 5:00 am. We worked a five-day week; on Sundays, only a couple of hours.

It took me a while but I finally figured out that there were payoffs being made to members of the vice squad. A few sergeants would take off by themselves every so often, usually around the first of the month. I found out later that they would go to Chinatown to see the main man involved in organized gambling. Every club in Chinatown had gaming going on and they could not operate without police protection. The games were very rarely hit. It was an unspoken rule. From our perspective it was not that they were protected, but it was more of a cultural accommodation.

Some members of vice kept pretty much to themselves. Traditionally narcotic guys do not talk much about their contacts. Drug investigations are by nature a secret business and drug officers tend to keep their informants to themselves. In other vice operations such as gaming, it seemed that everybody kept their mouth shut.

This fact hit home the first Christmas I was in vice. My team and I found a minor drinking in a notorious Combat Zone club and processed a violation against the club. I sensed that my two partners were not enthusiastic about the complaint. They had long faces on but said nothing. When I got back to the office I found out why. When I gave my report to the lieutenant, he remarked that I did not have to harass the owner of the club. He was obviously not pleased. It was then I realized that the club owner had recently given the officers a Christmas present and now they were embarrassed because I busted him. I was very disappointed in the lieutenant. He should have known better.

***

There were some sections of the city where drugs were prevalent, including parts of Beacon Hill. There was a lot of action on Anderson Street near Sal's Market. It was tough going for us to catch anyone, though. The streets were narrow, there were no available dwellings where we could set up and just no places to hide. A sale could be made right in front of us and we would not know it. The primary drug in this area was heroin. It could be hidden a short distance away, perhaps in a drainpipe or discarded cigarette package and the buyer would pick it up when the coast was clear. We had to watch from a distance while sitting in a police car. Buyers and sellers knew when we were around even in an unmarked car.

One night we seized a modest amount of marijuana in executing a search warrant. The culprit was taken to the office for processing by uniformed officers. Before we went back to our office we executed a second search warrant. When we left the car to make this second raid we left the drugs from the first raid in the unmarked police car. I thought that we had locked car but we may not have. The second raid was unsuccessful. We found nothing and returned to our car. When Detective Bird checked the rear seat for the seized drugs, they were gone.

We were trying to figure out where the drugs went when the lawyer for the culprit asked to talk privately. He said that his client's friend had witnessed the first raid and arrest. This friend saw us place the drugs in our car and then followed us to where we executed the second warrant. While we were doing so, this friend got into our car and stole the seized drugs. Now we had to decide what to do with this information. We could easily have replaced the marijuana to make the case go to trial, but the defendant would have been able to say that they were not the drugs we seized from him. None of us would ever have gone so far as to commit perjury, so the case was dismissed. Nevertheless it was embarrassing and we were careless. Another lesson learned.

***

Detectives, especially inexperienced ones, sometimes get the attitude that they are invincible and I fell victim to this syndrome one Sunday night. Both of my partners went home early but I hung around and drifted down to a disco dance club in the South End called the Boston Tea Party. I saw a dancer out on the dance floor who appeared high on drugs and I decided to arrest him. There were about 150 patrons on the dance floor. I walked out on the floor and identified myself and told him to come with me. Junkies were generally not aggressive but there were some exceptions and this fellow was one. He resisted arrest him and I grabbed him. The next thing I knew he was yelling, "Don't let this f---- guy take me!" The crowd moved in but I was able drag the suspect to a nearby office. It was a scary scene. I was plenty worried and called for help. Uniformed guys arrived quickly and I was able to get out with the prisoner, but it was a stupid thing to do. When making an arrest it is better to have several officers present.

Other times we made big scores. One night we raided an apartment on Westland Avenue in the Back Bay and got bundles of heroin. After the raid, we held the occupants in another room and set up shop, posing as dealers. As buyers came to the door we would invite them in and then arrest them. When the phone rang we made contracts to buy and sell. That night we arrested five or six buyers before we closed down.

One of the buyers was carrying a gun. This guy kept looking at us as if he were trying to tell us something. It was obvious to us that he was an undercover cop. Once we figured it out we signalled to him that we knew he was with the DEA. Then he started to play the tough guy so we would arrest him too. He was arrested, booked and went to court with everybody else. He was using a fake ID and defaulted at trial time. We dismissed his case and made sure his gun was returned. I never knew his name but we met several years later and he told me that after that arrest he had great success in infiltrating the drug network and made major buys on his own. Later I also came across the dealer that we had busted. He told me that he had completely fallen for the federal officer's undercover scam and had only heard of it much later.

***

Detective Joe Smith, who had come with me from District 11 still had many informants in Dorchester and we were able to put them to good use in an investigation involving the death of a fellow police officer. This officer, Charlie McNabb, had recently been killed in Brighton. He was a motorcycle officer and a 10 year veteran on the force. He had walked into a bookie operation on Commonwealth Avenue near Brighton Avenue when three armed men came in with the intent to rob the bookie. Charlie apparently tried to prevent the robbery but was shot to death by the holdup men. The investigation was going nowhere and there were no suspects.

Joe Smith got a call from one of his informants who said that he knew of three men, William Lydon, Lee Grantham and Abbot Blake who were doing a lot of holdups in the Boston area. The informant also said that these three men were living in a house in East Boston owned by a shady individual named Al. Joe Smith knew Al as a guy who had cooperated with the police in the past. Al had his own operation going, pills, pornography, maybe counterfeiting, who knows what else.

We got in touch with Al who told us that he did have three guys renting his third floor apartment. He said he thought these guys were the ones who shot the police officer. He also told us that the three had orchestrated a holdup in Lynn the previous day and that one of them had been shot in the hand. We checked with the Lynn Police Department. There had been a holdup the day before and one of the holdup men had indeed been shot in the hand. The informant's information checked out in all respects. Joe Smith knew that Billy Lydon had a reputation of being a dangerous guy.

We knew that as vice officers, not homicide guys, we were operating way out of our area. But police officers do not like giving up an opportunity to grab a cop killer, so we made our plans and moved ahead. The date was November 26, 1968; the time was 2:00 am. We discussed our options for about an hour. I made the decision that we would hit the house about 5:00 am. This is a good time for a forced entry. Occupants would be asleep, maybe half drunk, giving us every advantage. I called Lieutenant Rowan and brought him into the picture. I also called Detective Bob Fawcett, a very good detective from East Boston and the homicide officer who had the case, Sergeant Frank Whalen.

At that time it was within the law to make a forced entry without a warrant and make an arrest for a felony. I was a little concerned that homicide might be offended that we were moving ahead in this matter, but I need not have worried. They were pleased to pass this dangerous and dirty job to someone else. I got shotguns and bulletproof vests. Jake Bird and I put them on. We were ready to go.

We got to the house right on schedule. Al gave me the keys to the apartment and promptly disappeared. Jake, Fawcett and I crept up the stairs. Fawcett opened the door and he and I entered the apartment. I went right and Fawcett went left. Jake Bird followed me with a shotgun into a bedroom. All of us had our guns drawn and our adrenaline was really pumping. I stood right over a guy sleeping in a bed and put my gun to his head. It was Billy Lydon. He was stunned and for a second, did not move. On a table next to the bed was a .38 caliber revolver. I did not see it but Jake Bird did and went for it. Lydon lunged for it too, but Jake got it before Lydon did.

Lydon went crazy and there was a wild fight. By this time there were more cops in the room and we were able to get him under control and in handcuffs. There was one other guy in the apartment, Lee Grantham and he came easy. Two days later we got the third man, the one who had been shot in the hand.

Once the police have control in these situations they have a tremendous advantage but it only lasts for a short time. There is a window wherein the suspects are confused and frightened; this is the time to get information without hurting anybody. We shout at them and threaten them and can usually get the information we need. I put tremendous pressure on Grantham. He admitted that Lydon was the one who shot the officer and that he and Lydon had been involved in a holdup the day before and another guy with them had been shot. None of this was admissible but the defendants now know that we know we have the right culprits. It also gives us the opportunity to get one suspect to turn against the other. These scenes are not pretty but they are effective. Police officers cannot always be the good guys. If you don't have the stomach for these operations you are in the wrong business.

Even though we believed that these men had been responsible for McNabb's murder, we were never able to gather sufficient evidence to prosecute them for the killing. Actually, that was homicide's responsibility and they did not come through. We were able to stick them with four armed robberies and they all did long jail terms. Like I said, vice took any case that came along. At least my squad did. I found out later that when I put the gun to Lydon's head, he thought I was a killer sent by bookies to murder him, which under the circumstances was a reasonable assumption.

***

The longer we stayed in vice the better investigators we became. If I wanted to get close to a suspect or a location, I would put on my work boots and work clothes; carry a lunch bag and sometimes a newspaper under my arm. Construction workers are everywhere and no one thinks of them as undercover police officers. It never failed to work.

Complaints about drug usage, gambling and illegal drinking came in on a regular basis to the commander of the vice squad. The drug complaints were distributed among us. The gaming and illegal alcoholic beverage complaints were kept secret. The vice commander would have his closest associate (sometimes an undercover guy) investigate these complaints to see if they were valid. If they were, warrants were obtained. When the decision was made to hit one of these places, members of the squad were instructed to meet the commander at a place like the Greyhound Bus station parking lot. It was always a surprise to get one of these orders. We never knew where we were going until the last second. Ten or twelve of us would be present. The target location would be disclosed about 15 minutes before we moved. From that time on no one left the group until the warrant was served.

There was a good reason for all this secrecy. The information had to be protected until the last minute so it wouldn't be compromised. You never knew if there was a member of the unit who might try to pass the information along. Secrecy was also important for the safety of those involved and for the success of the operation.

Life continued in vice. One night Joe, Jake and I walked into Jacques Bar and Lounge in Bay Village on a routine inspection. It was and still is, a popular gay bar. It was crowded as usual. I am not sure of what happened next. One of the owners, Henry Vara, asked Jake and me for help throwing out a troublesome customer. Meanwhile Joe was snooping around the bar looking for violations of their license. As we neared the door with the unwanted customer, another bar patron started a fight with the guy we were trying to throw out. At that point Joe re-entered the picture. He decided that the guy Jake and I were throwing out was the real problem and Joe started fighting him.

There was a uniformed police officer doing a detail in the bar who did not know Joe Smith was a police officer, as we were in plain clothes. When he saw Joe fighting he thought that Joe was the problem and started swinging his nightstick at Joe. It was chaos and finally, when we got it all straightened out, Henry Vara was screaming that Joe Smith could start World War III. I think there was an element of truth in that.

A similar scene occurred one night in the Combat Zone in the Downtown Lounge. Joe wandered off and got into a dispute in the men's room. This time he did very well and came out with a prisoner and a fistful of pills.

One night we were just finishing our tour and heading back to headquarters when we passed a notorious after-hours spot called the Pioneer Club on Tremont Street. It was a jazz club that had been operating for many years. It had been allowed to operate with no interference and seemed to have some kind of immunity. A guy named Shag Taylor whom I did not know ran it. As we passed the club, there were four or five people in line waiting to get in. On impulse, I stopped the car, got out and went to the back of the line. Joe and Jake remained in the car.

The door opened and I entered with the group into a hallway. There was a second locked door leading into the club and this door had a window where those inside could see who was in the hallway. I started to get some suspicious looks from guys inside who apparently worked for the club and were observing me through the window. They were stalling and asking who I was. It seemed that no one knew me, so they refused to open the door. I finally announced that I was the police. That did not work. The group standing with me was getting very nervous. I did not get in and neither did anyone in the group, at least not when I was there. In retrospect, I never should have tried to get into the club without a lot of preparation. I moved on impulse and showed bad judgment.

Once I started on the Pioneer Club, I did not have the sense to stop. I made out my reports and the next morning I was in Roxbury Court seeking a complaint against the club for denying entrance by an investigator of the Licensing Board, which I was by statute. The clerk of court and many other court personnel, along with lawyers, reporters and musicians, all hung out at the Pioneer Club. He denied my complaint and suggested that I should go after the Harvard Club. The case was not important to me and I had no desire to go over the head of the clerk of court. Nevertheless, it caused quite a stir in police circles. It turned out the Pioneer Club was a sacred place.

***

On the drug side of vice, I found I had to have complete confidence in the officers I worked with. One key reason was that it is so easy to steal at a drug raid. Drugs and money can easily be concealed in one's pockets and it is impossible for the officer in charge to watch everybody. I can only imagine the effect of ordering all officers present to empty their pockets. But if you can't trust them, they should not be there.

When we seized money it was my practice to lay it all out on a table and then count it out with the defendant standing there as well as all the detectives at the scene. In that way there was never a dispute as to how much money was seized. Once in awhile we would have so much money that we could not get the count right. At that time we were not required to deposit seized drugs into a central depository. Instead, we kept all the evidence in our lockers. It was the honor system.

***

One of our detectives, Arthur Lynsky, had been in the business for a long time and was very successful at dealing with drug addicts. He had an incredible army of informants. He was off one night when a young man came in and asked for Arthur. He said that he wanted to give him some information. I told him that Arthur was off that night and asked if I could help. He hesitated and then launched into his story. The informant said that he had just come from an apartment in Brighton. The occupants of this apartment had a good stash of marijuana and plenty of cash. The cash was in the form of $10,000 bills and they had seven of them. He told me that one of the guys in the apartment had stolen a Porsche sedan and had found the money in the glove compartment. It was a wild story, but the informant insisted that it was true. I decided to act on the information. It never entered my mind to call Arthur, though I was criticized later for not doing so.

I sat down with my two partners, Jake and Joe and we talked the situation over. There was no question that a search warrant was needed. Once I completed the search warrant application we called our two favorite detectives in Brighton, Kennedy and O'Malley, got a clerk of the court out of bed and the warrant was issued. We arrived at the apartment about 10:30 pm and got in with little trouble. In the apartment were three men and one woman. There was evidence of marijuana use. We looked everywhere but found no money. We were in the apartment a long time, perhaps two hours. I did not want to give up but it was getting to the point where I had no other choice.

Joe Smith took one of the occupants of the apartment aside and asked me if he could have few minutes alone with him. I said sure. Joe took him into the bathroom and had him strip naked. Joe checked him out all over and found nothing. Just before he told the guy to dress Joe noticed that he was curling his toes. Joe reached down, straightened out his toes and a $10,000 bill fell out. Now we knew that the informant had been telling the truth. We put some pressure on the other occupants and found two more $10,000 bills.

They told us that three other men had been in the apartment before we got there. Of these three, one of them, a man named Howard, had stolen the Porsche; the other two were brothers. After they stole the car, the three of them headed back to the Brighton apartment where they dumped the car, smoked a few joints and divided up the money. The two brothers took $20,000 each and Skar took $30,000. The two brothers promptly left for Logan Airport where they purchased tickets to Los Angeles using one of the $10,000 bills to pay the fare and left on the next flight.

Howard had left the apartment on an errand shortly before we got there. Before he left he gave his share of the money to a friend, one of the apartment occupants, to hold until he got back. We continued to gather more in information and learned the identity of the two brothers. We notified the FBI in California and the brothers were arrested as fugitives from justice upon their arrival. It took us a few days to find Howard but we did and he was taken into custody.

When we returned to our office that night some of the 911 operators came down to see the $10,000 bills as there were very few in circulation. I myself had never seen one before. No one wanted to take responsibility for the money, so I put the $10,000 bills in my wallet and went home. I woke up my wife and told her that I wanted to give her a present. I gave her one of the bills but made sure that I got it back from her by the morning - before the store's opened.

The next day I went to court carrying $30,000 in my wallet. I met a charming old rogue detective, John Flaherty, and he asked if he could see the bills. I handed him one. He checked it and handed it back to me. A second later I looked and he had given me a $1 bill. He soon surrendered the big bill and we all had a good laugh.

The Porsche was recovered a couple of days later a short distance from the Brighton apartment. Though the car had been stolen a week earlier, the owner never reported it stolen. We were able to track down the owner in Boston. I had a long conversation with him and he told me that he was in the process of getting a divorce and decided to convert some of his assets to cash to conceal them. He chose $10,000 bills. He was under the impression that these bills were registered and could not be used by anyone but the rightful owner. Unfortunately he was mistaken. The bills were bearer bills, just like a one-dollar bill.

Apparently he felt that reporting the car and money stolen would jeopardize his scheme to hide assets. He was happy that we could give him three of the bills back but did not seem too concerned about the rest of the money.

The case against the three men was not major. Using a motor vehicle without authority, simple larceny of the $70,000 and possession of Class D drugs (marijuana). None of these charges was likely to result in a jail sentence. The major case was the federal one: transporting stolen goods (the $10,000 bills the brothers took) across state lines. The brothers were to be tried in California. The case got a lot of positive press for the department.

The night squad boss, Lieutenant Rowan, complained that I did not give Arthur a chance to become involved in the case. At that point I didn't care about not involving Arthur. We had made the arrest and it made sense to follow the case through to its conclusion. Arthur was even upset when Joe and I received federal summonses to appear in Los Angeles and testify, all expenses paid. This was the second trip I made in the course of my police duties and I was destined to make many more.

My wife, Eleanor, was struggling to take care of our five children and needed a break so I elected to take her with me. Howard also was summoned to Los Angeles, but he was going as a prisoner in custody of federal marshals. He did not want to go and said that if he was forced to, he would not testify. He made threats to the effect that a bomb would be planted on the plane. This made my wife very nervous. I assured her that Howard would not be on the same plane as we would be on.

When we got to the airport I was stunned to see him getting on the same plane. My wife was a good sport and got on the plane anyway. She later told me that she kept hearing the ticking of a bomb the whole trip. She was terrified all the way across the United States. On arrival she started shaking and could not stop. She had to stay in bed for 24 hours before she recovered.

I had a good relationship with the FBI and had a friend in the Boston office. When we arrived in LA we were met by a local agent who took us to a local hotel and gave us every attention, even inviting us to his home. My wife liked LA and so did Joe Smith. We stayed in LA for the duration of the trial, about ten days. Both defendants were found guilty. During the trial they were allowed out on bail. When they were found guilty the judge allowed them to go home before sentencing them. They both disappeared.

Friends of the defendants had cashed a couple of the $10,000 bills in California at a local bank. The owner of the stolen car sued the bank to try to be reimbursed for the stolen bills but the bank prevailed since the bills were legal tender. After the case was over the victim got back about $45,000 of the $70,000 stolen.

***

We continued to chase down prostitutes. Jake Bird was pretty good at picking them up. He was a young guy with a new sports car. Escort services were also easy targets because they had to advertise. The ads were obvious, so it just remained for us to call the published telephone numbers, act like customers, make the date, line up the hotel room (always available to us) and wait for the hookers to arrive. I played the customer one night in the Hotel Essex. The girl arrived in remarkably tight clothes. The idea was to have a conversation about the price for having sexual relations and then make an agreement. When that was done, the arrest was made and the support team called into the room.

There were always horror stories where the support team was late in arriving at the scene and the sexual activity had gone too far. The detectives involved called it "taking one for the city." It was all in the line of duty. I told my wife of my encounter with the prostitute in the Essex. She was not amused.

Days in vice had different priorities than nights did. Bookies were the big target in the daytime. To get the bookies, undercover officers had to be sent into barrooms and had to drink. A cardinal rule for these guys was that, if served a bottle of beer, don't drink out of the bottle because of a fear of drinking beer from a dirty glass. This was a dead giveaway that you were a cop. Pour the beer in the glass. Many officers were harmed by this duty because they spent so much time in bars. Some became alcoholics. It took me a long time to find out who the daytime vice officers were. Lieutenant Jordan had a penchant for secrecy and kept these operations close to the vest.

There were cases and cases of seized beer and whiskey stored in a cage in the vice office. I never saw any of this stuff leave. I assumed that it would be hauled out of the office from time to time but it never was. There is a legal process to get rid of this stuff, but I never saw it implemented. The booze was there when I came to vice and it was there when I left.

Lots of other stuff gets seized, too. Police officers, particularly those in plain clothes, accumulate all kinds of junk in their careers. Knives, whips, starter pistols, guns, fake and real, badges, suitcases, briefcases, ammunition, etc. These are just some of the things that police officers end up with. Much of this stuff is found on suspects, in their homes when search warrants are served or in their cars. We sometimes have to figure out what to do with it. If we find a big knife, do we give it back? If we find property that is obviously stolen, do we let the suspect keep it even though we will never know the true owner? The answer to both of these questions is no. We would take it and with the exception of something of real value, such as jewelry or a fur coat, store it in our lockers. Valuable items are turned in and recorded, then held for a year and sold by the city at auction. The vast amount of items seized has no value, so they just keep accumulating. I had a couple of briefcases, owner unknown, and I used them to carry evidence and reports to court.

Each station had an evidence room where seized items would be kept: bicycles, tools, tires, etc. Some items from these rooms disappeared over time and never made the auction. Recovered typewriters generally ended up in the detectives' office. The recovered ones were much better than the city issue and a lot newer. Plain-clothes officers sometimes borrowed bikes from the evidence room and used them in undercover work. I know of one such officer who got off his bike to make an arrest. When he returned to patrol he could not find his bike. It had been stolen a second time. The situation was somewhat better later in my career when a specific officer in each station was put in charge of the evidence locker and had sole access. At least there would be some accountability.

As we changed assignments we would empty our lockers and get rid of the junk.

***

I had been in vice almost two years when I was asked if I was interested in going to homicide. I liked the idea. Homicide was and is, a prestigious unit and it was the unit's custom to invite officers to work there. I asked Lieutenant Jordan if I could go and he turned me down. I was stuck in vice for the time being.

My team continued to be very productive. We knocked out a would-be motorcycle gang (they did not yet have any motorcycles) called the Iron Cross in the South End and seized a lot of Nazi-themed items along with guns, daggers, whips and drugs. We did this by spending time on foot in the Public Garden talking with hippies, junkies, bums and panhandlers, all of whom could give us valuable information. The gang had taken over the area of the Public Garden at Boylston and Arlington Streets. The gang leader had been convicted of multiple drug and firearms offenses. He said he knew me but I didn't remember him. He told me that I had arrested him in Dorchester when I was in District 11 for similar offenses.

About this time I was taking some courses at Northeastern University along with my old friend, Jim McDonald. We both signed up for a drug-oriented course Lieutenant Jordan was teaching. The information Jordan was presenting was more of a drug history lesson and it was clear that he was bluffing his way through it. If you asked him a question he would have a hard time answering it. I made the mistake of asking such a question and he wasn't happy about it. He always remembered my asking the question and he'd remark to Jim McDonald, "How is that smart aleck friend of yours?"

At the end of the course I got a B. Jim got an A. He never asked any questions.

A few months later I received a second invitation to go to the homicide unit and this time Lieutenant Jordan agreed to let me go. It was time to clean out my locker again. Into the trash went the whips,   daggers,   briefcases   and   Nazi   items.

Photos

(Extras and additional Photos can be found at bostonsfinestbook.com)

The author, left, poses with fellow officers.

Shootout in the bank basement

The author is in the black raincoat. The suspect is returning fire from the end of the hallway. Officer Jack Gallagher was fatally wounded by the suspect.

Bringing a prisoner to the nearest callbox.

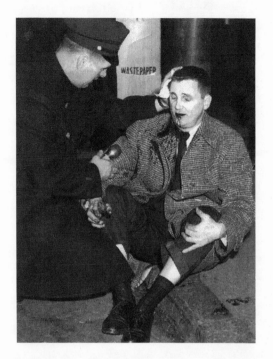

The author assisting an assault victim.

Break Not Yet Linked to Cops, Slattery Finds

Top officials of the Boston police force said last night that their nearly completed investigation has failed to uncover any evidence implicating Hub officers in a month-old break in a Park sq. lounge.

Some 10 policemen and scores of civilians have been questioned in the probe of allegations that policemen broke into the Leonardi Cocktail Lounge at the Greyhound Bus terminal early on Dec. 21, 1961.

The probe is continuing, according to Deputy Supt. John J. Slattery Jr.

Slattery conferred at police headquarters with Supt Francis J. Hennessy, Capt Edward Mannix of Station 16, and Lt Joseph Jordan.

Meanwhile a separate probe

News coverage of the break-in at Leonardi's Lounge.

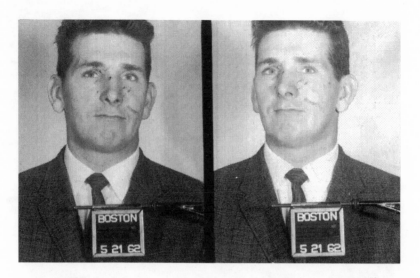

Photo taken after the iron workers brawl.

Promotion to sergeant.

Clockwise, the author, wife Eleanor, John, Anne and Richard.

The author, left, with Bob Harvey and Lawrence
O'Donnell, discussing the Jackie Washington case.

Singer to Shun Hearing

(Continued from First Page)

Washington charges he was beaten by two policemen Dec. 3 while on his way home from a friend's apartment in the Back Bay. The police officers, John J. Dailey and Robert X. Harvey, booked Washington for assault and battery and were sustained in municipal court Dec. 10.

Washington's appeal from the guilty finding and $$10 fine is pending appeal before superior court.

Following the district court finding, Barshak requested a Police Review Board public hearing from McNamara, which was yer because the city, not the citizen bringing the charges, is considered the plaintiff in the cases.

A conference on Barshak's suggestions was held at the office of Atty.-Gen. Edward J. McCormack, Jr., Dec. 27, with McCormack, Asst. Atty. Gen. Gerald Berlin, Barshak, McNamara, Atty. Lawrence O'Donnell and Asst. Corporation Counsels William E. O'Brien and Thomas Roche present. O'Donnell, a former police officer, is counsel for the two accused officers.

O'Brien, who will represent the city (and Washington) at tomor- a district court hearing' are to apply at the hearing, then Mr. Washington is ready to go forward with the hearing."

His reference to the district court pertained to a quotation from McNamara's letter which appeared in The Boston Herald Aug. 5, in which he wrote, "These hearings are conducted in compliance with all the legal standards of a district court hearings."

Barshak buttessed his letter with a memorandum on the legal points involved, which touch on Reg. 54 of the police rules.

McNamara's reply, delivered to

Example of news coverage of the Jackie Washington case.

Working Vice.

Carnival Ride, Flaws
Underscored in Test

TEST FATAL MACHINE— Boston police test "Hurricane" ride (photo above) in Charlestown, and a police photographer (right photo) takes pictures of the machine's air compressor. *Staff Photos by Dick Thomson*

A Boston police-conducted test of the "Hurricane" ride on which a woman was killed and 19 persons were injured at a carnival in Charlestown proved yesterday that the machine is capable of malfunctioning under over-pressurized conditions.

"A n official report on the test will not be issued until early next week, and no charges were made.

The ride was examined at the John J. Ryan, Jr., Playground by Det. Sgt. Jack Daley and Det. Jack Spencer of the Boston Police Department's homicide unit, with the aid of Prof. David Wilson, head of the mechanical engineering department at the Massachusetts Institute of Technology, and Richard Giampaolo, a Weymouth carnival operator.

Earlier yesterday in Charlestown District Court, Judge James J. Mellen denied five motions by attorneys representing the owner of the ride, Lawrence Carr of Wilmington, that authorities be restrained from examining the "Hurricane."

The ride was seized by police Monday on a search warrant issued by Judge Mellen following the Sunday mishap.

Black Market in A

Proposed new regulations   children's agency had con-,   aft

News coverage of the carnival ride, death investigation.

A seized handgun.

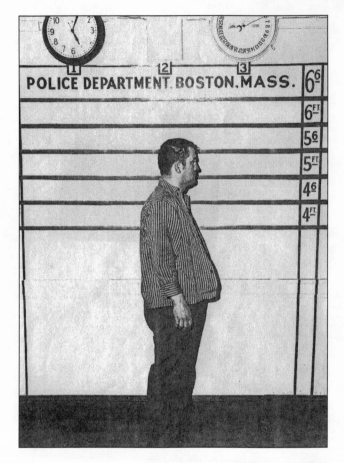

Serial killer Kenny Harrison, AKA 'The Giggler'.

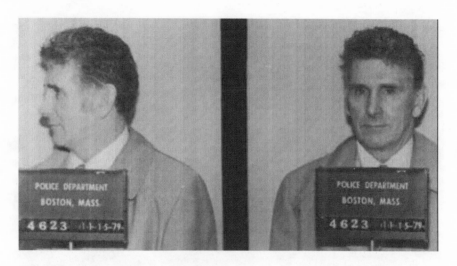

The author's police ID photo from 1979.

Gangland slaying later attributed to John Matorano.

Police Bulletin

(For Circulation Among Police Officers Exclusively)

EDMUND L. McNAMARA
POLICE COMMISSIONER

CITY OF BOSTON
POLICE DEPARTMENT

Wednesday, May 13, 1970

W A N T E D

FRANK TARVER   Colored, male, 29 years, date of birth,
9-16-40, 6'1", 195 lbs., a receding hair line, brown eyes, flared
nostrils and a pronounced scar near the right side of his right eye.
His last known address is 61 Waverly Street, Roxbury.
      It is very likely that he may no longer wear a mustache and/or a
beard or goatee in order to change his appearance.

      Roxbury Court Warrants # 5195, # 5196 and # 5197, issued 5-5-70,
for Assault by means of a Dangerous Weapon, Unlawful Confinement
and Unnatural Acts (with children) are at District Nine.
      West Roxbury Court Warrant # 77696, issued 3-10-70, for Default:
Assault and Battery by means of a Dangerous Weapon is at District
Thirteen.

**Police bulletin for Frank Tarver, wanted for the murder of
6 year-old Theresa Pina.**

ton Herald American

Complete AP, UPI and New York Times News & Feature Services

Largest Morning Circulation in New England

LATE		
COMPLETE		

0   MONDAY, MARCH 24, 1975   30 PAGES   FIFTEEN CENTS

al Slaying Placed Under Police Guard at Hospital

Investigators said yesterday they believe robbery could have been a motive in the assault, which began inside a stolen 1970 gray sedan and ended on the sidewalk of a South Boston street corner.

Police based their belief on information that the four assailants demanded their victims' wallets as soon as the two MIT students—reportedly hitchhiking—entered the car.

At Peter Bent Brigham Hospital yesterday, two uniformed Boston police officers were stationed outside Moses' room. Inside, Moses reportedly was able to arise from bed occasionally and walk about the room. A spokesman said his condition was "stable."

his arm in front of his face as his assailant fired at him and thereby saved his life.

Asinari had been stabbed at least 50 times while in the car and clubbed savagely after being dumped out of the vehicle near Emmet and East Second sts., South Boston.

"I've seen a lot of cases since I've been working homicide cases—but this is the most vicious of all," said Det. Sgt. John J. Daley of the Boston Police Homicide Unit. "The damage to these two kids was awesome. It could only have been the work of animals."

Daley and Det. Sgt. Frank Whalen and Det. John

(Continued on Page Five)

JOHN ASINARI   ROBERT MOSES

**News coverage of the murder of John Asinari and assault
of Robert Moses.**

114

Reviewing a case file with Jim McDonald.

A police family

Richard on the left, John on the right.

Richard and John promoted to sergeant

From left, Maryellen, Richard, Linda, Richie, Mary, John, Shayla, Jeanne and Anne.

Boston Magazine article.

Promotion to captain.

Bill Bratton, left and Mickey Roache on the right.

Retirement

William Broderick on the left. Mickey Roache on the right.

Homicide

Sergeant Detective

I arrived in homicide in February 1969 and I was to stay there for 6½ years with the rank of Sergeant Detective. As much as I liked working in vice, I loved working in homicide. It was mostly day work with plenty of night work mixed in. Homicide was a group of 15 officers headed by Lieutenant Sherry. There were three lieutenant detective investigators: Barry, McCallum and McDonald, four sergeant detective investigators: Whalen, Hudson, Kelley and now, me; and seven detectives: Harrington, Whitely, Spencer, Madden, Mulvey, Dewsnap and Daly. There were also four civilian stenographers: Byrne, Stapleton, Godfrey and Kraus.

Everybody in homicide was honest. They were considered a monastic group by the rank and file. For years they had never been paid for working overtime, though right before I started, they began to get overtime pay. It was a strong unit with plenty of informal leadership.

People have asked me which of the police television shows was closest to reality. My time in homicide coincided with Barney Miller and it was pretty close.

The detectives were all good workers and each had his strengths. Some of the most notable ones included Jack Spencer, who was a very big and charming guy. Everyone liked him, including judges and visiting dignitaries. He loved publicity and had contacts with various detective magazines. He often appeared in these magazines and it was always Jack playing the principal role in solving the case. When we would ask him what happened to our names, he would just laugh and so would we. Detective Mark Madden was an old acquaintance of mine from my patrolman days in District 16. He was a conscientious worker, content to be a support figure and he did a good job. Detective Bob Whitley was an older detective when he came to homicide. I knew little of his past history on the department but he seemed to have drifted through different jobs in headquarters. He was a very pleasant guy and could be depended upon. Detective Frank Mulvey was a different kind of cat. He had been in homicide many years before I got there and had many stories. His legs were giving out on him and his pace had slowed. He

---

121

would go out on a case and come back with all kinds of information and then make out long and detailed reports.

Cases were assigned equitably in accordance with a schedule. With the exception of Lieutenant Sherry, each lieutenant or sergeant took a 24-hour period every seven days. When on call you took a department car home with you. We only had three cars assigned to the unit and Lieutenant Sherry had one of them. When you were on call, you took all incidents. On occasion there would be multiple murders on your watch and a second investigator would have to be called. The detectives had a similar schedule and also responded. A homicide investigator responded to all actual or possible homicides where a victim was in danger of death. We also responded to many suicides.

***

The homicide investigator was free to investigate each case as he saw fit. He had complete responsibility and a lot of autonomy. This was fine if the officer was competent. Some investigators had a talent for finding legal reasons why they should not move ahead and did nothing. Because there was little oversight, failures would slip through the cracks. The real work begins when a case is solved and an arrest made. It was a lot easier for the investigator not to solve the case.

Because of my experiences in vice I was well prepared for homicide and brought my freewheeling and chance-taking style of investigation with me. I got my first major case right away. There had been a series of unexplained deaths over the previous two years including a ten-year-old girl found drowned in the Fort Point channel; an elderly woman found under the Broadway bridge, also drowned; and a Combat Zone drunk found dead in an excavation at Washington and Stuart Streets. There did not seem to be any connection between them. The victims were young and old, male and female and there were few reasons to believe any of these deaths were homicides. There was little or no trauma on the bodies so they were thought to be accidental.

About this time a nine-year-old boy, Kenneth Martin, was reported missing from his home in Dorchester. The boy was linked to a person of interest named Kenny Harrison, 31 years old. The juvenile officers in Dorchester: Olbrys, Kinneally and Murray, investigated the circumstances of the boy's disappearance.

Two long weeks went by with no luck in turning up the boy or Kenny Harrison. Then the detectives in Dorchester received an anonymous call stating that the boy could be found under South Station. This is a vast area of tunnels, catacombs, storage rooms and in one area, a bowling alley where the boy sometimes worked as a pinsetter. Kenny Harrison hung around the bowling alley. The information received was that Kenny was in the alley at about the time the boy disappeared. The three juvenile officers came to the homicide unit for assistance. Sergeant Hudson was the officer on call and went with about 15 officers to search beneath South Station.

I declined to go, partly because I was not running the show and partly because Hudson and I sometimes clashed. If they were unsuccessful in finding the boy's body, I told myself that I would go back with a detective and make another search myself.

They did not find the body. A day or so later I went back to the area with Detective Whitley. We split up, each of us in different areas and made an intensive search. Within 20 minutes Detective Whitley called to me that he had found the boy. His body had been wedged into a corner and covered with a canvas. He had been strangled.

I notified the homicide office that we had found the body. Sergeant Hudson returned to the scene and set the crime scene process in motion. The medical examiner responded as did fingerprint technicians and photographers.

Sergeant Hudson stayed at the scene (as he should have) and I chose to run down the suspect, Kenny Harrison. I went upstairs to the train station with some detectives and spoke with everyone who might have knowledge of Kenny Harrison. I found a train conductor who knew him. He told me that earlier that day, Harrison had boarded a train at South Station and got off in Providence. No one could tell us where he might go in Providence, not even his family. His sister was afraid of him and was concerned for her own family as she had small children of her own.

We went back to the homicide office and had a conference. I wanted to go to Providence right away before the word was out that Kenneth Martin's body had been found. It was my feeling that Harrison would be found in some fleabag hotel. Every city has them in their seediest areas. I thought we should check every cheap hotel and rooming house. There was a lot of resistance to my plan since most of us had been working since 8:00 am and it was now 10:30 pm. Jim McDonald supported me, so we decided to go. Two teams were set up and we left in two cars. Murray, Olbrys and Kinneally knew Harrison so they had to go. The second team was Mahoney, Butler and me. We got to Providence about 11:30 pm, picked up a local officer to help us out and started searching areas where we thought Harrison might be. Within an hour Detective Olbrys saw him standing on a street corner. Harrison made a run for it but Olbrys was faster and caught him.

Harrison was taken to Providence police headquarters where I had a conversation with him after giving him his Miranda rights. He made some admissions but not a confession. The admissions convinced me that he killed the boy, so we arrested him as a fugitive from justice and locked him up. I called Boston and told them that we had Harrison in custody. They were incredulous. The officers that stayed behind had given us little chance of finding him.

The next morning I returned to Providence to appear in the local court on the fugitive charge. Harrison elected to return to Boston without a hearing. He had done some thinking while in his cell and wanted to tell his story. A night in jail can work wonders. I am not sure what motivated him. I liked to think it was because I gained his confidence but I think it was more likely that he was a classic psychopath and just wanted to tell all. He suffered from no feelings of guilt and could be very charming. He waived his Miranda rights and agreed to go back with us to Boston.

His story was incredible. On the way back to Boston, he told me that he had killed Kenneth Martin but it was an accident. He said that he was the unknown caller who described where Martin's body could be found. To my surprise he continued talking and confessed to other murders. He told of walking on Dorchester Avenue alongside the Fort Point Channel with a 10-year-old girl a few months earlier. He got an urge to throw her in the channel and he did. It had been thought that her death was an accidental drowning.

He told me that another time he was walking across the Broadway Bridge from South Boston to the South End. It was winter and there was ice on the sidewalk. An older woman had fallen on the icy sidewalk and as Kenny came along she asked him for help getting up. He helped her up and then threw her over the railing into the water. Her death was also thought to have been accidental.

Just a week before Harrison's arrest, an anonymous phone call was received on the 911 line. The caller stated, "At the corner of Washington and Kneeland Street, in a construction site... There'll be a man down in the water, dead". The caller then said he was "The Giggler" and he giggled crazily over the telephone line.

There was a construction site at Washington and Kneeland Streets. When it was searched, there was indeed a man's body in the hole. Harrison told me that he was The Giggler. He recounted matter-of-factly that he had killed this man and thrown his body in the ditch.

I asked Harrison about Kenneth Martin and he told me the following: He had a falling out with his own sister and had made up his mind to kill her and her whole family. He killed Kenneth Martin for practice; a sort of dry run before he made his assault on his sister's family.

He also mentioned the Paramount Hotel on Boylston Street near Washington Street. It was a second rate hotel but it had a bar and lounge and occasionally I would have a drink there after work with a fellow sergeant. It had burned down about six months prior to Harrison's arrest. Harrison told me that he set the fire. I learned later that Harrison had a history of arson. Eleven people lost their lives in that hotel fire. He claimed to have killed 15 people but he was to revise this up later. Many of these confessions took place in the back seat of the police car as we traveled back to Boston. At no time did he show any signs of remorse for his actions.

The case received a lot of publicity. It was not often that a certified serial killer on the scale of Kenny Harrison was arrested. I brought him into the homicide office for further interrogation. I was feeling pretty proud of myself because I had pushed the case and made it work. But Lieutenant Sherry was the head of homicide and I was the new man. Sherry said a few words to Harrison and then came over to me and said, "Jack, I seemed to have established a good relationship with Harrison. Do you mind if I conduct the interrogation?"

I was not wild about the idea but I didn't have a choice. Lieutenant Sherry wanted a share of the stage. The case drifted away from me towards Sergeant Hudson, as it should have, since he was the original investigator assigned to the case.

Harrison never went to trial. He pleaded guilty to multiple murders and was given a life sentence. There was a question as to where he should do his time. He could not be sent to State Prison as child murderers do not have a good life expectancy there. It was agreed that he should spend the rest his life at the Bridgewater State Hospital for the criminally insane. There was no doubt that he was insane. He spent the rest of his life there. I had an occasion to talk with him while he was there. He was working in the hospital kitchen and was as charming as ever.

He committed suicide in 1989 by saving up his medications and overdosing. Just before he committed suicide he wrote to his sister telling her that she and her family would all be killed by an accomplice.

I had established my reputation in homicide. It was a good one, though I did bruise a few egos along the way.

***

Each of us developed our own style of investigation. Some officers were methodical, some cautious, some always caught up in legal problems, others, like me, were impulsive and acted on instinct, while others were just lazy or borderline incompetent. Some were great record keepers and very good note takers. I was not one of them. I would make notes on any piece of paper I had in my hand and afterwards try to make sense of them when I wrote up my formal reports.

When cases are solved and are being prepared for court, the paperwork must be in order so the district attorney can make a judgment on whether to go forward or not. This meant creating formal reports from rough notes, summaries of what witnesses will testify to, technical evidence, etc. This phase of the investigation was a lot of work; we actually had to sell our case to the DA.

There was an old French detective who once said that if you want to find the murderer, look at the victim. This is the absolute truth. Almost 75 % of murder victims know their assailant.

There is no perfect style for the investigator. Cautious investigators have a better conviction rate because they do not seek murder complaints unless a case is rock solid. The downside of this approach is that they have a lot of unsolved cases. If you play it too safe, a lot of people are going to get away with murder. That was not my style. If I was sure that I had the right person I might make an arrest on evidence that was not enough to convict but strong enough to meet probable cause. Many times when a suspect was arrested and spent a night in a jail cell, the case would strengthen and a good case could be made. The effect of being arrested and charged with murder is traumatic and tends to focus one's thoughts. If nothing changed after a suspect's night in a cell and the evidence didn't improve, I would make arrangements for his or her release. If further investigation implicated the suspect we could always arrest him or her again.

I recall two cases where this tactic was successful. The first involved a suspect named Strothers. He was a big man who, I believed, stabbed another man to death. He was a disturbed and dangerous man. I took my shot and locked him up. The next morning he asked to speak to a homicide officer. I was not available so Lieutenant Barry interviewed him. Strothers not only confessed to killing the victim in my case but also to another murder, which Lieutenant Barry was investigating. Strothers had not even been a suspect in Lieutenant Barry's case. Strothers was convicted of both murders. While serving his sentence of life imprisonment he killed his cellmate with a broken toilet.

The second case was a lot more complicated. It involved the shooting and killing of two escapees from the Deer Island House of Correction. Lieutenant McCallum was the duty officer when this case came in so it was assigned to him. I happened to have the day off. When I returned, I worked as the duty officer. It was a quiet Sunday so I looked into Lieutenant McCallum's folder regarding this double murder. Four days had passed since the murders had occurred and I saw that there was much to be done. I decided to look into the case and perhaps give Lieutenant McCallum a hand. I probably should have called him at home to tell him what I was doing, but I didn't.

Detective George Whitely and I headed over to East Boston where the murders occurred and talked to the victims' families and friends. We very carefully checked out the crime scene: two important and elementary tasks in any investigation. We then located some girlfriends of the victims. We were able to find out where the victims were on the night of their deaths and who they were with. We discovered that they were with two local kids and we got their names. One of these kids was Anthony Malerba, age 18. Malerba and one of the victims were romancing the same girl and Malerba was apparently jealous. Jealousy was a possible motive but certainly no evidence of guilt. The case was stalling.

We went to the homes of the subjects last seen with the victims. Malerba first. No one was home. The second subject, a 17 year-old named Angelo, was at home and alone. We brought him to the East Boston police station where he denied any knowledge of the murders. I did not believe him. I made it plain that if he did not come up with more information I was going to arrest and charge him. I told Whitely to get me some booking sheets. I meant to follow through even though the case against him was weak and would not lead to a conviction. This was the good cop-bad cop routine. For some reason I was always the bad cop.

At that point Angelo asked if he could speak to Whitely alone. That was okay with me. He told George that he did not want to get arrested and wanted to tell him something. George Whitely brought him back into the room where I was and we both listened to what he had to say. He gave up the whole story. He said that he was with Malerba the night of the murders and that Malerba shot both victims dead with a rifle. He told us where the rifle was hidden. He took us there and we recovered the murder weapon. He stated that Malerba was high on pills at the time of the shooting and that he was jealous of one of the victims. We sat down and tied Angelo in tight with stenographic statements. The next day we went back and arrested Malerba.

With the witnesses' statement and the recovered murder weapon, the case was pretty strong and Malerba was eventually convicted, but it did not come as easy as I had hoped. We had trouble tying Malerba to the murder weapon.

Fortunately our witness remembered that Malerba had fired the same rifle out the back window of his house a couple of years earlier.

We canvassed the houses in the rear of Malerba's and one occupant remembered a bullet hitting her house a few years earlier. She had called the police and reported it. She turned the spent bullet over to the responding officers but heard no more about it. A search was made and sure enough, the spent bullet was found in the detectives' files. A ballistic examination revealed it was fired from the murder weapon. Our witnesses' story was confirmed.

Malerba ended up in State Prison and was later involved in a murder in the prison. Eventually he himself was a murder victim while serving his time.

The pretrial and trial was very difficult for our witness, Angelo, but he hung in there all the way. He came from a good family and joined the Marines when the trial was over. He served his hitch and upon returning to East Boston, married and became a solid citizen.

The assistant DA in the case was Phil Beauschene. When we reported the result of our search for the spent bullet to the trial judge, Phil told the judge that he had made a personal investigation and had located the bullet himself. I kidded him for years about his "personal investigation."

This case was a rare instance of an original duty officer not following through on a case. Had George and I not moved on it, the murders were destined to have ended in the unsolved file. The accolades we received were tepid at best. Lieutenant McCallum would have liked to give us a few knocks but could not because we were successful. I deserved a D for interpersonal relationships.

***

Life in homicide continued. Most of us were always studying for promotional exams. I had taken the Lieutenant's exam and had done well. One of our homicide investigators ran a promotional school and made some serious money at it. He was a hard worker but had difficulty separating the academic side of the police business from the practical side. He was always finding legal reasons why he could not move forward and he never took the Lieutenant's exam himself. I once asked him why. "Suppose I fail?" he told me.

If a case came into the office and the duty officer was busy, Sergeant Hudson and I would fight over who would take it. The other officers in homicide were more than content to let us battle it out. Whichever one of us got the case stayed with it. There was a good reason for this. First, there was no diffusion of responsibility. Second, even with good notes, it was very difficult to transfer the whole feeling of the case to someone else. Third, the officer taking over the case tended to have a lot less interest in it than the original investigator.

Starting in 1969 the number of murders in the City of Boston increased each year until it hit a high of 130 in 1973.

We worked closely with the medical examiners: Doctors Ford, Atkins, Curtis and Katsas. Some of the doctors were easy to deal with, while others could be difficult and at times unreasonable. Some doctors discouraged the presence of police at an autopsy but most wanted us there, which made sense to me. Autopsies are not pleasant experiences but it is important that an investigator be there so that both the police and the medical examiner get the whole picture. There were some officers in homicide who seemed to enjoy being there. One detective used to watch the dissections and, as the doctor checked each organ would feel the corresponding area in his own body.

I was very uncomfortable at my first experience in the autopsy room. Dr. Ford was the pathologist and his words to me were, "You have to remember, dead bodies don't bleed. You must treat the body as a piece of meat." That advice always stuck with me. I was soon able to tolerate the autopsies but I never really liked being there.

One of my earliest cases took place in Dorchester near Geneva Avenue. This particular night local kids were harassing an older resident of the neighborhood. The older man, about 60 years old, came out of his house with a gun and fired one shot in their direction. The young men were getting into a car at the time. Once in the car, one of them realized that he had been shot. His companions took him to the Carney Hospital where he died. I distinctly remember viewing the body of this 18-year-old kid in the morgue with Dr. Ford. The doctor shook his head and remarked, "What a waste."

I was the duty officer and I responded. It was a nice summer evening and lots of people were outside so there were many witnesses. I was taking statements for hours. It did not take long to figure out what had happened. I went to the home of the alleged shooter and had a conversation with him. He admitted having a few drinks that night but made no confession. Six witnesses identified him as the shooter. I had no misgivings about arresting him and charging him with murder. I searched his house with a warrant but did not find the gun.

The case went through the lower court and on to the Grand Jury, where he was indicted for the murder. A strong case was presented at the trial. He was found not guilty. I was shocked. I had a conversation with the DA and he was quite sympathetic to the defendant because he had been harassed.

***

Prostitute murders are difficult. Many have pimps looking out for them, though often it's the pimp that is the murderer. I recall going to an alley off of Columbus Avenue at about 4:00 am one morning where the body of a young woman was found. It was a bitterly cold night and the body was frozen stiff. Her age and dress suggested that she was a prostitute. Frozen bodies cannot be autopsied until they thaw out. The body has to sit in a warm room until it is practical to examine it. There were no microwaves in the mortuary. In this case the girl had been missing from her home for a long time and her family did not know her associates. Her pimp had shot her, possibly, but we never received any further information. The case remains unsolved.

In another case, a man named Jimmy Murphy picked up a prostitute and took her to his room in a basement apartment on Commonwealth Avenue. It appeared that he caught her stealing money from his wallet and there was a struggle. She had a small .22 caliber gun and she shot and killed him. His wallet, with an unknown amount of money, was missing. The prostitute left in a hurry but she left her distinctively large underpants at the scene. Because of their size we were able to identify a potential suspect but that is as far as we got with the case. We were never able to get enough evidence to arrest her.

Murders of prostitutes could be very tough to get a conviction on, but every so often we could make a case. A girl nicknamed Cat was found in a third floor room on Massachusetts Avenue on a Sunday morning. She had part of her head blown away by a shotgun, which was still in the room. The detectives were on the scene when I arrived there. They had done some canvassing of the building but had not developed any leads. The room was a trick pad for the local prostitutes; they paid a fee to the janitor for every guy they brought up there. They were not expected to spend too much time with the customers as the janitor had to make a living on volume. The janitor told me that he was awake that Sunday morning and had been up most of the night listening to religious music. I didn't doubt that he was up all night but rather than listening to music I suspect he was keeping count of the number of customers using the room. It would never do to have one of the girls slip a customer in without paying him.

The janitor did not remember the last customer Cat brought up to the room. We canvassed the whole building and the adjoining buildings with negative results. The case lay dormant for a couple of days until after the autopsy was done and we were able to identify the girl through fingerprints. We learned that she came from a good family, but as is often the case, they had lost track of her. A short time later I received a telephone call from an individual who wanted to talk about Cat. He lived on Commonwealth Avenue at a pretty ritzy address and I agreed to meet him there. I suspected he was Cat's pimp. We made an implicit agreement that I would not move against him in his prostitute business nor would I give him up to the vice officers. These assurances are routine in homicide if you want to solve the murder.

He promised to provide information. He said that Cat was a friend of his and he wanted to get the man who killed her. He brought out another girl who worked for him and who was with Cat the night she was killed. This girl recalled seeing Cat go up the stairs with a fellow known to her only as Country. She did not see Cat again that night. She described Country as a guy who always dressed in overalls, like a farmer.

Another detective and I spent several evenings hanging around Massachusetts Avenue and Columbus Avenue. We discovered that Country was a regular in the area. We were able to get his real name then after some digging at the station we found that he had a police record and that his photo was on file. We alerted the district detectives and a short time later they had him in custody. He was wearing his trademark overalls. I talked to him and he made some damaging admissions, but it was a little short of a confession. By now we were very much aware of our obligations under the Miranda decision and I always stayed within the limits of the law.

Country was not a very bright guy however and he said enough to get himself convicted of murder. The girl who was working with Cat that night testified and was a very good witness. Country apparently carried the shotgun concealed in his overalls when he went up the stairs with Cat. After he shot her, he panicked and left the gun in the room.

Good investigators have a terrific advantage when talking to suspects like Country because of the tactics they have learned over the years. The steno record shows that all legal safeguards were observed but not the psychological pressure, the inflections in the voice of the interrogator or the body language used to obtain the necessary information.

***

Soon after that I had another late night/early morning investigation as part of a 20-hour day. William Macomber worked in a bowling alley on American Legion Highway in Roslindale as the night manager. He had been sleeping on a couch in the bowling alley for about four months.

About 3:00 am a car drove into the parking lot. Two people, a male driver and his female companion occupied the car. The male driver got out, went to the front door of the bowling alley and called to Macomber to come out. He then returned to the driver's side of the car. Macomber came out and walked to the passenger's side of the car. It appeared that he knew at least one of the car's occupants. There was a conversation among the three of them that lasted about 20 minutes. Three gunshots were then heard and the car took off. William Macomber lay dead in the parking lot.

Detective Bill Smith and I arrived about 3:45 am. We had one witness to the murder, an employee of the bowling alley. He was some distance from the shooting but was willing to do his best to tell us what he saw. He described the car and its occupants—a man and a woman. He did not get a registration number for the car.

We checked into Macomber's background. He was married with one child but had been separated for about four months. He was 42 and his wife Nancy was 24. We checked into Nancy's life. She had been left a large sum of money and she felt that her husband had swindled her.

Bill and I went to the house in Lexington where they had last lived together. The house had been sold and Nancy was gone. We talked to some people who knew her and they told us that before Nancy sold the house and moved, she took in a boarder named Ralph. She was presently living in a small town in New Hampshire with Ralph. Bill and I had been working this case for at least 15 hours at that point but I felt that we had to continue. We headed up to Warner, New Hampshire to look for Ralph and Nancy.

We arrived in Warner about 8:00 pm. Before we got there we checked motor vehicle records to see if Simpson owned a car. He did. The car was similar to the one described by the witness at the bowling alley. Once we arrived in Warner, we went to the local police station where we met an officer who knew where the couple was living and he took us there.

The car registered to Simpson was parked outside the house. We walked in without warning. Both Nancy and Ralph were there as well as several children, which surprised me. Nancy was blonde, roughly fitting the description given by the witness at the bowling alley. Simpson fit the description of the man. We separated them immediately. I took my best shot at both of them, coming on very strong but always staying within legal bounds. I was convinced that Simpson had shot Macomber and that Nancy was with him when he did it. Ralph Simpson was a tough nut and he did not fold. Nancy was shaky and wavered and almost gave Simpson up but stopped just short. I arrested Simpson for the murder. Since he was now in New Hampshire he was also a Fugitive from Justice.

Simpson went to the local jail and Bill and I went back to Boston. The next day we were back in Warner with our witness. We showed him Ralph's car and he said that it looked like the car. I put Ralph in a lineup at the Concord, New Hampshire police station. The witness picked out Ralph but said that he was not 100% sure. That was good enough for me and enough to satisfy New Hampshire requirements for rendition so he was returned to Massachusetts. While in New Hampshire I also got a search warrant for their home in the hope of finding the murder weapon but did not locate it.

I was able to get the case through the grand jury and got an indictment. Without physical evidence to back our witness up, though, the case was in trouble. I wasn't able to gather any further evidence and the indictment was dismissed.

Some years later I received an inquiry about Ralph from another police department. It seems that he was the prime suspect in a murder that they were investigating. Then about 20 years after William Macomber's murder, I received a letter from a lawyer in Rhode Island. He had been retained by some of Macomber's children, including the one he had with Nancy. He asked questions on their behalf about how their father died, saying that Nancy refused to give them any information. The lawyer demanded that I furnish the facts of Macomber's death under the Freedom of Information Act. I checked with our legal department. They said I had to comply. It must have been quite a surprise to learn that their mother or stepmother was very likely involved in the murder of their father.

***

There are rules dictating the use of deadly force but the rules cannot cover every conceivable situation that a police officer may encounter. In some situations the officer has to rely on his common sense. I encountered such a situation when Detective Jack Spencer and I were charged with looking for a guy named Billy who was a murder suspect. We did not know his full name but we did know who his common law wife was and that she lived in the Bromley Heath Housing Project. We paid her a visit and she turned out to be an extremely moral person. She couldn't tolerate an individual close to her who was a murderer and she knew that Billy had committed this murder.

She called me a few days later and told me that Billy would be in the project at a certain time, told me what apartment he was going to and what he would be wearing. I decided to go over to the project a couple of hours ahead of time to look over the area and make plans for the arrest. Spencer and I drove over and parked our unmarked vehicle. I told Jack to stay in the car while I walked through the courtyards checking out the apartments where we might find Billy and make the arrest.

While I was walking around two guys came walking in my direction. One of them was wearing the clothes described by our witness. When they were within 25 feet I drew my gun, identified myself and ordered them to halt. I called out Billy's name and the one who I thought was Billy said, "You got the wrong man Buddy." They kept on coming in my direction. They were very close now and it was decision time for me. If I let them get closer they could jump me and take my gun. I gave one more order to stop. If I fired and killed the wrong man I would be the one to go jail. My gun still raised, I again ordered them to stop. Perhaps there was something in my voice that alarmed them and they stopped and raised their hands. All this took place in a matter of seconds.

I marched them at gunpoint back to where Jack Spencer sat in the police car. With Jack's help, both men were handcuffed. I brought them both up to the apartment where they were supposed to be going, according to the tip we had. The suspect kept arguing that I had the wrong man. When we got to the designated apartment I told both suspects to say nothing and I knocked on the door. A man answered and I asked if he knew the two men we had in custody. He identified the suspect as Billy and the other man as Thomas. Thomas was released and Billy arrested and brought to headquarters. He got some serious time.

**

The assistant district attorneys who tried murder cases were often pretty good. The job did not pay well but they gained invaluable experience. At that time ADAs could practice civil law as well, so some had thriving civil practices and tended to stay as ADAs a long time. Because the position was a political appointment there was a range in their level of competence. Some were born to be prosecutors; Tom Munday was the best of these. Others who stood out were Paul Buckley, Joe Nolan, Phil Bauschene, Newman Flanagan, Jack Gaffney and Huck Riordan. They were a cadre of good lawyers who worked hard and wanted to win. They demanded a lot from the police and sometimes expected more than we could produce. Nevertheless we all shared a common goal and did our best.

The DAs took no part in the investigation of homicides unless they were asked. Only in exceptional circumstances in matter of law were they consulted. Homicide investigators were responsible for all aspects of the investigation. It was their duty to put a case together and present it to the DA's office at the appropriate time after the arrest was made. The case was then assigned to an ADA. If that ADA determined that our case was too weak to go to trial or that an egregious error had been made, he (as they were all males at the time) would not move forward with it. If the police felt differently they could shop the case to another ADA who might be willing to take it on. I did this on a couple of occasions and came out a winner.

I had many cases with ADA Tom Mundy in the early 1970s. I recall having two homicide cases on trial at the same time and in the same building. Tom was the ADA for one of them. I spent a few days shuttling between the two courtrooms testifying.

I got off the stand in the one Tom was prosecuting thinking I had been a pretty good witness for the government. I asked Tom how I did. His answer was that I had screwed up the whole case. Unwittingly, I had mixed up the two murders and fouled up the chain of evidence in Tom's case. This would not have happened had I stayed in the courtroom with Tom during the whole trial, which I ordinarily did. Nevertheless the jury brought in a guilty verdict. Tom Mundy did not lose many cases.

Many years later Tom and I went to Worcester to attend a hearing sought by a prisoner convicted of murder in one of the first cases that I brought in and that Tom tried. The prisoner was claiming that he was not given adequate representation in his original trial. I went to leave the courtroom to attend to some personal business and Tom grabbed me and told me not to leave. He said, "The last time you left you screwed the whole case up." I stayed. The petition for a new trial was denied. Tom had a long memory.

***

Homicide officers spend a lot of time in courtrooms and in DA's offices. It's a long process from the murder arrest to the time the suspect is placed on trial. The police become friendly with the Assistant DAs, court personnel and sometimes with the defense attorneys. They experience the drama and the tedium of a trial over and over. They know what different judges expect. We were present usually from the beginning to the end of a trial. I enjoyed the opening statements and the closing arguments. Many a case is won or lost in the closing argument.

At the conclusion of a murder trial, when the jury was charged and sent out to deliberate, it was our practice to stay in the courtroom-- or at least in the courthouse--to await the jury's verdict. The jury did not go home, the judge did not go home and neither did the ADA or defense counsel. It was not uncommon to be in the courthouse at 2:00 am. This practice put pressure on juries to come up with a verdict. This practice no longer exists. The Commonwealth pays for their lodging and meals and jurors are not pressed to come up with a verdict until they are ready. I guess the theory is that well rested and fed jurors will come in with a more thoughtful verdict.

If the verdict was guilty of murder in the first degree the defendant was immediately sentenced. At that time, the sentence was death, though in 1984 capital punishment was abolished in Massachusetts. I recall an old Yankee judge, Judge Hudson, reading a death sentence. His words were still clear in my mind years later. He said, "You shall be taken from this court to the State Prison in Walpole and be held there until a certain date at which time a current of electricity shall be passed through your body until you are dead."

The court officers responded with the usual, "God save the Commonwealth of Massachusetts," and the prisoner was removed from the courtroom. Then Judge Hudson took a 20-minute recess and then called for the next case. The previous defendant was ancient history.

When a not guilty verdict came back I was always surprised. It was difficult to get a homicide case all the way through the system to a trial in Superior Court. The case had to be pretty well put together to get this far. When the verdict was not guilty or when the trial ended in a hung jury, I would make an effort to talk with some of the jurors to find out why they found as they did. Some of the reasons they gave were astounding. What we thought was significant and important evidence, the jurors completely disregarded. They would tend to latch on to some insignificant detail and base their decision on it.

DA Mundy always finished his argument to the jury with these words, "Ladies and gentleman of the jury, the police have done their duty, the district attorney has done his and now it is time for you to do your duty." It was a powerful appeal, a reminder that as citizens, it is the jury members' duty to take their task seriously. There were no thank you's. It was almost an order to find the defendant guilty.

He also said, "The victim may not have been a good person but he had a right to his life. He had the right to speak with a priest before he died and this right was denied to him by the defendant."

What Tom was saying was that the defendant not only killed the victim but denied him or her any chance of absolution and caused that person to spend eternity in hell. Powerful stuff. Very effective before Catholic jurors and Boston was still a very Catholic city. Tom's style worked very well.

***

The year 1970 arrived and with it more senseless murders. One of them involved a man named Gonzales who was unhappy with his supper. The dinner was cold and he was upset with his wife. They argued. He got up and went to another room, got a revolver and came back and shot her dead. He put his hat and coat on and walked over to his brother-in-law's house. I found him there and placed him under arrest. When I tried to talk to him about what happened and why, he made no excuses and showed no signs of remorse. Later, he cried a little bit.

He spent just one day in jail; the day I locked him up. He never served another day in spite of pleading guilty to manslaughter. In court his lawyer argued that the defendant had great sorrow. He also said that he was given to wild outbursts of emotion. When in the grip of these emotions he could do things that he did not really mean to do. The defendant did not really mean to kill his wife when he shot her in the chest. Justice would be best served if he could be allowed to go home to the children. He said that the defendant was not a threat to anyone. The judge actually bought this nonsense and allowed the defendant to go free on personal recognizance. In the trial court his sentence for manslaughter was suspended. I wonder if the judge would have found differently if the case had happened in more recent years, in light of our increased awareness of domestic abuse.

***

Many police officers get involved in two or three cases which play a major role in their careers and whose resolution gives them a great deal of satisfaction. One that gave me that satisfaction ended with the conviction of a killer. It was the murder case of Theresa Pina, a 6-year-old girl from Roxbury.

Theresa was a bright girl from a close-knit family. One Sunday afternoon in April, 1970, she and her two brothers, Michael, 10 and Richard, 8 went to a local movie house at Warren and Waverly Streets. After the movie the three children crossed Warren Street heading home. As they did, they were approached by a man who asked the two boys to go back across the street to a variety store and get him some cigarettes. He gave them some extra money for themselves, so the two boys left their sister, crossed the street and entered the Sunrise Variety Store. When they returned a few minutes later the man was gone and so was their sister.

They went home and told their parents, who called the police and reported their daughter missing and the circumstances. A sergeant and two patrolmen responded from the local station, District 2. They made a search but could not locate the missing child or learn any information as to her whereabouts.

The next day, Monday morning, a park employee found the body of a young girl in Franklin Park. I went there with Detective Mark Madden and other District 2 officers. There was no question that this was the body of Theresa Pina. We checked the body as closely as we could without disturbing the crime scene. The child had been strangled. She appeared to have been dressed carelessly and was wrapped in a white sheet. Word quickly spread. The grandmother arrived and there was an emotional scene. She identified her granddaughter. Other members of the family arrived to share in the horror of finding their kin dead.

The scene was processed and no significant evidence was found. The body was taken to the morgue. Dr. Curtis was the medical examiner. I viewed the body in the morgue but was not present at the autopsy. (Dr. Curtis was one of those ME's who did not want company when he did the post mortem).

Theresa Pina had been strangled with a cord. She had been raped. The murderer apparently dressed her after death as some of her clothes were put on backwards. It appeared that the murder took place elsewhere then she was wrapped in a sheet and brought to the park. There were about a dozen male hairs found on her body. They were carefully taken and preserved. Semen was found and preserved, though DNA evidence was unknown at that time, so we could not do much with it. Nothing of any evidentiary value was found on her clothes. Before the body was buried I realized that we had no hair samples from the victim. There was a brief flap but I contacted the undertaker and he got samples before she was buried.

At that point there were no suspects. The two brothers were at least able to give us a description and that gave Mark and I a starting point. The younger brother told us that he had seen the man who took his sister before. He had been hanging out near the variety store. I am not a fan of composite sketches because they usually don't come out looking like the suspect and that can really hurt a case at trial. In this murder we had no choice and a sketch was made and circulated. It didn't generate any responses.

Because the murder of a child is so terrible and shocking there was a lot of publicity. Many tips came in. Every single one of them was checked, not once but several times. None proved fruitful. All known sex offenders in the neighborhood were checked but nothing turned up. A canvas was made of the area but no new information surfaced. The case seemed like it was dead in the water.

I decided to do a cold canvas of the neighborhood at night. Cold canvassing is rarely successful and cops do it reluctantly. It is tough, tiring, tedious work. However we had no other leads and I felt like we had to give it a try. So Detective Madden and I went back one night and went cold turkey, from house to house, showing the composite, explaining our mission and asking questions.

At one house we showed the composite and asked if they knew the individual. The occupants said they did not. The mother did tell us that her nine-year-old daughter was the subject of a sexual assault some time earlier but never reported the incident to the police. I asked the girl if she remembered where the assault took place. She did and was willing to go with us and point out the house.

She took us to a house on Waverly Street and told us the assault happened on the second floor. She described the inside of the house and the man who assaulted her. She told us that this man had approached her and promised to give her some money, so she went with him. He gave her a dime, took her upstairs and abused her, forcing her to comply at knifepoint and threatening to kill her. Eventually he let her go but not before he taped her eyes and mouth shut. He then left her out on the street. She was able to get the tape off and made her way home. Incredibly, she said that she had seen this man after the attack at the variety store in the neighborhood-- the same variety store where Theresa Pina was last seen.

It was easy to find out the identity of the occupant of that apartment. His name was Frank Tarver. He had moved from that apartment the day Theresa Pina's body was found, leaving no forwarding address. The landlord allowed us to enter. It had not been rented since Tarver left. We found nothing of any value. Tarver had a minor record so we had a photo of him on file. I put together a photo array of nine photos including Tarver's. The girl who showed us the address picked him right out. I got an arrest warrant for Frank Tarver based on her identification charging him with rape of a child and kidnapping.

I entered the warrant into the NCIC system and started running Tarver down. We were able to locate a brother who lived on Devon Street in Dorchester. I interviewed him but he was not cooperative and denied knowing Frank's current whereabouts, though we got him to admit that he had lent his car to his brother the day Theresa Pina was murdered. In spite of our efforts we could find no other family and were at loss as to Tarver's whereabouts.

I felt strongly that Frank Tarver killed Theresa Pina. I did not want to show his photo to the two brothers of Theresa Pina yet. I decided to wait until Frank Tarver was in custody so the boys could view him in a line up. I reasoned that an in-person identification would be more compelling.

A few months later, in October, Frank Tarver was arrested in Las Vegas. He had applied for a job in a casino where his fingerprints were taken and a routine check made to see if he had a criminal history. My warrant showed up. He was arrested by the Las Vegas police at a girlfriend's house without incident. I went to Las Vegas to bring Tarver back, accompanied by a detective from the DA's office, Jack O'Malley. We got through the rendition process and prepared to return to Boston with the prisoner in custody. It was evening when we arrived back in Boston. I took Tarver to the homicide office and called for the department chemist. I had Tarver strip while the chemist took hair samples from all parts of his body. I then had him sent to Charles Street jail to await trial.

The taking of the hair samples was an issue brought before the State Supreme Court later. The defense claimed that it was an unlawful search and seizure. The court ruled that it was not.

The body hairs taken from Frank Tarver were sent to the FBI lab for comparison with the hairs taken from the body of Theresa Pina. The FBI lab report stated that they could not make a 100% commitment that the hairs on the girl's body came from Frank Tarver. They did find that the hairs were similar in all respects and there was a very high probability that the hairs on the Pina girl came from Frank Tarver. Again, this test was before DNA technology.

Two weeks later a lineup was held in the homicide office. The Pina boys viewed it independently. One boy, the younger one, made a pretty good ID of Frank Tarver. The older boy could not.

I now had to sell the case to the District Attorney and it was a hard sell. The first DA I went to was Joe Knowland. He showed a group of photos to the Pina boys over my objection after the lineup had taken place. They picked out Frank Tarver. This photo identification caused many problems. It turned out that Frank Tarver had been the only one in the lineup wearing a cap. It was argued that this made the identification suggestive and tainted the identifications already made. As a result, Knowland refused to take the case.

I knew that the case was not a powerhouse but still pitched it to another DA, Huck Riordan. He thought that we had a chance but he wanted a little more evidence. He sent me back to Las Vegas. I interviewed Tarver's girlfriend out there and learned that Frank had a brother living in Las Vegas, which the brother in Boston had neglected to tell me. The brother in Vegas was Jonathan Tarver, married to an Englishwoman named Dianne Tarver. Jonathan was not a cooperative witness but his wife was and she was glad to help out because she did not like her husband's brother.

She said that Frank Tarver's arrival in Vegas was completely unexpected. He had traveled there by Greyhound bus from Boston. She remembered what he was wearing when he arrived, including a V-necked sweater similar to one described by the Pina boys. She still had the clothes Tarver was wearing when he arrived and she delivered them to me. I returned with the clothes and the names of two strong witnesses: Dianne Tarver and Kurt Kenny, the Las Vegas police officer to whom Frank Tarver made some admissions at the time of his arrest. Now it was a pretty good case.

I found out why Dianne Tarver did not like Frank Tarver. Frank stayed in her house for some time after his arrival, just hanging around and drinking and she got tired of it. She distinctly remembered that Tarver smoked Marlboro cigarettes, the same brand that he asked the boys to get at the variety store. She turned out to be a moral person who could not lie. She would be a dynamite witness at the trial.

The trial date was set. The judge assigned to the case, Judge Roy, was a no-nonsense law and order type who maintained strict discipline in his courtroom. Kurt Kenny, the Las Vegas police officer and Dianne Tarver were standing by. Besides me, the other witnesses were the technical witnesses (photographers, the chemist and the medical examiner), the Pina boys, members of the Pina family and lastly, but very importantly, the FBI hair expert.

The trial itself was a spectacle. The Pina boys, when on the stand, had trouble identifying Tarver. This was understandable because two years had elapsed since their sister was murdered and they were still only children. Dianne Tarver was terrific as was Kurt Kenny. In the end the case rested on the testimony of the FBI hair expert. These expert witnesses can be dynamite and this guy was. He was a bona fide FBI agent from the forensic lab and he knew his area. He knew how to dress and how to testify. Witnesses like this impress juries far out of proportion to the evidence they are presenting. He testified that the hairs found on Theresa Pina's body came from a black male and compared exactly with hairs taken from Tarver's body upon his arrest. He could not say with absolute certainty that they came from Tarver but he did say that he was 95 % sure that the hairs from Theresa's body came from Frank Tarver.

Frank Tarver was found guilty on all counts, was sentenced to death and taken to Walpole State Prison. He was saved from electrocution by the elimination of the death penalty. To my knowledge he is still in prison.

The Pina family, grateful to me for my diligence on the case, called The Boston Globe and told the story to one of their reporters. The paper did a complimentary article on me. I kept in touch with the family for years afterwards. They moved out of the city to the suburbs in search of a better life. Later, one of the Pina boys had some minor trouble with the law. They called and asked me for help, which I gave. It was an extremely rewarding case for me. I truly made it happen. I loved being personally responsible for a major case like this one. I made my own decisions, dictated the course of the investigation, took a chance here and there and commanded the resources of the police department as necessary. Much of homicide investigation is intuitive but often the most important element is effort.

***

Officers are trained in the rules of obtaining dying declarations although their use in trials is rare. Second-hand statements are generally not admissible in court under the hearsay rule. But there are exceptions and dying declaration is one of them. The assumption is that a person who is dying will tell the truth. In order to have a dying declaration get into evidence the person making it must be told that he or she may be dying. For example, "You're not going to make it, tell us who shot you."

On Northampton Street one night, a young man was shot after leaving a barroom. A police officer walking in the area heard the shots and ran to the scene. The shooter had fled and the victim was lying on the street. The police officer asked the victim who shot him and the victim gave the name Richard Jones. Seeing that the victim was in very bad shape, the officer said, "Look, you may be dying. Are you telling the truth?"

The victim said yes. The officer then asked again, "Are you sure that Richard Jones shot you?"

The victim grabbed the officer's hand and told him, yes, he was positive. The shooting victim died that night. Richard Jones was soon arrested. We were able to place him in the vicinity of the shooting and he was convicted on the strength of the dying declaration.

I know of only one instance where a dying person lied in the last moments of his life. Lieutenant Sherry had this case before I came to homicide. A naval officer was badly stabbed at the corner of Beacon and Berkeley Streets. He was taken to Massachusetts General Hospital where the lieutenant interviewed him. The victim said that

145

he was stabbed by a reporter from The Boston Globe and named this individual. The statement met all the requirements of a dying declaration. The victim died shortly afterwards.

Lieutenant Sherry was not completely convinced that the naval officer was telling the truth so he held off on arresting the reporter. It turned out that he was correct in his reservations. Further investigation disclosed that the naval officer and the reporter were romancing the same woman who lived on Beacon Street. The investigation revealed that the girlfriend had stabbed the naval officer in her apartment. Then he somehow made it outside to the corner of Berkeley and Beacon Streets where he was found. When he made the declaration to the lieutenant, he was lying, trying to protect his girlfriend and put his rival in jail. His hatred of the reporter was so great that he was willing to lie in the face of his impending death. The girlfriend was arrested and tried.

***

Sometimes we were able to convict one person involved in a murder, but not the other, or others involved. One summer morning a young man was found dead on the railroad tracks under Blue Hill Avenue near Simco's, an old hot dog stand in Mattapan. I was on the scene with Detective Ballard. It was a hot day and the victim had been dead for some time so there were maggots crawling all over the body. It was unpleasant but maggots can be a useful tool for determining how long a person has been dead. They lay eggs in the eyes of the corpse soon after life ends. By determining what stage the larvae are in it is reasonably possible to determine an approximate time of death.

Based on the wounds, I believed the man had been hit by a train, likely by accident. I was surprised when the medical examiner called the next day and said that the victim was killed with an axe. I found that hard to believe but Detective Ballard and I went to work. We came up with a suspect and brought him to our office. He claimed that he was innocent. We talked him into taking a lie detector test, which he failed. We put more pressure on him and led him down the garden path, convincing him that it was in his interest to tell us the truth. He made a complete confession. He told us that he and a friend had lured the victim down to the tracks with the intention of robbing him. Once on the tracks this friend hit the victim with a machete and robbed him. All our suspect did was go down to the tracks and take some of the victim's money. He said that he never hit the victim himself. The plan was to use this suspect's testimony against the principal offender. Unfortunately we were never able to find him and our suspect took the weight of the case. He was convicted of second-degree murder.

***

Arson deaths can be very difficult for the homicide investigator. The first problem is determining if arson was truly the cause of a fire. To get that determination we depend on the arson investigators in the fire department. Typical indications of arson include the presence of accelerants or a fire originating in several places in a building. Other factors include the financial stability of the building's owner, over insured buildings and irreplaceable items such as photographs and jewelry removed from the fire scene.

Charred and burned bodies are tough down at the morgue. It is a difficult autopsy for the medical examiner to perform. The skin falls off, the eyes pop out. It can also be difficult for the fingerprint technician, since among other things, the skin comes off as the fingers are rolled over the fingerprint paper.

One morning Jack Spencer and I responded to a house fire in Dorchester near the McKeon Post on Hilltop Street. It was July 4, 1970. A fire had started in the basement of this single family home. The basement was divided into furnished rooms and the father and three sons slept there. Two of the sons and the father died in the blaze.

The mother and a daughter slept upstairs. The mother went to bed about 11:00 pm and awoke after smelling smoke. She heard someone yelling fire. She was able to get out of the house with other members of her family who slept upstairs. No one got out of the basement.

The mother believed that her husband and three sons had perished. After the fire was put out a firefighter approached the mother and told her that he had found one of her sons alive in the backyard. He was the only survivor from the basement. It did not take long for us to consider him an arson suspect. Both his mother and sister indicated that he may have set the fire.

147

I brought all parties to District 11 and set up shop in the captain's office. Detective Spencer was with me as well as a department stenographer. I sat the boy and his mother down in the office and explained to them that I was going to ask the boy questions about the fire and I expected truthful answers. I told the mother and son that our conversation would be recorded. I read the boy his Miranda rights and made sure that the mother and son understood. I had set the stage very carefully.

I asked the boy if he was willing to tell me how the fire started. He answered no. I was stunned. I stormed out of the office and Jack Spencer took over. It was the classic good-cop, bad-cop routine. He told the boy, "Watch out, that guy's crazy, if you just tell the truth I will get him to calm down."

A few minutes later Jack called me back into the office and told me that the boy was willing to talk. He explained that he wanted to kill his parents and some of his brothers and sisters. First he lit a fire in his sister's closet. After the fire started to spread he tried to wake up one of his brothers but the brother would not wake up. The boy ran out of the basement to the backyard and climbed a tree. He stayed there for three hours and watched the house burn down.

The family was not wealthy but they somehow managed to hire one of the best criminal lawyers in the state, Dan O'Connell. The case never went to trial. A deal was made and the boy was sent to an institution where it was hoped that he could be treated.

***

I had a lot of experience in homicide by now but I still could make the occasional rookie mistake. A man known as King Solomon owned a variety store on Shawmut Avenue in Roxbury. It was a small store in a row of brick buildings with apartments on the second and third floors. The store was called, appropriately, King Solomon's Mines. One night in April 1970, King Solomon closed his store as usual about 9:30 pm and left with an employee. They had a brief conversation and went their separate ways. As King Solomon got to his car a shot rang out, quickly followed by another one. King Solomon drew a gun from his coat but apparently could not figure out where the shots were coming from.

A witness heard him cry out, "Please don't kill me! Please don't shoot me again!" More shots were heard and King Solomon fell to the ground fatally wounded.

As soon as he fell dead, the local kids were on him. They didn't take his gun but they did take his wallet. When I was called in, I leaped to the conclusion that it was a street crime. The very capable detective sergeant in the station came to the same conclusion and had his detectives talk to the kids in the area. We quickly identified the two who took King Solomon's wallet. They readily admitted taking his wallet but denied taking part in the shooting. That was as far as we got and the case stalled.

Four months later a man named Edward Armour walked into a police station in Decatur, Georgia. He told the officers he recently killed a man in Boston by the name of King Solomon. Armour was brought back to Boston and this is what he told me: He lived in the apartment directly above Solomon's store. On the day of the shooting, he ran into Solomon on a back stairway and they had an argument. Solomon wanted to borrow a .22 caliber rifle that Amour owned and Amour refused. They called each other names and threats were made. Solomon could be difficult, he said and it was known that he carried a gun. Amour saw a gun in Solomon's belt during their argument.

That night when Solomon closed the store and walked to his car, Amour watched from his second floor window. From the window, he yelled out, "I'm ready."

Armour saw Solomon draw his .38 caliber revolver in response but Solomon couldn't see Armour standing back from his window. Armour fired five or six shots with the .22 caliber rifle and killed Solomon. Armour was shooting through his screened window so it would have been difficult for Solomon to see him.

After shooting Solomon, Armour told his live-in female companion that he had just shot King Solomon and was going out for awhile. He never came back. He took a cab to the Greyhound Bus Terminal in Park Square then hopped a bus to his sister's house in Decatur. Eventually the murder started weighing on his conscience and he turned himself in to the local authorities.

I realized I had made two significant errors in my investigation. First, I arrived at the crime scene at night and failed to go back in the daytime for a second look. I went back to the scene after hearing Armour's story. When I looked up at his apartment over the store, the screen was still in the window. Seven bullet holes were clearly visible. Second, I had failed to canvass the shooting area. I have no doubt that the lady friend of Armour would have told the truth if we had asked her. Despite the fact that he had given himself up, Edward Armour was convicted of manslaughter and got 5 to 10 years.

***

Bodies dropped from a car in a lonely area at night can present investigators with a challenge. All you have is the body.

Once investigators make an identification avenues tend to open up. One September night in 1970, the body of a 30-year-old man nicknamed Poison was found in Franklin Park near the Shattuck Hospital. He had been shot twice on the left side. We checked into his background and tried to determine where he had spent his final hours but nothing of significance turned up.

A month later, a woman named Mildred was riding in a cab in the Fenway, high as a kite on cocaine and carrying a sawed-off shotgun and two other guns. During the cab ride the shotgun somehow discharged, blowing a hole in the taxi roof. The alarmed cab driver called the police. Mildred was brought to the homicide office where she told us a story of drugs, prostitutes, booze, binges - and murder.

It begins with Charles "The King" French, a Florida native who had spent the last 10 years in Boston. He was dangerous and ambitious but not very smart. French wanted to wrest control of the drug trade from the Saunders brothers and their associate, Deacon Chambers, but needed help. French had a friend named Pickles, also a Florida native, who at that time was picking apples in New Hampshire. French went to New Hampshire, got Pickles off his apple picking crew and brought him back to Boston. Now French had a partner. Unfortunately Pickles didn't bring much brain power to the effort.

One night French and Pickles decided to challenge Chambers and the Saunders brothers. They drove to their rivals' headquarters on Blue Hill Avenue with two prostitutes and a guy named Baynon. One of the prostitutes with them was Mildred. The other was a woman named Candy.

They pulled up and saw Chambers and started firing at him with the two guns and sawed off shotgun they had brought. They were shooting from inside the car and were terrible shots so Chambers escaped unscathed.

Later that night, they made a second attempt on Chambers' life at the Dudley bus terminal, again missing their targets. The Saunders group was getting tired of French's shooting sprees so when they later found Banyon alone in a nearby bar, they killed him. Banyon was Mildred's and Candy's pimp and they were upset at what the Saunders crew had done.

A few days later French and Pickles met at the girls' apartment on Forest Hill Street in Jamaica Plain. They were frustrated. All of their attempts to kill Chambers and the Saunders brothers had been unsuccessful. Candy was looking out a window and saw the guy named Poison walking toward the building. Poison was an associate of the Saunders brothers but more on the fringes.

Mildred and Candy were suspicious of Poison because they had heard he ended up with a watch belonging to their dead friend Banyon. If they couldn't manage to kill Saunders or Chambers, they would at least try to kill Poison. As he came down the hallway he was lured into the girls' apartment. A shotgun was put to his head.

Mildred took a .32 from Poison. Then they marched him down the back stairs and into Mildred's car. Mildred drove, Candy sat in the middle of the front seat and French sat next to her. French kept his sawed off shotgun pointed at Poison who was now in the back seat with Pickles. After some back and forth, Candy shouted, "Kill him! Kill him!" Pickles fired two shots, killing him. Mildred stopped the car. French got out and threw Poison's body out into the street.

As they drove away Mildred began to panic and French had to take over the driving. A short distance away they ran into the police who were at the scene of an accident. More panic, but they held it together. They all returned to the girls' apartment. The next day French and Pickles decided that it was time to leave town so Candy drove them to the airport. French went to New York and Pickles returned to Florida.

151

Candy and Mildred stayed in their apartment in Jamaica Plain and became increasingly nervous. About three weeks went by, then one day Mildred was in the apartment by herself when she received a telephone call from Alvin Saunders. He told her that he was at the Sheraton Boston and he wanted her to come down and see him. She tried to refuse but he told her that if she did not come he would come to her. That made her even more nervous.

She agreed to meet him at the hotel. She threw the sawed-off shotgun over her shoulder and under her coat. She also put Pickles' .32 in her purse and took a cab to the hotel. When she got to the hotel she found that Alvin Saunders had company. Candy was already there. Was she now working for Saunders?

Mildred was afraid of Candy because she knew that she always carried a gun in her handbag. When Candy left the room for a few minutes, Mildred stole her gun and put it in her own bag. Mildred was now a walking arsenal. Mildred said she wanted to leave. Then Saunders' wanted to know if she was going home, but she was afraid that she was being set up and refused to tell him. She left the hotel room and got into the cab carrying the handguns and the shotgun. She was so worried and distracted that she accidentally blew a hole in the roof of the cab.

Before telling this story to the police, Mildred was read her Miranda rights. She seemed glad to be in the hands of the police and we had every indication that she would continue to cooperate. Mildred told us where Candy was. We brought in Candy and she too gave a full statement. Her statement corroborated Mildred's. She gave us French's address in New York. Surprisingly she also admitted her part in the shooting of Poison, though not the part when she shouted, "Kill him!" She said more than enough to get herself arrested and likely convicted of murder.

Two arrest warrants went out for French and Pickles. I did not have the power to offer immunity to Mildred or Candy but I suggested that I would recommend a deal to the DA for their cooperation and I did.

Once I had French's location in New York I called the precinct where the address was located and spoke with a detective. I told him about French, described how dangerous he was and asked him to bring French in as a fugitive from justice. This detective was terrific. He called me back in two hours and told me that he had our man in custody. The NYPD have never disappointed me.

I did not know where Pickles was in Florida. I entered him into the NCIC system. A short time later Pickles was arrested in Florida for a minor offense and his name popped as wanted in Massachusetts for murder.

Both Mildred and Candy testified for the government and were given deals. They were great witnesses. When Mildred was cross examined she would answer in a way that was especially effective to the jury. After each response she would cross her heart and say, "And that's the truth, so help me God."

French and Pickles were convicted of first-degree murder and got life. Mildred and Candy got far lesser sentences.

***

In September of 1970, Joseph Sherman reported his 21-year-old daughter, Rhonda, missing. She was last seen near the Fenway. Detectives questioned her friends, including her boyfriend, George Marshall. No one had any idea what happened to Rhonda. The river in the Fens was dragged but no trace of Rhonda Sherman was found.

Over a year later, George Marshall went to visit a friend in Newton. As he got out of his car he was assaulted and kidnapped by three men. At the time of the assault he heard one of the men say, "I want to make your parents suffer."

He lost consciousness. When he awoke he found himself in a car with the three young men traveling on the turnpike. He remembered one of the men paying a $1.75 toll. He was taken to an isolated cabin somewhere in western Massachusetts. At one point when the three kidnappers and Marshall were in the vicinity of the cabin, they were approached by a local police officer who asked what they were up to. The group assured the officer that all was well. Marshall made no attempt to escape or to tell the officer that he was a kidnap victim.

He was beaten, held for about 24 hours and then brought back to the Boston area and released. He ended up at Massachusetts General Hospital where he was admitted for head injuries.

Three days later police received a telephone call. The caller stated that Rhonda's body could be found alongside the railroad tracks on Park Drive. The caller sounded very much like Joseph Sherman, Rhonda's father, but the mystery caller's identity was never established. Detectives went to Park Drive and found what appeared to be a corpse in a shallow grave alongside the tracks.

I responded with the medical examiner and officers from the DA's Office. I viewed the body, now just a skeleton, buried just below the cinders of the track bed. I saw beads around the neck similar to those that Rhonda was said to have been wearing the night she disappeared.

Rhonda Sherman was no longer a missing person case. Now it was a homicide. Other officers had done a lot of work on the case but now I was the investigator in charge. The crime scene was processed and the body was removed to the mortuary. It was now about 4:00 am.

I learned that Marshall was at Mass General Hospital. This seemed like more than a coincidence; his being beaten about the same time that his former girlfriend's body was found. I wanted to speak with him right away. I went to the hospital with Detectives from District 4 and brought a stenographer. What better time to question a suspect?

I advised Marshall of his rights in his hospital room and put all the pressure I could on him but I couldn't get him to roll over. It was now almost 5:00 am. I stopped and waited for a short time and then went back to his room and tried again. This time he agreed to talk but refused to allow the stenographer to take notes. It made no difference. The stenographer typed up the confession as he heard it. On that basis I applied for and was granted a murder complaint against Marshall for the murder of Rhonda Sherman.

Rhonda was identified by dental records and the beads around her neck. We learned later that Marshall was kidnapped and beaten by members of an organization who acted on behalf of Rhonda's father Joseph Sherman. This group forced Marshall to give up the location of Rhonda's body. We also learned the identities of the three young men who kidnapped Marshall.

These men were never arrested nor charged with any crimes. What they did, however, caused serious complications in the case against

Marshall. Coercing him to give up the location of Rhonda's body was troublesome. If we couldn't get the body into evidence the case would go nowhere.

The judge ruled that Marshall's statements to his kidnappers were voluntary. He reasoned that the appearance of the police officer at the camp gave Marshall the opportunity to escape his interrogators and he chose not to do so. The judge also ruled that the statement made to me at the hospital was admissible. That statement was in effect a confession and Marshall was convicted of second-degree murder. All attempts to have the verdict overturned failed. The assistant DA who tried the case, Newman Flanagan, was later elected District Attorney for Suffolk County.

***

When a police officer is shot, a huge effort is made to catch the shooter. Homicide is generally called upon to investigate. Such was the case in the shooting of two police officers on Massachusetts Avenue in the South End in March 1971. This was a high crime area frequented by prostitutes, drunks and thieves. Two uniformed officers, Peter Muise and Dennis Ross assigned to the police wagon, had just started a last half tour when they attempted to make an arrest near 410 Massachusetts Avenue. The suspect was resisting arrest as Officer Muise was trying to get him into the wagon. The prisoner continued to resist and Muise yelled to his partner Dennis Ross to call for help. Ross did so after calling an officer in trouble alert on the radio, which is guaranteed to have every available officer respond.

As this was going on, a man named Eugene Knox stepped out of a nearby building and approached Officer Muise from behind. He grabbed him, spun him around and shot him three times in the chest. Muise's prisoner took off but later turned himself in. He did not know Knox and had no desire to get mixed up in the shooting of a police officer.

Officer Ross had just radioed for help when he heard gunshots coming from the rear of the wagon. He walked back along the driver's side. Knox walked to the front of the wagon along the passenger's side and finding it empty, walked back to the rear. He and Ross arrived at the rear of the wagon at the same time and there was an exchange of gunfire. Ross was hit in the chest and went down. Knox, uninjured, put the gun back in his pants' pocket and casually walked away.

I arrived at District 4, along with my boss Lieutenant Sherry and other homicide officers. A lot of suspects' names came up and photos and records were collected. An anonymous witness had fingered Eugene Knox as the shooter. My partner Detective Madden and I worked through the night chasing down every possible location for Eugene Knox with no luck. Following a lead, we knocked on the door of the house of a black militant group. The members refused to let us in or talk with us. I tried to bluff my way in but they stonewalled us, which was probably for the best. By this time we were the only ones still working the case. I am not sure if I was the duty officer. I don't think I was, but there was no question now that I was going to end up with the case.

In the morning I went to the hospital with a photo array that included a photo of Eugene Knox and showed it to Ross and Muise separately. Officer Ross could not identify Knox but Officer Muise was able to. He made a positive identification of Knox as the shooter without any hesitation. I sought warrants against Knox and entered them locally and into the federal system. The case lay dormant for several months when we got word that Knox was in Baltimore. There were two officers in District 4 who knew Knox, Patrolmen Hank Sheehan and Ed Phalen.

The three of us went to Baltimore and tried to locate Knox but were unsuccessful. The members of the Baltimore Police gave us great assistance but we didn't find Knox. We later learned that in January of 1972, Eugene Knox was in another shootout with police in New Orleans. This time his luck ran out; he was shot dead by the officers, both of whom survived.

***

Occasionally we have to do business with bad people. If two people commit a crime and there are no credible witnesses, it's in the government's interest to use one of the culprits against the other.

One summer evening two men drove down Broadway in South Boston in a stolen car looking for a man named Otis Wood, a well-known local thug. As they passed Sonny and Whitey's cafe, they saw their target in the doorway. They drove around the block and came back a second time, but Otis was gone from the doorway. Nevertheless both men fired into the café through the open doorway. They hit several patrons including a young man named Nicky Papadopoulos who was sitting at the bar. He was hit in the head and killed. Two other patrons were wounded but not seriously.

The local detective sergeant from District 6, Jim Dolan, did some good work before I got there. He had put together a list of suspects. Two names on his list were Rick Dennis and Ken Keegan. The detectives in South Boston knew Dennis. There was a warrant outstanding for his arrest charging him with armed robbery in the nearby town of Malden. However there were no witnesses who could identify the suspects, so even with their names the case did not look promising.

The night after the shooting a savvy District 6 officer, Jack McGill, was off duty and in a bar in Dorchester. He saw Rick Dennis in the bar. McGill moved to question him despite the fact that he was alone and in plain clothes. After a bit of a struggle Dennis was taken into custody. McGill should have been given an award for his initiative and effort.

Dennis was brought to District 11 and held in one of the dungeon-like cells in the basement. Right away he said that he wanted to talk to someone from homicide. I was called and went down to talk with him. He was offering information on the Papadopoulos shooting but was looking for immunity. I really didn't have the authority to offer him immunity but I made a pitch. I told him that I couldn't guarantee him immunity but if he cooperated with me I would tell the DA that he did and there was every possibility that he would be treated leniently.

He decided to talk. He told me that he was having an affair with Otis Wood's wife. Wood had moved out and he had moved in to his house. Wood was unhappy with the arrangement and was giving his wife and Dennis, a hard time. Wood had a violent history, which worried Dennis.

Rick Dennis decided that the only way he could keep Mrs. Wood safe was to get rid of her estranged husband. He asked his friend, Ken Keegan, a real brute at 6'3", 250 pounds and something of a psychopath, to help him kill Otis Wood. Keegan had just been released from Walpole State Prison and signed on to the effort.

157

Rick Dennis and Ken Keegan got together the day before the shooting and did some serious drinking. Both had guns on them. Now drunk, they had a disagreement with one of Keegan's neighbors and beat him up. Keegan hit the neighbor over the head with the barrel of his gun in the dispute and bent the barrel.

Dennis described how he and Keegan drove past Sonny and Whitey's twice. The first time Wood was in the open doorway and on the second pass he wasn't. They fired into the café anyway, killing Papadopoulos. They continued to drive a while but then abandoned the car, leaving it running and in gear. It rolled into a building and crashed.

Dennis and Keegan then decided it was time to split up. Keegan went to a relative's house in Medford. Dennis went to a friend's house in Dorchester taking the two guns they had just used with him. He carefully took the guns apart, wrapped them in paper and threw them into a dumpster nearby. He needed a drink and went to a local bar, The Sands, a short walk from where he was staying. It was there that Officer McGill spotted him.

Dennis's story was complete but I had to have more to make the case stick. I took him out of the cell and had him take Detective Madden and I to the dumpster where he dumped the guns. It was full to the brim with rubbish. We contacted the refuse company and had them empty the dumpster right out on the street. After a lengthy search we found the two guns wrapped in paper. The ballistic tests came back positive. The bullets recovered in the café were shot from the guns found in the dumpster. It was now a solid case.

Before we'd brought him back to his cell I had asked Dennis if he knew where Ken Keegan was staying. He said he did and gave us the address. A few detectives and I went to the address in Medford and to my surprise, Keegan was there and he came easy. I was lucky. We were able to verify every aspect of Rick Dennis' story.

There is a long interval between arrest and trial and that is when my troubles with Rick Dennis began. Keegan and Dennis had to be kept in separate jails for obvious reasons. I had promised Dennis that I would recommend leniency and I was obligated to follow through. He began calling the homicide office almost daily, complaining that he was being threatened by other prisoners. I had him moved to another jail. Then it was something else. As soon as I solved one problem for him another would come up and I would have to act on his behalf. It got so that no sheriff or warden in the state wanted to take him because of all the problems he was causing. Somehow he got my home address and I got a Christmas card from him.

Finally the case came to trial. Dennis and Keegan were to be tried separately. Keegan went first. Dennis had to testify as a witness against him if he wanted the deal from the government. Rick Dennis did very well on the witness stand. He was a great witness because he told a story that was believable. His testimony was disturbing because he didn't minimize his own role in the murder.

ADA Tom Mundy, a young prosecutor, presented the case. At one point the defense called a female witness whose purpose was to discredit Dennis. As she approached the witness stand she winked at the defendant, Ken Keegan. Tom Mundy saw her do it.

When his turn came to cross examine her, the first question he asked was, "Did you wink at the defendant as you came up to the witness stand or did you have something in your eye?" That question pretty much destroyed her credibility. After the evidence was all in, the defense and prosecution made their final arguments to the jury.

Tom Mundy had the last word. He urged the jury to do their duty and find this murdering bum guilty in the first degree. Hearing these words, Ken Keegan became enraged. He came charging out of the defendant's chair heading for Mundy. I got between the two of them and as I did, Tom whispered in my ear, "Let him come." Keegan stopped short and went back to his chair but the jury had witnessed his behavior. That surely had negative effect on his chances of acquittal.

Ken Keegan was found guilty of first-degree murder. The jury was dismissed. He was removed from the courtroom. He was history. The irony was that the government witness, Rick Dennis, had instigated the murder. His accomplice got the chair. Dennis walked.

The defense appealed claiming that Tom Mundy's argument was prejudicial. The issue eventually went to the Massachusetts Supreme Court. Tom Mundy received a mild chastising from the justices but the verdict was upheld.

Besides the murder charge there were several armed robberies against Rick Dennis in different jurisdictions. He remained in a county jail for about eight months and was brought before a judge in a closed session where his cooperation was detailed. The judge decided that he wouldn't be tried for the murder. He pleaded guilty to all the robberies and, in a package deal, received a mild sentence. The only ones present in the courtroom were Tom Mundy, the judge and the court reporter, and me. I told Dennis that we were now even. Nevertheless, he continued to call me whenever he got into trouble. At least there were no more Christmas cards.

My last contact with Rick Dennis took place about 12 years after the murder. He was back in jail. He called from Worcester Police Headquarters where he was being questioned by detectives regarding what he knew about a murder that had taken place in a local jail. He asked me if he should talk to them. If he thought I was his lawyer he was mistaken. As far as I was concerned it was fine for him to talk to the Worcester police.

I believe he was convicted of that murder. I never heard from him again.

***

The following was Lieutenant Barry's case. My involvement started when I passed on some information from my old partner in vice, Joe Smith. In June of 1971 he received information about a missing man named John Fahey. Fahey had been reported missing in March and had not been seen since. He had a minor record and had been living in a rooming house on Deer Street in Dorchester with his wife. There were also two brothers, Richard and Robert Adams, living in the same rooming house. Both had violent records.

One March night John Fahey returned to his room on Deer Street very drunk. He was drinking with a friend, Mark Olson, who he brought home with him. For some reason Rooney went into Richard Adams' room. Adams was in bed at the time. Then Olson heard gunshots. He ran into Adams' room to see what had happened. When he got there he saw Richard Adams getting out of bed with a gun in his hand and John Fahey lying on the floor. Adams pointed the gun at Olson and told him to leave. Olson hesitated so Adams said it again. This time he got the message and left.

John Fahey was never seen again.

This information was sent up through channels to Lieutenant Barry. He had done all the routine work so far. Unfortunately he had no body. Then we received a call that a body had washed up on a Dorchester beach. Lieutenant Barry and I went to the tidal pool off Morrissey Boulevard near the Boston Globe headquarters. A torso had washed up on a mud bank. It was headless, both arms and the right leg were gone. The left leg extended only to the knee. The torso had been burned, apparently with a blowtorch, removing any tattoos and scars. There was a small hatchet still stuck in the chest.

Because there were no hands there were no fingerprints. Because there was no head, no visual identification was possible and no dental work could be checked. There was nothing on the torso that could be tied to Fahey. DNA testing had yet to be discovered. Still, we suspected this body might be Fahey's since he was missing and was last seen less than a mile away.

I knew Richard Adams because I had arrested him for accessory in a previous murder. I decided to question him. I went to his house and brought him into the homicide office for questioning. The questioning went nowhere and Adams walked out.

The torso was brought to the autopsy chamber and examined by the medical examiner. Lieutenant Barry and I stood by watching. I remember the doctor asking, "What do you expect me to do with this?"

"Your best," was all I could think to reply.

The M.E. suggested that we X-ray the spine. It was a good suggestion and an X-ray was made. I made some inquiries at Boston City Hospital. I thought that if Fahey had ever been a patient there perhaps there might be X-rays in his medical file. Sure enough, there were. They had X-rays of his back on file.

I got in touch with a forensic radiologist, Dr. Susman, at the Brigham Hospital. He compared the X-rays that had been on file with those of the torso. Looking at details in the bones he was able to determine that the X-rays of the torso found on the beach was John Fahey. Lieutenant Barry now had a pretty good case.

The M.E. did a post-mortem on the torso. A bullet was found in the heart so the cause of death was determined to be the fatal gunshot wound. The hatchet buried in his chest was put there after death and was probably used to dismember the body.

Warrants were issued for the arrest of Richard Adams for the murder of John Rooney. We learned that he had fled the area but eventually he was picked up in New York City. He was tried and convicted. He did no more than 12 years because I noticed that he was arrested again in 1983.

***

Morgues are never pleasant places and the one in Boston was no different than any other except that it was old. Bodies are held on trays, stacked about five feet high in refrigerated boxes covered with a sheet. There is always the odor of death and disinfectant. The bodies often have a lot of blood on them.

It is not fun bringing a victim's relative, friend or acquaintance into the storage areas for identification purposes. The tray is rolled out, the sheet pulled down and the witness is asked if they know the person lying there. Occasionally they don't recognize the body on the tray even when they know the person well. Burn victims can be dreadfully disfigured. Drowning victims too, especially if they have been in the water for some time. A body floats head down and any blood left ends up in the head turning it black. If the body has been in salt water, the odor is quite foul. I always made an effort to stay upwind when a body was placed on the dock. No one tells you these things at the academy. It's unpleasant on-the-job training that comes with working in homicide.

***

The Boston Police Department had a policy of sending officers to assorted courses for extra or specialized training. The FBI Academy was one of the most sought after but there were several others, including the Babson Command Training Institute at Babson College in Wellesley and the Dale Carnegie School of Public Speaking. I was fortunate enough to attend all of them.

The course at Babson College was three weeks long and gave us great insight into management practices. It also gave us the opportunity to meet police officers from all over New England. Some of my fellow students knew I was from Boston and that I had just finished a tour in vice and narcotics. They expressed a desire to see some of the seamier sights of the city. I made the arrangements and they spent a night riding with officers of the vice squad.

The Dale Carnegie School was fabulous. We met one night a week for 10 weeks. Every student had to speak at every session; there was no escape. At the first meeting all we had to do was stand up, state our name and where we were from. It was done in such a way that each pupil's confidence was gradually built up so that by the end of the 10 weeks, most of the members of the class were dying to get on their feet and speak. I recommend this course to anyone who has to speak in public—be it to small or large groups.

I was called upon to speak to different groups about homicide investigation. I spoke in high schools, middle schools, college classes and private organizations. I talked about interesting investigations, our successes and failures. Well before Power Point, I illustrated the talks with photos passed around and by playing audio recordings. Prior to the class I would rather have died than speak in public but because of the Dale Carnegie course I grew to enjoy it.

My old friend Jim McDonald recommended that I attend the FBI Academy, a six-week course held on the Marine Corps Base in Quantico, Virginia. It was a prestigious school and the Boston Police Department sent only one or two officers a year. I expressed my interest and was admitted in the fall of 1972.

It meant a financial sacrifice. No details, no court time, no overtime, though the City of Boston still paid my salary plus an extra $300. I was willing to take those hits for the opportunity to study there and fortunately my wife understood and supported me. The FBI does a check on all candidates and I passed though I know of other candidates who did not.

The mission of the school was not only to teach the latest developments in law enforcement, but also to expose us to others in law enforcement throughout the country and world, thereby creating a vast network of officers with ties to the FBI and to each other. The US government paid airfare, room and board. Books and other study materials were also furnished.

I arrived in Washington at the appointed time and went to FBI headquarters. There I met about 40 other candidates, all bound for the academy. A bus came along and drove us the 40 miles to Quantico. The school consisted of a cluster of new dormitories and classroom buildings in a beautiful setting. On arrival we were taken to an auditorium and given an orientation lecture by the man in charge of the school, Jim Cotter. He made it plain that we had to play by the rules of the academy and if we did not we would be dismissed and sent back. None of us could stand that kind of disgrace so we took his remarks seriously. The students were police officers from across the US and from other parts of the world. I met students from Japan, Malaysia, Mexico and Vietnam. There were 250 students in our class, the 99th class to go through the academy.

We lived two to a room, the roommates chosen alphabetically. I lived with a man named Darrell, a state trooper from the Mississippi Highway Patrol. He turned out to have a deep hatred of Northern liberals. He particularly hated the Kennedys. We tolerated each other but never became fast friends.

Classes started at 8:00 am each day and ended at 5:00 pm. The school was a first-class training facility. They even had a full-size plane fuselage where officers were trained to overcome hijackers. Shooting was an important part of the training. We spent hours on indoor and outdoor ranges where different crime scenarios were presented and targets popped up electronically.

The students in the academy were, for the most part, not working police officers. They seemed to be from management and training. They were mainly from small towns, sheriff departments and park agencies. There was an officer from the NYPD and he impressed me. The big cities seemed to send fewer officers; perhaps this was because of financial problems. I gave a talk on search warrants to my section. I don't believe that anyone in my group had ever sought a search warrant or an arrest warrant.

Living in groups can get close at times and we all needed some solitude. I would take a bike furnished by the academy and go for a long ride. They had a good library and I enjoyed finding a good book and reading it. Some students worried about the academic side of the school but I never did. It was not that I was so smart, I just could not see the academy failing anybody and sending him back to his department hostile to the FBI. Nobody failed.

There was a large swimming pool, a gym and handball courts nearby. The academy placed great emphasis on physical fitness. We had to run every day. The length of the run was gradually increased day by day. At the end of the term we were all required to run for 40 minutes, stopping and doing exercises on demand.

Graduation was a major event and we were all awarded certificates by the head of the FBI, Clarence Kelley. It was a wonderful experience. I maintained ties to many of my fellow students throughout my career and even after retirement.

***

In 1972 Mayor Kevin White decided to bring in an outsider as police commissioner, Robert DiGrazia. He was charged with making much needed change. His focus was to turn the department from a rather corrupt operation to a reasonably honest one. One way he did this was by removing every detective sergeant in the station houses in one mass transfer. These detective supervisors were traditionally the ones who controlled the cash flow from all illicit activities. They had many political connections and they tried to use them to stop some of the transfers. But DiGrazia made them stick. Many of these officers had funnelled cash into Mayor White's campaign and felt that White owed them. White solved that problem by leaving the city and going on vacation during this period of upheaval. The detective sergeants were never able to regain their power. DiGrazia brought a young team with him, including Joseph Jordan as superintendent of police. Initially DeGrazia's team was very successful in its reform efforts although he often clashed with the culture of the department.

A lieutenant's examination had been held before I left for the FBI Academy. I was second or third on the list but did not get promoted. In fact very few promotions were made in spite of an obvious shortage of ranking officers. It took me only a short time to realize that the failure to promote officers was intentional. The police commissioner started appointing acting lieutenants and captains. There was a perception that those chosen were politically connected to the mayor. About this time a position opened up in the vice unit for an acting lieutenant. I was still suffering from naiveté and applied for the job but it soon was made clear to me that I was not going to get it. The man who did get it was a sergeant who, I understood, was a political organizer and fundraiser for White in East Boston.

Over time DiGrazia began to suffer from hubris and this was to be his undoing. When he started making noises a few years later about running for mayor, Kevin White declined to reappoint him as commissioner and he faded from the scene.

So I stayed in homicide and continued to take cases. The average number of murders in Boston in the years I was assigned to homicide, 1969-1974, was about 100. There was a dramatic increase in the early 1970s jumping to 130. These numbers were caused by gang wars involving the Charlestown gangs, the North End Mafia, the Winter Hill gang and Whitey Bulger's South Boston group. Much of it was internecine. Eventually they decided to calm things down and make accommodations with each other. The clearance rate for the unit was about 68%, which was a little lower than the national average. My personal clearance rate was somewhat higher. We used the same FBI reporting system that was standard throughout the country.

***

Once in a while a court case would interfere with vacation plans. A trial that I would testify in had been on and off the schedule many times. I was the principal witness in the case. With no scheduled trial date I made plans to go to Florida with my wife. I bought plane tickets. I had just purchased a condo and was anxious to show it to Eleanor. I told the DA of my plans but apparently there was a misunderstanding between us. I got off the plane in Fort Lauderdale and went to the car rental agency. As I was filling out the rental forms I received a call from the FBI telling me to contact the DA's office at once. I did so reluctantly. I was ordered to return the next morning and be ready to testify at 10:00 am. I didn't have much choice. I drove across Alligator Alley with Eleanor to our new condo on the West Coast. Early the next morning I caught the first flight back to Boston. I was on the witness stand at 10:00 am and finished and excused at 11:00 am. I headed right back to Florida. It was a pretty expensive hour of testimony.

***

It is amazing how many shootings occur in barrooms and when the police arrive the only one present is the victim. A patron in a Charlestown bar shot the bartender to death one night. When the police arrived the bar was empty except for a drunk who was asleep in a corner and the bartender, who was dead. The drunk did not see or hear a thing and had to be awakened by the responding officers. No one in Charlestown would admit to being in the bar at the time of the shooting. No witnesses. A tough start to any investigation.

Even when patrons haven't had the chance to flee from the scene of a shooting, witnesses are rare. Everyone seemed to be in the men's or ladies' room when the murder took place. Those restrooms can get mighty crowded at these important times.

***

There were many old elevators in the city. Warehouses and industrial buildings had elevators that were controlled by wires or ropes. There were no doors, just gates on each floor. To operate one of these freight elevators you had to either pull down on the wire or pull up. To stop at a floor the operator of the elevator snapped a lock as the elevator approached the desired floor. The elevators had only the most rudimentary safeguards which employees or residents often modified. Out-dated and damaged elevators were tough on the police who routinely responded to emergencies that took place in older buildings and the officers had to use the elevators to reach their destinations.

Shortly after World War II many housing developments were built in Boston. Some of the buildings had as many as seven floors. Ideally the elevators in these projects would be child-proof but as the buildings aged the elevators were subjected to neglect and abuse. Elevator safeguards started to fail. Maintenance was inadequate. Usually elevator accidents aren't homicides but an investigation still had to be made. Civil suits associated with these types of accidents were common and generally not resolved for many years so the investigator had to keep good records.

In April of 1974, a nine-year-old boy was found dead in the elevator machinery at the Annunciation Housing Development in Roxbury. The boy apparently crawled up on top of the elevator car and was crushed when the elevator went to the top floor. The cause of death was pretty straightforward.

Mayor White established a task force to look into the circumstances of the death. The mayor was a good politician—this was a hot issue in the city. I was a member of the task force and we met in City Hall on several occasions. I was asked to write up a report on our findings. We had several meetings and at the last one they accepted my report as the official record of the incident.

The boy's parents sued the city and a large settlement was agreed upon. Sometimes only a tragedy can force change. I don't know if elevator maintenance has improved in Boston housing after this but I assume that it did. I do know that there have been no more children's deaths in elevators in the housing developments since.

***

In June 1974, a girl was thrown from an amusement ride called the Hurricane at a carnival in Charlestown near the old Schrafft's candy factory. She died as a result.

The Hurricane took patrons up in cars and revolved them around a center post at different speeds and elevations. On this particular evening the carnival was crowded and the Hurricane had a full load. The operator set the ride in motion. The cars went up to the highest elevation and began to revolve very fast. The passengers soon started screaming in terror. The ride machinery began to shake and literally fly apart. Riders were thrown from the cars. Many were injured, some seriously and one girl was killed. The operator finally managed to shut the ride down but it was too late.

I arrived at the scene the next morning with Detective Jack Spencer and began the investigation. The facts surrounding this death were completely new to the unit so there were no guidelines on how to proceed.

It was easy enough to get witnesses to describe what happened but to actually visualize it was difficult. A lawyer representing the owner of the ride was on the scene. He forbade me to touch any of the machinery belonging to his client. I feared that they were preparing to break it down and cart it away. I couldn't allow the investigation to be frustrated so I went to Charlestown District Court and sought a warrant to seize and search the ride. My rationale was that the ride was possible evidence in a crime and thus subject to search and seizure. It was new ground for the court but the judge, Chief Judge Mellen, agreed with my argument and issued the warrant.

I went back to the carnival site and took control of the ride, then continued to the homicide office and called a conference. There was a great deal of concern as to where the liability lay and if there was any criminal responsibility. Was the owner of the ride responsible? It might be the ride manufacturer. Or perhaps the carnival company? Or the operator himself? Everybody had something to say and I respected their opinions.

None of us was qualified to examine machinery. Before we could make any charges we had to find out why the ride malfunctioned. Someone suggested that we contact the engineering department at the Massachusetts Institute of Technology and we did. We were referred to Professor David Wilson of the Mechanical Engineering Department and he agreed to help us.

Professor Wilson turned out to be a real prize. He was thorough and competent. Detective Spencer, Professor Wilson and I went back to the scene of the carnival a couple of days later. The carnival had moved on but the Hurricane and a generator truck were still on site. The professor spent a full day going over the machinery of the stationary ride. The three of us returned the following day determined to get the ride moving so the investigation could continue. But we found the generator truck padlocked. The same lawyer representing the owner of the ride was at the scene. He told me that if I touched the generator he would sue me for every nickel I had. He threatened me with the loss of my home and all I possessed. I called the Police Emergency Unit and had them cut the locks. I got on the generator truck and tried to start the generator but it soon became apparent that Spencer and I were not going to get the rig started without some assistance. I called around for help and found a man who worked for another carnival who was interested in finding out why this particular ride malfunctioned. I offered him twenty bucks if he would get the machinery working. He agreed and promptly started the power. The lawyer was livid at this development.

Once we got power, Professor Wilson took over the controls and put the Hurricane through its paces several times. Each time the ride worked normally. Local television stations had camera crews at the scene and filmed each test, but nothing dramatic happened. After a while they got bored and stopped videotaping.

The professor had an idea as to why the ride malfunctioned and he decided to let the ride sit at rest for a short time to see if air pressure in a certain tank would build up beyond normal levels. About 20 minutes went by before he took the controls again and set the ride in motion. Then it happened. The ride began flying apart. Glass and debris flew all over the place. I was close enough to be nervous about getting hit with one of the flying pieces. The professor, clad in his coveralls and wearing his hard hat, stood his ground at the controls and calmly shut the ride down.

Now we had the answer. The professor had found a mechanical defect that probably should have been obvious to the operator. Unfortunately operators of rides at carnivals do not get much training beyond the basics of starting and stopping rides and collecting tickets. The professor wanted to do another test. I vetoed that as being too dangerous. The television camera crews who had shut down their cameras missed the previous test run. Only one station got the dramatic footage of the ride self-destructing, Channel 5.

An inquest was held in the Boston Municipal Court before Judge Mellen. The Channel 5 video was admitted in evidence. The judge ruled that there was no criminal responsibility. The matter became a civil case. I never heard about the case again. I do know that I was never sued and I assumed that all injured parties were compensated out of court.

**

The first time I experienced the murder of a police officer was when my friend and colleague Jack Gallagher was shot. The second was the shooting of officer Charles McNabb in Brighton, which I investigated. The third was the murder of John Schroeder. He came on the force with me so I knew him well.

Jack Schroeder was assigned to the South End, District 4. One night in November of 1973 three armed youths went into a pawnshop on Washington Street to rob it. Jack tried to prevent the robbery and was shot to death. The robbers took his gun as well as money and jewelry from the pawn shop.

The case unfolded very quickly. Three juvenile officers in District 11, Murray, Kinneally and Olbrys, received information about the

170

identity of the thieves from a street contact. Soon after, Sergeant Bob Hudson learned that the suspects had fled the state on a Greyhound Bus. He was able to get the bus stopped in Virginia where the suspects were arrested. They still had Jack's gun.

It was Sergeant Hudson's case but he did not want to go to Virginia. I was familiar with rendition procedures and I took his place. Detectives Olbrys and Kinneally went with me. There were three of us and three suspects to bring back. We interviewed the suspects in Virginia. They talked and made incriminating statements, just short of confessions. The statements were recorded and became part of the record. The three suspects waived their rendition rights and agreed to return with us to Boston.

I had only brought a few dollars with me because we left on short notice. The town in which the suspects were arrested was a short distance from the North Carolina border so the nearest airport was in Greensboro, North Carolina. The local police took us there and I bought six airline tickets back to Boston using a personal check. I had nowhere near enough money in my account to cover the checks but I assumed I would be reimbursed as soon as I got back to Boston.

We boarded the plane before the other passengers and sat in the rear of the plane. When the pilot came on board he refused to take us and asked us to get off the plane. He gave no reason. We checked our prisoners into the local jail in Greensboro. The two detectives and I had to spend the night in a local motel. Again I paid using a personal check. The next day we returned to the airport with our prisoners but two other pilots refused to take us on their aircrafts as well.

I was getting desperate. The only avenue left was to rent a van and drive it back to Boston. I did not want to do that. I finally found a veteran Eastern Airlines pilot who agreed to take us on his flight to Newark. We jumped at this chance to get out of Greensboro. On arrival in Newark we were met by a large contingent of local police requested by our lieutenant. They helped arrange a connection back to Boston.

When we arrived back in Boston there was a lot of publicity. The local TV stations covered the event as well as the print media. I was reimbursed promptly for my expenses and was happy that no checks bounced.

All three suspects were convicted.

Jack's brother Walter, also a Boston police officer, was killed in the line of duty several years earlier. A double tragedy.

***

Some detectives form an exaggerated idea of their skills and importance and tend to look down on uniformed officers. This is self-defeating. The officers in uniform make contacts every day on the street. They are on the front line and they know what's happening on the ground. If a detective alienates these guys the information is going to stop flowing. I always tried to keep officers involved in a case if they showed interest or provided us with information. And I always thought it was important to make sure that they got credit as well.

Early one October morning 26 year old John Labanara was found shot to death on Newbury Street. He worked as a lawyer in the DA's office and had some connections to City Hall. He was found seated in his car shot in the head.

Sergeant Joe Kelley was the on-call officer. He took all the routine steps but had no strong leads and none developed later.

I entered the case a few days later. I received information that a certain junkie, who I had done some business with when I was in vice, knew something about the murder. We questioned him on and off for three days before we realized he was conning us. That lead went nowhere.

Two uniformed patrolmen, Knave and Boylan, were sector car officers covering the Greyhound Bus Terminal. They made it their business to know what was going on in the terminal. One night soon after the murder they noticed a young man named Michael Wilson hanging around. He was a drifter, AWOL from the army. He told the officers a wild story.

He said that he had been hitchhiking from Hartford, Connecticut to Durham, New Hampshire recently and was picked up early one morning by a young woman near Portsmouth. Her last name was Zelda. She asked him if he had a place to stay and when he told her that he did not, she suggested that he stay at her house for a few days as a babysitter. This was agreeable to Wilson.

Zelda had three children, ages 3 to 11. She was married to an Air Force man stationed at Pease Air Force Base in New Hampshire. He was on extended duty for long periods of time so she was alone with the children a lot.

Zelda, with Wilson, stopped at a friend's house on the way home. This friend, Peter Yankun joined them and the three of them continued on to Zelda's house. Zelda and Peter Yankun had a conversation about an armed robbery that they were planning. Having this kind of conversation in front of someone they only knew for about an hour was not wise.

The next morning Zelda asked Wilson to babysit her children while she drove to Kittery, Maine. A few hours later she returned home with a .32 cal revolver. Yankun took it to another room and ground off its serial numbers. Michael Wilson saw and heard all of this. He also saw a lot of ammunition. He learned that they were planning a robbery for that night but changed their plans because they couldn't get enough people to take part.

The following evening, a young man named Bernie arrived at Zelda's house. Then, at about 11, Bernie, Yankun and Zelda set off for Boston in Zelda's car. Michael Wilson continued his babysitting duties.

They returned about 3:00 am. Zelda was very upset, almost hysterical. Bernie had the gun and unloaded it. One round had been fired. Michael Wilson asked Zelda what happened. She told him that they drove to Boston, saw a drunk man and decided to rob him. But the drunk put up a fight. Bernie shot him in the head, then ran back with Yankun to where Zelda was waiting in the car. The trio headed back to New Hampshire.

The next day Zelda told Michael Wilson that her husband was getting off duty and his services as a babysitter were no longer needed. Wilson left that morning and took a bus to Boston, arriving at the Greyhound terminal. Before he left he saw a television account of the murder and realized that everything he had been told was factual. He did not contact the police and probably never would have talked about it had it not been for Patrolmen Knave and Boylan asking a few basic questions.

The officers called homicide after hearing Michael Wilson's story. They brought Wilson into the office and he told the same story to me. I headed immediately to Portsmouth with Michael Wilson and Detective Bill Smith.

Once in Portsmouth, Wilson was able to direct us to Zelda's house. No one was home so we went to police headquarters in Portsmouth where we met Lieutenant Detective Bill Mortimer. I told him of our mission and like any good detective he pumped out the names of possible suspects. One of those was Bernie Jordan. He got out some mug shots and Michael Wilson identified Jordan as the man with the gun who was with Zelda and Yankun the night of the murder.

I wanted Jordan arrested at once. The Portsmouth police went to his house but it was not an easy arrest. He gave them a good battle before they got him into custody. He refused to talk and was locked up for the murder. Since it was late, Bill Smith and I stayed overnight in New Hampshire, joined by several others from homicide, including my old friend Lieutenant McDonald. It was a high profile case with plenty of heat from above and we took great pleasure in wrapping it up. We dined at the city's expense that night.

The next day the Portsmouth police went back to Zelda's house and this time found her home. She gave it all up including Peter Yankun. The case was a lock and it was time for me to step out of it. Sergeant Joe Kelley came up to New Hampshire the next day and took over the details.

Both Jordan and Yankun were returned to Boston and convicted of murder. They got life. Mrs. Zelda was given a deal for her testimony and walked. Yankun did not live long after the trial. When he was given a physical at the jail he was found to have terminal cancer and was dead within months. Needless to say, this case would not have been solved as quickly as it was without the information provided by officers Knave and Boylan.

***

Too many murders go unsolved. 22-year-old Janet Sparks lived in an apartment on the Riverway with two other young women. She worked nights as a nurse and her two roommates worked days so Janet slept during the day.

One afternoon a barely audible call came into the police dispatcher. The woman on the line asked for help and was able to give her location. Officers from the district responded and banged on her door. The line was still open to the dispatcher. He could hear officers knocking on the door but nothing more from the woman. The officers got in and found Janet Sparks on the floor, dead.

I was called to the scene and picked up the case. I entered the apartment and saw the victim lying naked on her side, covered with blood. She still had the telephone in her hand and up to her mouth. I could see stab wounds.

The apartment showed no signs of forced entry. Her lunch was still on the table partially eaten. The autopsy showed food in her stomach. She had been stabbed to death with a pair of scissors which were found in the apartment. It appeared that someone had come to her door and she apparently had let them in. Her friends told us that she was a trusting girl but not a stupid one.

It was the kind of case that would stir anyone's emotions. We did the usual canvas of the crime scene area. In a nearby apartment we found two young men who I knew casually because they were handball players like me. One of them gave me a bad feeling. I felt that he was a potential suspect after talking with him even though he said nothing incriminating. It was a hunch, nothing more.

I spoke with my boss, Ed Sherry and told him of my suspicions. He also knew the handball player and believed that he could not possibly be a killer. I was relatively new to homicide and I was swayed by his opinion so I did not question the handball player any further.

The consensus among the investigators was that Janet Sparks confronted a random person breaking into apartments. The investigation went in that direction. We staked out the building where Sparks lived in the hope that another B&E might be attempted. None was. I traveled out of state checking witnesses but I never turned up any real evidence. The case was never solved.

My theory was that the handball player, a neighbor of the victim, came upstairs and knocked on Spark's door. She probably knew him, he was a very charming guy and she let him in. Maybe he was looking for sex and she was not receptive. Maybe he became enraged, picked up the scissors and stabbed her.

But I couldn't convince the boss and there was no real evidence against him. It's a case that stayed with me. I held onto the recording of Karen's last words, recorded over 911, for many years.

***

Even though I was striving to get promoted to Lieutenant, I still enjoyed being a homicide investigator. I had been doing the job for almost six years when I connected with another major case.

I was on duty the night of March 24, 1975 when a 21-year-old young man, John Asinari, was brought to Boston City Hospital and pronounced dead. I was called at 4:15 am and went to the hospital, picking up Detective Jack Spencer along the way. At the hospital I met with a sergeant from the South Boston station, Jim Dolan and he gave us a rundown of the events that brought Asinari to the hospital.

At 3:40 in the morning, officers responding to an anonymous 911 call went to East Second Street in South Boston. There they found Asinari apparently dead in the street and a second man, Robert Moses, age 20, shot, lying nearby. Both Asinari and Moses were MIT students.

John Asinari's father arrived at the hospital and identified his only child. It was an emotional scene. He asked me who was responsible as he pointed to his son's body. At this time I had very little information to give to the father. I told what little I knew and moved on with the investigation.

When, some time later, I looked back on my encounter with father in the presence of his dead son, I realized that I was insensitive to the situation. I looked upon bodies only as evidence. I was almost completely directed towards solving this crime and getting the persons responsible. I was unable to empathize with the father. All I could think of was getting to the surviving victim, Robert Moses. He could help me solve the crime.

Moses had been stabilized and was able to talk when I got to him. He told me an incredible story.

Robert Moses and John Asinari studied at MIT and lived in Cambridge. That night they had gone to Kenmore Square in Boston to have a few drinks, hit some nightspots and relax. This area is surrounded by colleges and is packed with students every night. After midnight they started back towards Cambridge. They walked down Beacon Street to Massachusetts Avenue. When they got to Massachusetts Avenue they stood out on the street and put their thumbs out hoping that someone would pick them up and give them a ride across the bridge to Cambridge. It is a long cold walk across the Mass. Ave. Bridge in March.

Four guys stopped and picked them up. Asinari and Moses got into the back seat of the now crowded car.

The driver started towards Cambridge but suddenly made a right turn from Massachusetts Avenue and went down Back Street, staying on the Boston side of the river. The car was a two-door model and Asinari and Moses were squeezed in the back seat between two others. The driver and passenger sat in the front. Suddenly the driver stopped the car in the alley. The front seat passenger turned around and faced Asinari and Moses. He had a gun in one hand and knife in the other. He started shooting and stabbing the two students. Moses put up his hand to protect himself against the gunshots. One bullet entered the palm of his hand and traveled up his arm to his elbow. The bullet was clearly visible when I was shown the X-ray.

The driver of the car wanted a little sport too. He got a hold of the knife and stabbed Moses and Asinari a couple of times. The two students were trapped in the back seat with no way to exit. The driver started the car again and started driving around Cambridge and Boston. The man in the front seat continued to fire shots at the two students.

There didn't seem to be any motive for this bizarre attack. Moses and Asinari were unknown to their assailants. There was no real attempt to rob them. Moses remembers the guy with the gun in the front seat saying, "You guys think you got it made, don't you?" A telling remark--the sentiments of someone who resented another with brains, talent and good prospects for the future.

The group rode around for about 40 minutes and ended up in South Boston. They stopped at one house and the man with the gun went in and got more bullets. He came back and the nightmare ride continued. Finally the torturers got tired. The driver stopped the car on a small street near East Second Street in South Boston. By this time Asinari had been stabbed about 50 times and shot several times but he was still alive. An opportunity arose and both students fled the car and ran down the street. They split up. Moses ran into a backyard and hid in a pile of wood pallets. Asinari continued down the street. He was pursued by one of the men in the car who caught up to him and then hit him over the head with a two by four. This was the fatal blow. The medical examiner said he probably would have survived had he not suffered this final attack.

Robert Moses said that he could identify the men in the front seat but not those in the back seat with him. He said the man in the front seat, who did most of the shooting, was young, blond hair, pimple faced and acted like a mad man. He described the man driving the car as good-looking, clean-shaven and also about 19 years old. Moses was also able to describe some things about the car they were riding in.

In homicide investigations you must move quickly to insure that witnesses are not compromised. You must get statements from as many people as possible as quickly as possible; otherwise they could become alibi witnesses for the suspect. Jack Spencer and I were back in South Boston at first light and checked the area where Asinari's body was found. We did some canvassing and talked with residents but got no significant information.

As was my usual custom I sought out the officers in the local station who were most likely to know something. Every station has these officers; they are the ones who know all the players. We received some good information from a few detectives and uniformed officers.

We started checking them out. After a couple of false starts we hit upon a person named Robert Shaughnessey. He fit Moses' description of one of the attackers. Jack and I went to his house, got him out of bed and spoke with him. Something did not seem quite right to me. I decided that I was not going to let him walk without Moses taking a look at him. I had enough probable cause to arrest Shaughnessy. I told him that I was taking him to a hospital where

Moses was a patient. He objected but I was determined to move forward.

I told him to get dressed because he was coming with us. He put on his sneakers and I noticed that they had some brown spots on them. As soon as we were out of the house I took his sneakers away from him. Later that day I took them to the lab where tests showed that the stains were human blood.

At the hospital I talked with Robert Moses and explained that I was going to set up a lineup so he could try to identify one of his captors. He was upset and emotional but I was intent on the process going forward.

A lot hinges on the eyewitness identification of a suspect. I did not want to take any chances and allow a defense attorney to claim that the lineup was unfair or improper. I gathered eight young men who worked at the hospital and who agreed to stand in the lineup with Shaughnessey. They were all white, all about the same age as Shaughnessey. I arranged for a hospital attorney to view and attend the lineup to guarantee the fairness of the procedure. The attorney was not happy to be pressed into service in this way but he complied. My guess is that he was not looking forward to being a witness in a later trial. Lawyers, in my experience, do not like getting on the witness stand where you are under oath to tell the truth.

I asked all of the men who would be in the lineup to put on white hospital coats including Shaughnessey. I asked Shaughnessey if he was satisfied with his position in the lineup and he said that he was.

Robert Moses was brought into an outer room in a wheelchair. He was then brought into the room where the lineup was being held. It was a tense moment. He looked the group over carefully and returned to the outer room where I met with him privately. He said nothing. He was distraught, reluctant and scared. I told him to go back and try again. Robert Moses went back in the room and returned, saying that the man who was third from the left was the man with the gun. He had identified Shaughnessey.

I went back into the lineup room and told Shaughnessey that he had been identified and that he would be charged with murder. He wilted a little but did not make any statement. We took him back to the South Boston station and booked him. I saw no point in delaying the process. I believed and still do, that the quicker the investigation moves forward, the better for the case.

Meanwhile, the South Boston detectives were busy on their end. A car had been found torched in South Boston with the keys still in the ignition. The torched car was a two-door sedan and it fit the general description provided by Moses. The detectives went through the burned-out wreck and found Asinari's wallet.

The registration was checked and it was determined that the car had been stolen some time before. One of the South Boston detectives, Sergeant Childers, located and talked to the rightful owner. Sergeant Childers showed him the keys found in the car. The owner admitted that he had left his keys in the car and identified his key ring and car keys. He also noticed an extra key on the ring that was not there when the car was stolen.

The South Boston detectives continued to pump out the names of possible associates of Shaughnessy. One of the names they came up with was John Blodgett who had dropped out of sight. It was known that he came from a big family in Lawrence, Massachusetts. Blodgett had a police record so I was able to get his photo. I also found an address in Lawrence where Blodgett was possibly staying with his brother.

Spencer and I headed up there. We found the apartment empty. Local witnesses said that John Blodgett had been living there but left the night of the murder and had not been seen since. I had the keys found in the ignition of the stolen car including the extra key. I fished out the mystery key and put it in the lock of the apartment. Bingo! The key fit the front door lock. I removed the door lock, purchased a new one and installed it, giving the new key to the landlord.

We talked to neighbors and one recalled seeing Blodgett driving a car similar to the one torched in South Boston.

The case was building well. Robert Moses' condition was improving. I showed him a series of police photos including one of Blodgett. He picked out Blodgett as the driver of the car. I sought a murder warrant for Blodgett's arrest. He had likely fled the state so I entered a federal fugitive warrant into NCIC.

As soon as Shaughnessy was identified we went to all known family, friends and associates to get statements about what they knew, if anything, regarding the murder of John Asinari and about Shaughnessey's whereabouts the night of the murder. If done quickly, people will generally tell the truth. People who otherwise could become defense witnesses are now neutralized and are locked into the statements they made to the police. Soon after questioning them, Shaughnessy's family hired a lawyer and everybody close to Shaughnessy refused to talk to us.

Shaughnessy was now faced with a probable cause hearing in South Boston District Court. Larry Cameron was Chief Justice of this court and it was he who presided. Albert Farese represented Shaughnessy.

The hearing went well until Robert Moses was asked to identify Robert Shaughnessy as the man with the gun.

When Moses looked around the courtroom for Shaughnessey, he was nowhere to be found. Robert Shaughnessy had ducked below the barrier and was out of sight. His brother who looked just like him and was seated in the public area now stood up. It was a blatant attempt by Attorney Farese to have Moses identify the wrong brother. Moses was hesitating. Farese was on his feet claiming that Moses could not identify his assailant.

In South Boston District Court the defendant stands behind a paneled wall about four feet high to the left of the Judge in an area called the prisoner's dock. I saw that Robert Shaughnessey was not even visible to the witness. In fact, he was lying on the floor. I finally got the judge's attention. He was furious. He ordered Robert Shaughnessy to stand up. When he did, Robert Moses identified him. I had seen attorneys use family before in attempts to weaken identification but I had never seen a defendant hide in a courtroom. It was a deliberate attempt to frustrate justice and it almost worked. The judge found probable cause and Robert Shaughnessey was returned to Charles Street Jail to await trial for murder.

John Asinari's father called me frequently, inquiring about the progress of the case. Because only two of the four involved had been charged, he was not happy. It turned out that John was their only son. He had been the family's pride and joy and hope for the future. His death was an enormous tragedy for the family. His mother also called me every day for weeks. Because arrests had been made and more were sure to come, I had more time to deal with the family and I like to think I was more compassionate than I had been at the hospital.

We had two of the assailants identified and in custody and thanks to some detectives in the South Boston District we knew who the other two were. Only one was likely to be charged because of identification problems. As chance would have it, one of these suspects died within a few months of Asinari's murder and the other 18 months later. I do not know the circumstances of their deaths but I do know they were not murdered. I was able to assure Lou Asinari that all the players involved in his son's death were identified.

The case against Robert Shaughnessy was a powerful one and I was looking forward to it. Unfortunately it was not to be. Shaughnessy committed suicide in Charles Street Jail by hanging himself before the trial began.

He had a brother working in the police department and I took a little flack from that direction. I was accused of railroading Robert Shaughnessey. I admit to going all out to arrest and prosecute him, but I could hardly do otherwise.

About a year went by and finally John Blodgett was arrested in California and brought back to Boston. Sergeant Childers and another South Boston detective flew out to get him. It was a suitable reward for all the good work they had done on the case. I brought the case file to the DA's office but I did not have to sell it. The first assistant DA, Jack Gaffney, wanted to be the prosecutor. Ordinarily he did not try cases but this case was going to get a lot of publicity and it was a strong one for the government.

The trial was the most dramatic in years. John Asinari's entire family came to court every day of the trial and seats were always held for them. Even my wife Eleanor came for a couple of days. She was fascinated by the trial. Blodgett was a tall, handsome guy and that accounted for much of the interest in the trial. The trial went well for the government and John Blodgett was convicted of murder in the first degree and sentenced to life imprisonment. In later years, when he was in Walpole State Prison, he became spokesman for his fellow prisoners and got a great deal of publicity. To my knowledge he has never been released.

I was driving home one day in June 1975 when I heard of a shooting on Morrissey Boulevard. I arrived at the scene and saw the body of an old friend, Eddie Connors, slumped in a phone booth. I had known the Connors family for about 20 years.

Eddie was a professional boxer at one time but somewhere along the line he took the wrong track. He was not a dyed-in-the-wool criminal but he associated with some who were. He had done time for attempted bank theft. He was with a group who were breaking into a Rhode Island bank. The burglars tripped an alarm, the police responded and made arrests. Eddie was up a tree acting as a lookout. He fell out of the tree and was arrested. As I say, not a very good criminal.

After he finished his time in jail he bought a tavern in the Savin Hill area of Dorchester. This tavern should have been a money maker but Eddie was a poor businessman and he got mixed up in all kinds of shady deals to keep the operation going. He renewed his association with the guys who got him into trouble in the first place.

The night Eddie Connors was murdered he received a call at his apartment instructing him to go to a pay phone and call a certain number. His assailants knew the location of the phone he was to use. As he was talking on the phone, three men pulled up in a car. Two of them got out, one wielding a shotgun, the other a handgun. They shot Eddie at least a dozen times, blowing off parts of his hand and legs. They blew out the glass in the phone booth. I was at the morgue when the body arrived. When it was transferred from the stretcher to the gurney, bullets and shotgun pellets fell to the floor like rain.

I made a special effort in the investigation because I had a personal connection. But it's very difficult to get results in gangland murders, which is what this likely was. These guys are generally not careless, though they can be. There are examples of guys running a red light with a body in the trunk, or killing the wrong person. In this killing they made no mistakes. I came up with all kinds of theories, none of which proved fruitful. There was no intelligence, not even from the department's organized crime unit, which had a pretty good crew. I made contact with Jimmy Murphy, a neighborhood figure who was a friend and relative of Eddie Connors and known in criminal

183

circles. I think he got more information out of me than I got out of him. He made it pretty clear that he would never meet me again and he never did.

It was 35 years before I knew more about Eddie Connors' murder and that came from John Martorano, a notorious member of Boston's underworld. Martorano was a killer and a teammate of Whitey Bulger and Stevie Flemmi. He was associated with the Winter Hill Gang in Somerville and the Jerry Angiulo group in the North End. At the time of Eddie Connor's murder, however, I had no knowledge of Martorano's existence or of the role that he played in the local underworld, nor did anyone else in the homicide unit. That was a colossal failure of intelligence.

In January 1995 John Martorano was in prison after many years on the run. He learned that both of his associates, Whitey Bulger and Steve Flemmi, had been government informants. He became a government witness and worked out a favorable deal for himself. His rationale was that you can't rat on a rat. He gave it all up and after he had served a modest sentence (considering the number of murders he admitted to committing). He actually wrote a book about his life as a criminal and provided an intimate picture of that life.

In his book he described the killing of Eddie Connors. Martorano was the driver of the car that night, a stolen car. Whitey Bulger and Stephen Flemmi were the shooters. The motive for Eddie's murder was unclear but, likely, it was that Bulger and Flemmi came to believe Eddie was talking too much about the December 1973 murder of Spike O'Toole. Bulger and Flemmi also learned that the FBI was talking to Connors about his involvement in a series of recent robberies in the Boston area. They concluded that he was cooperating with the FBI and decided he was a weak link and had to go.

In his book, Martorano also talked about another unsolved murder that I had worked on. He identified Bobby Palladino as the first man he ever killed. He left his body under the expressway at North Station. I happened to be the uniformed sergeant on scene that night, years earlier. That murder was never solved. I was also involved in the investigation into the shooting and killing of Michael Milano in Brighton. Martarano described what happened to him, too. Milano was mistakenly identified as "Indian Al," an enemy of the Winter Hill gang and marked for death. One night Martorano and two others pulled alongside Milano's car and opened fire. John hit the front seat killing Milano and his accomplice fired into the back seat, hitting a second man and paralyzing him. Milano's girlfriend, also in the front seat, escaped injury. We knew pretty quickly that the killing of Milano was probably a mistake, but got no further.

***

Some murders remain mysteries forever. A cab driver in East Boston named Romano was found shot to death in his cab about a mile from the East Boston Police station. He was 29 years old and a family man. He had done some betting with a local bookie, whose name we knew and had stiffed him. The bookie put some pressure on Romano to pay up but the pressure was mild. Time passed and Romano never paid. The bookie seemed to have accepted the loss. After all, it is a neighborhood business.

Maybe Romano resented being pressured to pay his debts, or perhaps he had a personal beef with the bookie but, in any event, he went to the FBI with his story. The FBI apparently liked the idea of getting the bookie before the Boston Police could. They wired Romano and sent him to the Suffolk Downs racetrack where he engaged the bookie in conversation. The bookie made no incriminating statements so the FBI had to let the case go. Even then everything would have been all right but Romano was a guy who could not keep his mouth shut. About six months after he went to Suffolk Downs wired he told somebody about it. Naturally organized crime could not accept this conduct.

Romano drove a cab nights. He was an easy target. A fare got into his cab, had him drive to a secluded area and then shot him in the head. We had a witness who saw a suspect get in the cab. I tried to get him to make an ID of this suspect. I am sure that we had some gangland members in East Boston worried. Unfortunately the witness could not positively identify the suspect. With the case failing I went directly to the suspect, lied to him about the identification and accused him directly. He was a recent release from the state prison and he called my bluff. I had to back off. I had taken my best shot and missed. Time to move on.

185

Romano's mother called me for years afterwards wanting to know if I had caught the man who killed her son. I never had good news for her and I was uncomfortable with her phone calls. She would cry on the phone. I told her that sometimes, long after a murder, new information comes to light and if that happened we would catch her son's murderer. As time passed her calls dwindled down to about once a year, usually coinciding with her deceased son's birthday. After many years I no longer recognized her voice when she called so she would have to identify herself. I always told her the same story.

District 1, Downtown

Detective Commander

I had been in homicide about six years and I was getting restless. I felt that perhaps it was time to make a change. The boss, Lieutenant Sherry, retired and the new boss and I seldom agreed on things. Also, two of my friends, Lieutenants McDonald and Barry, had been promoted and left. Ordinarily investigators would spend their whole career in homicide but I was getting a little tired of it. I had investigated about 100 homicides and had a respectable conviction rate.

I picked up on some buzz that the powers that be were dissatisfied with the Detective Commander in District 1, the downtown section of the city. I had no idea what the problem was but I let it be known that I was interested in making a change and would be willing to go to District 1. The Superintendent, Joe Jordan, called me into his office. He was surprised to learn of my interest but approved the move and I was transferred in late 1975.

It was a monumental change for which I was totally unprepared. I was coming from a job where I was responsible for working, with my squad of one or two detectives, at solving homicides to a job that required me to supervise twenty-two detectives, fourteen day detectives and eight night detectives. I now had direct responsibility for all the crime and vice problems downtown both day and night, including the Combat Zone, an area still swamped with prostitutes, peep shows, drugs and every kind of vice you could think of. It had become even more violent and dangerous since I had last worked there.

I was a very experienced detective sergeant and knew how to attack crime problems but I had no experience in delegating work. I was used to doing everything myself. But I realized that had to change. I gradually learned that no matter how hard I worked, the job could not be done unless I parcelled out the workload and made the detectives responsible. Fortunately I had a police clerk who helped me make the transition from investigator to supervisor. Because I had focused on nothing but homicides for the previous six years, I also had to do a lot of catch-up studying. My new job required a vast extension of my police knowledge.

I believe that when you get a new job it is unwise to make changes until you are well settled in and have had the opportunity to evaluate the capabilities of those working for you. After close observation, it seemed like the highest priority was the installation of a case management system. Up to that point, detectives were given assignments every day but there wasn't a formal way to monitor and manage the myriad of cases that we handled. The supervisor knew which detective got which case, but there was no follow-up mechanism to see what had been done and when. Naturally, many detectives did nothing, or the bare minimum and just coasted along. Because they got so many cases they could pick and choose the cases that had some promise. This actually worked pretty well but there was very little accountability. In many cases the victim was never contacted. The good detectives looked upon my new case management system as an annoyance and the lazy ones hated it. The system required a written closure report in 30 days. Computer systems in police departments were still in their infancy. This was a paper system and it required a lot of paper. But at least it was a start.

There were some upsides to being the detective commander. I had the police commissioner's old car, a big Buick, to commute in. I also had carte blanche as far as overtime goes and I could work overtime any time I thought it was necessary.

I soon settled into a routine. Each morning I would arrive about 8:00 am and would review all the incidents that had taken place the past 24 hours. I would assign cases to individual detectives as equitably as possible. The least we could do is contact crime victims and listen to their story. This took a lot of my time and I soon decided that a detective could do it as well as I could, so I had a limited-duty detective take over this chore.

It was a very busy office. Prostitutes were arrested every night and every day. Twenty-two detectives generate a lot of arrests and the office was constantly busy. This was real-world Barney Miller and I was Barney.

As I was responsible for conditions in the Combat Zone, I had to come in at night and see for myself what was going on. In addition, every major complaint that came into the station ended up on my desk. It was the hardest job I ever had. The workload was enormous and I was exhausted at the end of every day.

I couldn't get over how many personal problems I had to deal with. I found myself counselling detectives and taking action to forestall personal disasters. There was one team of night detectives who seemed to get along well. One detective on the team came to me and asked if he could be given a different partner. I was very surprised. He didn't give me a reason for his request and it took me some time to figure it out. His partner had a drinking problem. I knew this man personally and always thought of him as a good detective. I called him into my office and told him that he would have to enter the department's stress program designed to assist problem drinkers. He said he would think about it. It was painful for me but I told him that he had no choice. He had to do it right away, so he did. He completed the program and became an active and useful member of the department again. He never did get his partner back. I am convinced that had he not completed the program he would have drifted off into alcoholism, destroying his career and himself.

***

Gaming operations were no different from when I was in vice years earlier. They were still very hard to crack.

We had limited success in making good cases and often had to settle for just shutting the down the games. The deputy gave me free reign to hit any game I wanted. Police detectives could just walk into any club and see what was going on. The doors were open and there were no watchmen. This may have been because there was a steady stream of payoffs to certain officers giving the operators a false sense of security. But other than a token raid now and then, no one had moved against the Chinatown games for years. There was one man, named Harry, who dealt with the police and reportedly distributed payoffs.

One night, a few detectives suggested hitting some games in Chinatown. That sounded like a great idea to me. I decided in the interest of harmony and coordination, to inform the new acting lieutenant in charge of the vice squad of my intentions. The notification was a mistake. He asked me not to; he said he had just sought some warrants and was planning a raid soon. I think, in truth, he was nervous when he heard my plan because he would have been embarrassed. After all, he was the head of the vice squad and had not ordered any raids for years. He did indeed get warrants, hit some clubs and got a lot of publicity some weeks later. I never made that same mistake again. From then on, whenever I intended to raid a place I told no one until just before I executed the warrants.

In relative terms, gaming in Chinatown was not an evil thing and I couldn't really get upset at the gambling. It was the payoffs that worried me. Once I was able to get things going we served two warrants a night. I could walk into one of these clubs with a couple of detectives, or even alone and order all present to stand where they were. They would stop the game and comply. I would then call for the wagon, pick up the money and chips and send them all to the station.

Occasionally an elderly gentleman would ask to be allowed to leave and we always acceded. It was not unusual to have 30 players in the club. There were no problems making arrests in Chinatown.

However, processing the arrested at the station was a pain because of the language problems. It was an inconvenience to prisoners but it cost them no money. The club running the game (or Harry) would pay all bail fees and any fines ordered by the court. It was a good day for the bondsman. The more prisoners, the more money he made. His risk was close to zero. The bondsmen loved to come to the station when large numbers were arrested in Chinatown. They were always bailed out.

On rare occasions there would be violence. It happened when a group came from another city and tried to shake down the merchants or the gaming clubs. There would be shootouts, sometimes fatalities, but these conflicts were relatively brief and order always returned.

Like any other closed community the locals reacted sharply to outsiders in their midst who came to cause problems. The young local gangs would not hesitate to attack and beat outsiders who were unwelcome.

As we cracked down on the Chinatown games, over time, they resorted to elaborate security measures, using lookouts, TV cameras, double and barricaded doors. It made it much more difficult for us to gather sufficient evidence to obtain a search warrant. Nevertheless we continued with the raids.

In those years the Combat Zone was designated as an 'Adult Entertainment Zone' in an attempt to keep activities that took place there contained within a manageable zone. The problem was, it wasn't manageable.

Prostitutes multiplied like bacteria. Robberies and assaults skyrocketed. I saw the stats every day and told the deputy superintendent and the captain what was happening. But it appeared they were powerless to do anything about it. The Adult Entertainment Zone was a political experiment by the mayor and no one wanted to admit that it might have been a bad idea.

The captain made a point of never getting involved. Meanwhile it got so dangerous in the Zone that the operators of the X-rated movie theaters wanted to hire a detail officer to keep their patrons from being robbed or assaulted when they entered or left the movies. I thought it was a good idea but my bosses would not allow it.

I was charged with enforcing the vice laws in the Combat Zone and if I failed to take action I felt I would be open to suspicion that I was on their payroll. All the businesses in the Combat Zone know who the police are and they especially know those who were a threat to them. I would be recognized either with or without a detective as soon as I entered a club or bar. A signal would go out to the girls to cool the action until we had left the premises. Once in awhile, when the lookouts were careless, we could slip by and when we did it was not unusual to find bargirls engaging in sexual acts with customers in dark corners. Blatant misbehavior would cause us to make arrests and to prosecute the owners for license violations.

On one occasion I entered a bar undetected, the 2 O'clock Lounge, with Detective Ballard and observed a large crowd gathered around a rear stage. We got in close and observed a dancer lying on the floor naked and simulating sex with a dildo, which was a clear violation of the obscenity laws. We waited until the show was over, followed her to her dressing room and placed her under arrest. We sent her to the station where she was processed. I seized her costume and her apparatus. The case was an easy shot in the lower court. The girl was found guilty. She appealed to the Superior Court where obscenity and civil rights lawyers (hired by the clubs) sought to have the case dismissed. Apparently they were successful because I never heard about the case again. The dancer did call me later and asked if she could have her costume back. There wasn't much to them, just a Gstring and pasties. I gave them back to her. I guess they were expensive.

Movie theaters in the Combat Zone ran X-rated movies seven days a week. We would check them out every so often but there rarely was anything criminal going on. I remember getting a phone call that someone had planted a bomb in one of these theaters so I went in with a couple of detectives to make a quick search. We told the projectionist of our concerns and he allowed the film to continue but put the lights on in the theatre. The patrons in the theater were embarrassed as hell and there was plenty ducking of heads. We did not find a bomb.

Late at night the prostitutes in the Zone would operate in packs. They concentrated at Washington and Boylston Streets and very aggressively approached drivers of cars. If the cars were not locked they would get right in and rob the drivers. Pedestrians were also targets and got the same treatment. Only a small portion of these victims contacted the police. Who wants a public record of the fact you were in the Zone at 2:00 am and got robbed by a prostitute? There were always a few who did want to prosecute. They would go back to the scene with detectives to try to pick out the girls who robbed them. They were rarely successful.

Nevertheless prostitutes were arrested constantly. Not a night went by without two or three arrests. In spite of this we made only a small dent in the problem. When the weather got cold it was sad to see these girls standing on street corners hustling tricks, sometimes dressed in scanty costumes. They made a lot of money but most of it went to their pimp. In 1975, a thousand dollars a week would not be an unusual wage for a working girl.

The Combat Zone continued to prosper until street thugs murdered a Harvard student one night in 1976. The newspapers reacted and when they did, the mayor had the police cool down the area. It took the death of a Harvard student to expose the folly of the Adult Entertainment Zone.

***

The Boston Common was fast becoming a place where it was dangerous to walk, especially at night in the mid 1970s. It was a hangout for drug dealers, street hustlers and the homeless. In the daytime, con men would set up card games like three card monte. The card dealer worked with an associate who would win a couple of times, then a mark would be invited into the game and allowed to win a little. Invariably the mark's luck would go bad and he'd lose it all. It's illegal to gamble on Boston Common and we constantly tried to nab these street hustlers but with limited success. These hustlers were street smart, had good lookouts and could sense a cop coming. And they could run faster than we could.

***

Ted Landsmark was going into City Hall one afternoon for a community affairs meeting. Landsmark, who was African-American, was unlucky enough to wander into an anti-busing demonstration. The crowd turned on him and he took a beating. His nose was broken and he was taken to Massachusetts General Hospital. I quickly heard of the incident and went to the hospital with two good detectives to talk to him. He was all patched up around the face but still looked pretty rough. He told a straightforward story: He was walking into City Hall to a community organizers meeting when one the demonstrators attacked him. The demonstrators were all white. He said that one of demonstrators was carrying an American flag on a large pole that he used as a spear to attack him. Landsmark was cogent after the attack and said he appreciated our interest but he also said he would be unable to make any identifications.

There was no shortage of news media covering the anti-busing demonstration so there were good photos and even a video of the attack. I obtained copies and took them to South Boston, as that was the base of the anti-busing movement.

Two South Boston detectives recognized the man attacking Landsmark and identified him as a guy named Rakes who was well known in Southie. Others involved in the assault were also identified but Rakes was the major offender. Rakes was arrested and tried. There was a dramatic photo of Rakes attacking Landsmark with the flag. Unfortunately, the photographer, Stanley Foreman, who won a prize for the photo, refused to testify at the trial. The video cameraman, John Premack from one of the local televisions stations, had taken great footage of the assault. He testified and was a good government witness. Rakes was ultimately convicted and did time.

193

A group of condominium owners in a small six-unit building on Beacon Hill came in one day with a novel complaint. One of the first-floor owners refused to pay his condo fees and the other owners were trying to get him to either pay his share or move out. This did not make for a happy building. The delinquent owner would strike back at his fellow owners from time to time by disabling the only elevator in the building. We figured out that he did this by reaching up in the elevator and bending the control rods.

We told the disgruntled owners that in order to make a successful prosecution for malicious destruction of property one has to be caught in the act and that would be difficult. Surveillance cameras were not yet commonplace. I had an idea. I called the crime lab and had them go to the building when the owner was not at home. I asked them to paint the control rods with an invisible dye that would stain any human hand that touched it. The stain would be a deep purple and would be very difficult to remove. I then talked to one of the owners and told him to call me the next time the elevator was disabled. He called me the next day.

I went down to the building with a detective and knocked on the first-floor apartment door. The occupant was at home but refused to open the door. The next morning I sent two detectives to his place of employment. He hid so they could not examine his hands. I am sure they were violently purple. We were never able to get a case together but the tampering of the elevator stopped.

***

Politics continued to play an increasing role in the department. It was 1976 and an election year. Mayor White hosted a breakfast at the Ritz for a group of campaign contributors and was accused of putting pressure on the group for contributions. A scandal was brewing and The Boston Globe was pushing the story. The mayor responded by selecting a patrolman who worked in the DA's office, John Doyle, to investigate the charges. John Doyle's investigation found the mayor innocent of any wrongdoing. A short time later Patrolman Doyle was promoted to full superintendent. He was placed in charge of the detectives.

***

Card games aren't the biggest evil in the world but they are illegal and periodically we would plan a raid. Shortly after I came to District 1 I was walking down Hanover Street and met an old adversary in a bribery case, North End Nick. He was still a North End guy with Mafia connections and he remembered me.

Nick was known to be running high stakes card games and one night I found out he was running a game in a dingy club on Charter Street. I got a gaming warrant and waited for the weekend to serve it. Search warrants have a life of 10 days after which they are invalid. We checked the club at 2:00 am and it was in darkness with a lock on the outside of the door. It appeared that no action was taking place but all is not what it appears not be.

A short distance down Charter Street we observed a man asleep in his car. The car was parked up on the sidewalk close to an apartment building. A window in a first-floor apartment was open. It was a warm night. All this is not unusual in the crowded North End. What was unusual was that we knew the individual asleep in the car. His name was Peg Leg and he was a fringe criminal guy. We watched for a while.

When a player wanted to get into the game he would wake Peg Leg who would walk him up to the club. Peg Leg used a key to open the padlock and the player entered. The padlock was reset. When someone wanted to leave the game they called the apartment with the open window. Peg Leg heard the ring through the open window. He would go back to the club and let them out.

We grabbed Peg Leg, frisked him, took his key to the padlock and got into the club and game. There were six players but no money on the table. It isn't much of a gaming case if no money is found. Nick was mad as hell. He said "Daley, there's no money here. We play only for chips. We settle up the next day."

I seized all the paraphernalia anyway, but the case would go nowhere. A week later Nick came into the station and asked for the stuff that I seized. There was no case. I gave it all back to him.

***

I was working one Saturday night when I received a call from an old friend, Arthur Sutliffe. He told me that there was going to be an uncomplimentary story coming out in The Boston Globe Sunday morning about District 1. I was concerned but not particularly worried. I knew of no scandal and had been in the job for a little more than a year.

The story was on the front pages and portrayed a full-scale scandal accusing District 1 officers of having a cozy relationship with the Mafia and turning a blind eye to incidents of vice. It covered the period of time prior to my arrival in the district. Undercover detectives reporting directly to the police commissioner prepared the report. Now I knew why Superintendent Jordan was incredulous when I had volunteered to go to District 1 a year earlier; he was aware of this potential scandal but did not confide in me.

The three commanders at the time of the alleged scandal were Deputy Saia, Captain Casale and Sergeant Detective Al Savioli. Saia and Savioli had been transferred some time ago. The new team was Deputy Schroeder, Captain Casale and me. The story was a damning one and it knocked Saia, Casale and Savioli. Police Commissioner DiGrazia delivered the story to the press taking the position that he was in no way responsible.

Soon afterward, DiGrazia left for a new job in Maryland. During his tenure in Boston he made the mistake of turning the Patrolman's Union into a bitter enemy. Nevertheless he left the department in better shape. He eliminated the endemic corruption of the sergeant detectives. This was a major accomplishment.

The rank and file were optimistic when the mayor appointed Joe Jordan as police commissioner in November 1976. Now that Jordan was the commissioner he felt that he had to take some action in the District 1 scandal. He decided to transfer the command staff -- Schroeder, Casale and all the detectives, as well as me. Much publicity accompanied these transfers.

Traditionally, when scandals occur in police departments, everyone gets transferred, the guilty and the innocent. Nevertheless, I was surprised to find myself transferred since Jordan knew that I had no part in the scandal. No matter. I was sent to District 6 in South Boston as detective commander.

District 6, South Boston

Detective Commander

South Boston was much quieter than downtown Boston. It was essentially a residential area with businesses and some industrial areas. It was an insular, old-time neighborhood, predominantly Irish, consisting of housing developments, expensive waterfront homes and catholic churches. It was also a hotbed of anti-busing activity and the home of some major gangsters, including Whitey Bulger. In terms of crime, there was a lot of local gaming. They were still taking the dog and horse action in the bars and cafés. There was some minor corruption at the station house level, uniformed sergeants and old timers on the pad. Maybe some detectives too, but I never saw it.

My workload was drastically reduced. In District 1 I had two dozen detectives working for me. In District 6 I had six and a couple of clerks. In District 1 it took me two hours to go over all the police reports and in District 6 it took 15 minutes. I had a great deal of time on my hands so I did a lot of walking.

The captain, Joe Mills, was an old acquaintance. He and I got along well. We agreed what our targets would be and both of us were determined to do our very best to make things work. The detectives were of mixed ability but at least all were willing to work. There was considerable apprehension at the prospect of my arrival as I was known to be a straight-shooter and that was not the tradition in South Boston. Prior to my arrival at least one detective retired saying that he was taking no chances.

The courthouse in South Boston was a fascinating place. There was a real family atmosphere. Most defendants knew someone there. The chief clerk was John Flaherty, a South Boston native and charming guy who had held the clerk's job for many years. He was supported by an efficient staff of assistants. The Chief Justice was Larry Cameron, a former Assistant DA I knew from my homicide days. He was an honest and hardworking guy. One of the associate justices, Joe Feeney, was an old Southie guy. He had difficulty finding anyone guilty, especially a South Boston resident. If he absolutely had to find someone guilty he had an even harder time sending them to jail.

One of my duties was to go after the local bookies. Unfortunately for me, bookies in South Boston were not looked upon as evil people and the courthouse reflected this community attitude. The courthouse personnel never got in my way when I attempted to enforce the gaming laws but there were times when they were less than enthusiastic. When I would come in with a tricky gaming warrant the chief clerk would say, "See Ralph" who was the assistant clerk. Ralph would grumble but he always heard the application and granted the warrant. I was never asked to do anything unethical in my many appearances before the court.

It did not take me long to realize that as soon as I left the station house and started walking up Broadway the word would be passed to the bookies that I was out and lookouts would start setting up. Ironically, the bookies got this information from the patrol officers. Many of these officers had been in the district a long time and naturally knew all of the action guys.

There were about eight centers of illegal gaming in the district. One of the most notorious was a barroom called the Penn Café, located almost across the street from the station house. It had been in operation for many years and was one of the most difficult to crack. The owner, Hank, owned a big Cadillac, which he parked right at the front door. At least two bookies, Watson and Driscoll, operated out of the bar. When I first arrived at District 6 one of my first acts was to walk into the door of the bar and tell one of the bookies that I was going to do everything I could to knock him out of business. He was not happy. It was open warfare after that.

The café had unusual operating hours. It opened at 10 am and it closed every night at 6 pm. I never heard of anyone having a meal in this café and I never saw food in their kitchen. The proximity to the station was an asset back in the days when there were payoffs but now it was a nuisance for them.

Watson, Driscoll and Garrity ran a sophisticated operation. They never did any business when a stranger was in the café. This made it impossible to send in an undercover officer to drink and watch. If there was a new a face in the café, they would shut down the operation and not resume until that person left. When a stranger did come in, when they left they would be followed. A simple and very effective strategy because often an undercover officer will go to a very obvious unmarked police car parked around the corner.

Lookouts were posted, one inside the door of the café and one out on the street. The inside man sat at the front door and looked out through the venetian blinds. Every time I walked into the Penn Café, I would find about 40 middle-aged men sitting around drinking coffee. There was some alcohol being consumed but coffee seemed to be the predominate beverage. If I were quick enough getting to the front door, I could hear the lookout shout, "Duck!" just before I got through the door. I would go through the place checking everywhere -- including behind the bar and back office. I never found any betting slips. I found a lot of Armstrong Racing Forms, but I could not make a case solely on them. I had to have betting slips if I was going to get a case together. There were no telephones in the café. I was always checking for hidden wires and for drops. I never found them. I would go into the café about once a week and it was driving them crazy.

After awhile, it appeared everyone was more relaxed when I came into the café. They hadn't stopped booking, it just seemed that they had earlier warning. We figured out how. I noticed the same guy day after day hanging around a gas station directly across from the café. A detective and I walked up to him and searched him. He was found to be carrying an electronic device that looked something like a remote garage door opener. He was using it to send a signal into the café every time we came near. We confiscated it and had some fun sending the café false signals over the next few days.

For all our efforts, we were never able to get a strong gaming case out of the Penn Café. Gaming cases are difficult to prosecute, sometimes even harder than homicides. Bookies have money and can hire the best lawyers so we could be sure of an aggressive defense. There is also little satisfaction in getting a gaming conviction compared to a murder conviction. Nevertheless it is a job that has to be done, otherwise there would be a bookie on every corner and wholesale corruption.

Some bookies in South Boston were easy to catch. One was Lefty Johnson. Lefty was so named because he had only one arm, the right one. We could walk into his café just before the daily double went off and catch him right in the act of taking a bet. When arrested he would say, "What's a one armed guy to do?" Actually, he did pretty well.

***

South Boston has a history of violent and murderous gangs. During my tenure a couple of the worst gangs had left or were considerably weakened. The few that were left became quite powerful. The big man was Whitey Bulger and he maintained a very low profile. Nevertheless, he was the boss of all illicit activities in South Boston. His reputation was such that no one challenged him.

The dominant gang in South Boston for many years was the Mullen gang. The Mullens were involved in a violent and ongoing conflict with a Charlestown gang led by the McLaughlins, a Somerville group known as the Winter Hill gang and a North End Mafia gang lead by Jerry Angiulo. Only the smartest and quickest could survive these wars and Whitey Bulger was one. I never had any contact with Whitey Bulger during my time in South Boston, but as the detective sergeant I got a lot of feedback relative to some of his activities. I never came close to charging him with any violation of the law, but if I had, who would have been willing to testify against him?

One incident involving Bulger concerned an investigative reporter from the Herald American named Eddie Corsetti. Eddie's story dug deep into Whitey's criminal activities and was going to embarrass Whitey's brother Billy, a prominent politician. As the story goes, Eddie Corsetti was seated in a North End bar one evening before the story came out. Whitey came into the bar and sat next to Corsetti. He let Corsetti know that the consequences of printing the story would be devastating to the reporter. The story was never printed.

The Hogan brothers were a dangerous group in South Boston. I knew at least three of them. George Hogan was considered the most dangerous. He owned a small variety store on D Street where he sold groceries, beer and wine.

One night, one of the Hogans had a beef with Tommy Nee on East Broadway in front of a Legion Post that had a liquor license. Tommy Nee was acting as a bouncer for the Post and he gave this particular Hogan a beating. Nee was a survivor of gang wars and dangerous himself. The beating took place at 7 pm..

At 10 pm, Tommy Nee was shot to death on the sidewalk right outside the Legion Post. I'm convinced that one of the Hogan brothers shot Nee to death. I didn't arrive on the scene until some time later. When I did, the body was gone but George Hogan was there. He and I exchanged a few words. He was obviously there to see who was talking to the police. His presence was intimidating and despite the sidewalk being a normally busy place at that time of night no one came forward to talk to us.

After the Nee shooting I started looking into the ownership of the bars, cafés and liquor stores in South Boston. I was amazed to see the same names appearing on many of the licenses. There were about five names in general use, all associates of Whitey Bulger. These names would appear on the license, usually three names, in random combinations. It was clear that Whitey Bulger controlled a lot of liquor outlets. I met with FBI officials and advised them to buy the next liquor joint that came on the market in South Boston. If they did so, it would not be very long before Whitey would come to them with a deal they couldn't refuse. They had been after Whitey for years and had the patience and money to do this sort of thing. They didn't take my advice.

Years afterwards it became common knowledge that they already had Whitey as an informant and would take no action that might endanger this status.

***

Jimmy Matera was killed in Hap's Lounge on West Broadway, a dive bar owned by Louis Litif. I knew Louis. He was one of a group of handball players who used the courts at the YMCA on Huntington Ave. We weren't friends although he seemed to go out of his way to be friendly with me. I kept my distance. I knew him to be a minor racketeer.

I suspected that Louis had a gaming office and took a lot of sports bets in his bar, but I was never able to get further into his activities. I did know that one of his associates, some years earlier, betrayed Louis's sports action to the police. It was believed that before the case came to trial Louis shot him. The informant lived but refused to testify and the case collapsed.

Louis was not the sole owner of Hap's Lounge. He had members of organized crime as partners, including Whitey Bulger and his associates. Another partner was Jimmy Matera who was one of Whitey's collectors.

One night there was an argument between Louis and Jimmy over expenses; Louis was holding money back on his partners. He said the money went to pay the water bill. Matera didn't buy it and slapped Louis around in the bar. For a gangster like Louis it was humiliating for patrons to see this happen in his own place.

He fumed about his disgrace. Then, a few days later he and Matera were together again in the bar. It was morning and the place was quiet. The issue of the money came up again. Louis invited Jimmy Matera to go down to the cellar with him. He wanted to show him the broken water meter that would explain the missing money. It was a pretext and Jimmy Matera may have guessed it because he said to the bartender, jokingly, "If I don't come back in a minute, Louis shot me."

He was right. As soon as they got into the cellar Louis shot him four times, killing him. Louis walked out of the cellar alone and out of the café. The bartender apparently was busy because he didn't notice that Matera hadn't come up. Of course he didn't hear the shots. It wasn't until a couple of hours later that he had occasion to go down to the cellar where he found Matera's body and called the police. At least that was what he told me when I questioned him afterward.

The bartender, named Conrad, was a mild mannered guy and refused to make any statements, at least to me. He did later speak to Bill Smith from Homicide. Bill told me that the bartender knew what happened but that he was scared. I came down hard on the bartender. Eventually he told me what happened but said he would never testify because he was terrified of Litif. I wouldn't let the bartender off the hook that easily and put pressure on him to testify. He had to make a choice -- either he came with us, or stayed with Louis. He chose to stay with Louis.

Louis had a head start. He disappeared so we couldn't question him. A day or so later the bartender disappeared. I tracked down the bartender's girlfriend and got a copy of her phone bills. I saw calls from Las Vegas and she admitted that he had called her from out there. That was the last anyone ever saw or heard from him.

Louis was no dope. He knew that Conrad was the only person that could put him in jail. Louis had a place in rural Canada. The story goes that a while later, Louis tracked down Conrad, brought him to Canada where he killed him and buried him in the woods. I wanted to go up there to see if anyone remembered Conrad staying at Louis's place but the District Attorney's office would not go for it. John Connolly, Whitey Bulger's FBI handler, had contact with Conrad's family afterward. He assured them that Conrad was drunk and suffered no pain when Louis shot and killed him. Connolly did not share this information with me, even though I was the principal investigator.

I drove the case as far as I could. It went before a grand jury but without the bartender the case would go nowhere. Louis was back in town now and appearing very confident because he knew he had the case licked. He also knew he was in big trouble with Whitey because he had killed one of his guys, Matera. We couldn't get to Louis but Whitey and his partners in the bar could and did. About six months later Louis was found shot to death in the trunk of his Mercury Marquis. The case was never solved but there was little doubt as to who killed him and why. In January 2012, as part of the FBI corruption trial, a federal court awarded a sum in excess of $1 million to the Litif family.

I learned later that Louis went to the FBI and offered to give up Whitey and make a deal for himself. John Connolly and a high-ranking Boston Police officer turned him down. The FBI didn't share this with me. It's conceivable that Connolly passed the information about Louis's offer to Whitey.

***

I was still on the promotion list for Lieutenant. I had been jumped over by political appointees but was still in a good position to get promoted. In the meantime, a variety of cases came across my desk.

A cab driver was robbed one Sunday morning and because I was the only detective working, I went to the scene. I took the driver back to the station and had him go through our photo books to see if he could pick out the holdup man. The driver told me that he had seen the thief many times in South Boston and had had him as a fare before. He could not make an ID from the photo books. I continued the investigation and several days later a suspect's name was passed on to me. I checked our photo books and noted that this suspect's photo was not there. I found a different photo of the suspect and mailed it to the cab driver with instructions that he should notify me if the photo was of the man who robbed him. It turned out that it was.

A few days later the cab driver went to the station and spoke with a night desk lieutenant. He left the photo with the lieutenant with a message that the man in the photo was the robber. The lieutenant never passed on the message or the photo. Since I hadn't heard from the cab driver, I assumed that he did not recognize the suspect in the photo.

At that point I had been in the South Boston station for three years and was tired of chasing bookies. I took a vacation in Florida and while there I got a telephone call informing me that I had been transferred back to District 1, downtown and placed in charge of the night detectives. The cab robbery investigation would follow me there.

***

My days of volunteering for assignments were over. In this case I was just a piece on the chessboard. I was transferred back to the Downtown district neither as a reward or a punishment. Apparently the sergeant who was in the job got himself into a nasty scandal and had to be transferred at once. He was caught shaking down the Chinatown games, downtown bars and Combat Zone strip clubs. He was a politically connected guy and had to be taken care of. The word was that the police commissioner needed a legitimate guy to take his place and I was it.

The sergeant being transferred took my place in South Boston. His escape from punishment in District 1 did not change his habits. He immediately made it clear to his underlings that he was going to control the action personally. He was a corrupt guy and later was caught by the FBI extorting money. We later found that he was given immunity and cooperated with the Bureau in an effort to nail other corrupt cops. He wore a wire and enticed other officers into criminal conversations. He did not do one day of time and stayed on the job. It was a perfect example of letting the big fish go to catch the minnows. But this was all in the future.

Back to the South Boston cab robbery. In a public relations move, our superintendent, John Doyle, gave a newspaper team from The Boston Globe permission to look over the detectives files in South

Boston. While going through the file, they came across the cab robbery. They called up the driver and asked him about the case. He related that he had been robbed, had viewed photos but could not pick anyone out. He told them that he had then received another photo in the mail. That photo was of the man who had robbed him. He said he went back to the station and told the officer on the desk that the man in the photo robbed him. And he told the newspaper team that he never heard from the police again.

As I was no longer in the South Boston station. The newspaper team never asked me for an explanation. The corrupt sergeant who took my place was indifferent to my situation and probably resented my taking his place after he was kicked out of District 1. Charges were filed against me alleging that I showed a witness a single photo in violation of the department's rules and regulations. It was a technical violation of a new procedure. I should have known better.

The hearing officer, Captain Bob Bradley, admitted to me that he had no choice but to find me guilty because of pressure from the commissioner. I knew Commissioner Jordan was sore at me because I was allied with several captains who had confronted him about political promotions. I was given a reprimand, which was made part of my record. I was concerned that this reprimand would give Jordan an excuse for passing me over for promotion and promotions were now imminent. In the long run Joe Jordan did promote me to lieutenant.

In the meantime, I was back in District 1, back in the world of prostitutes, gaming, strip clubs and X-rated movies. I wasn't enthusiastic about it. I was the night commander with only 5 detectives where previously I was the overall commander. It was difficult to play a lesser role. Fortunately, the detectives were good officers and because of my reputation as a straight shooter they were on their best behavior. Professionally it was a boring time for me. I kept busy working my off duty sideline building houses on Nantucket Island. I made a buck and used up surplus energy.

District 3, Mattapan
District 2, Roxbury

Lieutenant

On October 27, 1980, I was promoted to lieutenant. My initial assignment was to Staff Inspection where my old friend, Captain Jim McDonald, was presently assigned. This was a dead-end assignment, a dumping ground for those out of favor. Fortunately, at the last moment, my assignment changed. I was sent to District 3 in Mattapan as night desk lieutenant. I assume that I was sent there because nobody else wanted it. It wasn't great but it was better than Staff Inspection. It was an old and decrepit station house in a high crime area.

I reported to District 3 just before midnight for my first tour of duty. In every new assignment there is a testing period. The officers under you want to see what your limits are. At my first roll call a sergeant lined up the men for inspection and assignments. As I went through the roster he gave the order for the officers to stand at ease. This struck me as inappropriate and I instructed the sergeant that the order should have been "Attention to roll call." I made this comment in front of the men. It was a rather chilly start but that is how the mood is set.

I was back in uniform after serving the previous twelve years in plain clothes. I was also back to working rotating evening and midnight shifts. This was tough on a 52 year-old.

The station was busy and getting busier all the time. The Sergeants in District 3 were a good lot, most of them very young. I had great sergeants; Pugsley, a very good worker from a police family; Gaughan, a real take charge guy; Cummings, smart and cool; Parlon, Reardon and Spring, new but willing to learn.

***

In the early 1980's the city and the police department were in a financial crisis. Mayor White reacted by slashing the police department's budget and ordering some stations closed, including District 3. Officers, some with up to five years of experience, were

206

laid off. Some ranking officers were demoted. Lieutenants went back to being sergeants and some were demoted two ranks to patrol officer. Many sergeants went back to being patrol officers.

When District 3 was closed I moved to District 2 in Roxbury. I was still a lieutenant working nights on the desk. It was high-crime and fast paced and I enjoyed it. I had only been in District 3 for eight months and I was still learning the ins and outs of running the station.

There was a steady stream of arrests coming in. The demand for police services was incessant. Citizens came to the front desk seeking assistance. The cells were always nearly full. The desk officer had to be alert. Decisions had to be made quickly and appropriately. The younger officers seemed to have a talent for getting into bizarre situations and they looked to me for guidance. I was a teacher as well as an administrator.

Before the layoffs we had 23 two-person police cars and wagons rolling out on a first half and 11 on last half. Afterwards it was nine on first half and eight on last half. Crime had not gone down -- it had in fact increased -- but our ability to respond had been cut in half.

Another result of the financial crunch was that the fleet was not kept up. Cruisers were dented, some with leaking mufflers and non-functioning heaters or air conditioners. The better cars were used by the sergeants, which some patrol officers resented. We just tried to keep the cars rolling from one tour of duty to the next. Driving beat up police cars in a high crime area only seemed to make things more depressing. Every day there was an accident with a police car.

***

Because District 2 was such a frantic place everyone had to chip in and carry their share of the load just to keep the place functioning. A long-time friend of mine from the District 16 days was working as a sergeant in District 2 when I got there. We had been friends for almost 20 years. He was a nice guy and we had had some great times together but unfortunately he was a lazy policeman. Now he was working for me and did not make the slightest effort to do the sergeant's job. He squeaked in at the last minute. Then he took out a newspaper and settled into the captain's office for some casual reading. Meanwhile everyone else was working at a frantic pace.

It exasperated me and as time went by I pressured him to do better. I ordered him out of the office and into the fray. His response was lackluster. As a result we had a falling out and he was transferred.

***

Every day in District 2 was like an episode of Hill Street Blues. The strain on the officers working the street was tremendous. Some tolerated it better than others. Occasionally there was a nervous breakdown.

An officer arrested a man for an armed robbery near the station. An accomplice, a woman, got away. During the booking the accomplice came into the station to inquire about her partner in crime and was taken into custody. As she was being brought to the booking desk she attacked the arresting officer, biting him as he struggled with her. Then she took out a knife that had been concealed in her dress and began swinging it wildly. An officer nearby grabbed the knife and subdued the woman. The arresting officer, overtaken by stress and flushed with adrenaline, ran into a corner screaming before being ushered into a private office by one of his colleagues so that he could recover his composure. This officer was otherwise exemplary, not prone to being overly sensitive. It was just that he was placed in an environment that put too much stress on him.

***

I no longer had a department car assigned to me and drove my own car to work each night. I parked in a large lot across from the station where it was visible. One night I looked out the window shortly before I was to go home and my car was gone -- stolen. Officers Hallum and Myer recovered it about five hours later with only minor damage. They were a great team with that distinct ability to diffuse many a dangerous situation. I was grateful to them for finding my car and on the next tour of duty I gave them each a box of candy.

***

A young officer named Cunningham was driving down Blue Hill Avenue near Talbot Avenue with his partner, a young woman police

208

officer. As they passed a small nightclub they saw a man shoot another man right in front of the club then drive off. Cunningham jammed on his brakes. His partner immediately jumped out and went to check on the man who had been shot while Cunningham took off after the shooter. He caught up with the suspect's car and ordered him to get out. The suspect came out shooting. Cunningham was hit in the arm. The patrol supervisor arrived. The suspect was still shooting and one of his bullets went through the supervisor's windshield. Cunningham returned fire and killed the shooter. It was amazing work by all of the officers involved. Unfortunately the incident was not too unusual an event for the officers working in District 2.

***

My sons, John and Richard, decided to follow in my footsteps and become police officers. In 1983 they enrolled in the Boston Police Academy. They were appointed to the Boston Police Department on July 15, 1983. Richard's wife, Linda pinned his badge on him and I pinned the badge on John. Commissioner Joe Jordan presided over the ceremony and he appeared surprised when I pinned John. I hoped at the time that he would not carry any grudges against me that would affect my sons. I shouldn't have worried. Jordan wouldn't be around forever.

Within minutes after leaving the graduation ceremonies, citizens seeking directions or information approached John and Richard. It was their first time in uniform in public and they were flustered by the questions but officers quickly adjust to their high-visibility roles and to public expectations.

***

Morale in District 2 was high but so was sick time abuse. Some officers called in sick 38 times in the first five months of the year. They used up all of their sick time early in the year and wouldn't get paid when they needed to take a real sick day. They didn't seem to care.

I asked one high performing officer why he had taken 15 sick days in the first six months of the year. He answered, "Because that's all they gave me." He went on to say the stress of working on the street in District 2 was so great that every so often he had to take a break to preserve his mental health.

Not long before he and his partner pulled over a car for a routine traffic stop. As the officers were approaching the driver pulled a gun and started shooting. One officer dove under a parked car to escape the bullets. His partner opened fire on the shooter. A dozen shots were exchanged before the suspect jumped in his car and drove off. No wonder these guys needed an extra day off every once in awhile.

***

One officer in District 2 told me that he won a hundred dollars in a card game and he wanted to keep it from his wife. He went to the bank and turned it into a one hundred dollar bill. He knew that his wife was desperately afraid of guns so he rolled up the bill and placed it in the barrel of his service revolver, which he promptly forgot about. He ended up firing his gun in the line of duty sometime afterward and blew his $100 bill to bits.

***

I received a telephone call from the girlfriend of an officer suspected of drug use. She told me he was getting deeper and deeper into drugs. She asked if there was anything I could do to help. The officer was at work and I called him to my office. I sent him to the hospital for treatment. I told him that was his only hope of keeping his job. It was non-negotiable. He went to the hospital but walked right back out. He was arrested several days later when he came back to work. He ended up being fired.

***

In early August, 1983, I got a phone call notifying me that I was being transferred along with two other lieutenants. It was a bolt out of the blue. I enjoyed working in District 2.

My next job wasn't as challenging or enjoyable. I was transferred to Staff Inspection. My job was to check on officers in the field and in the station houses to make sure they were following basic rules while on duty. It was something of a dumping ground for those out of favor. To make things worse the deputy superintendent who ran the unit was difficult to work for. I was put on nights and tried to make the best of it.

Although I didn't like the staff inspection job I did get the opportunity to visit the stations and catch up with people. I remained in Staff Inspections for fourteen months.

Homicide Commander

In 1985 the new mayor, Ray Flynn, forced Commissioner Jordan to resign. There was also an exodus of superintendents and deputy superintendents and other political appointees. Flynn announced a nationwide search for a new commissioner but he ended up picking one of his best friends, Mickey Roache, from down the street in South Boston. My old friend Jim McDonald was one of two finalists for the position.

In April I was transferred back to homicide as the commanding officer. My old friend Jack Barry was influential in the assignment. I suppose it didn't hurt that he was a friend of the new commissioner.

**

As the lieutenant in overall command of the Homicide Unit I had 21 officers and two civilians working for me. It was a very challenging job and one of the best in the police department.

In order to put the house in order I had to do a few unpleasant things so the first few months were difficult. First, I had to take cars away from 11 officers. From time to time we needed vehicles that were not available because they were parked at some detective's home. I also changed the night officers' hours in order to make for a better distribution of cases. Eventually the team got used to these changes.

There had been some changes since I was last in the unit. The District Attorney had much more input into homicide investigations. Some years previously, a District Attorney from Norfolk County, William Delahunt, moved to have prosecutors take more control of murder investigations. He sponsored a law giving the DA control over homicide investigations. It came to be known as the Delahunt law. After its passage, lawyers called the shots on whether to charge or arrest. I believe that it was because of this law that clearance rates went down, in some cases dramatically.

It was a matter of differing motives. A police officer wants to find and charge the murderer. The goal is a trial. For the prosecutor the goal is conviction. A trial that could go either way is a risk to a prosecutor's record and the tendency is to be risk-averse... to pull punches. Hence, less cases solved or cleared.

There was also a new system for the medical examiners. It was run by the state instead of the county. Under the old system some of the pathologists did not want the police present during autopsies. Under the new system the doctors welcomed the presence and participation of the investigating officers at autopsies whenever possible. Some of my investigators were not enthusiastic about being present for the autopsies. I encouraged them to do so but did not force them.

We responded to just about every sudden death where in the past we responded only to deaths that seemed suspicious.

***

Soon after I arrived I went out with the responding homicide officers on a call to Sparhawk Street in Brighton. We found a deceased man, about 55 years old, slumped over at the bottom of cellar stairs with a kitchen knife in his hand. He had cut his own throat. It was not a tentative wound by any stretch of the imagination. The throat was open to the windpipe leaving a gap about four inches wide. We found later that he had a terminal illness but I still wondered how anybody could do this to themselves.

***

A man named Bobo Barrett was shot to death in the Celtic Tavern in Charlestown. He and his partner had robbed a bank in Natick netting about $20,000. They spent some and used the rest, about $16,000, to buy cocaine from a bartender at the Tavern. It turned out that the coke was poor quality. Barrett returned to the tavern demanding his money back. When he persisted a patron fired two shots into his stomach.

Then the shooter reached into Barrett's belt and took a .38 cal firearm from his waist which he used to shoot Barrett three more times with his own gun, killing him. He then picked up his body and threw it out the front door. The shooter came back into the tavern, locked the front and rear doors and told the ten or so patrons still there that they had five minutes to finish their drinks and leave the tavern. I am sure that all were gone long before that deadline.

213

We got this information from the FBI. They had good pipelines into Charlestown and this was one of the rare occasions that they shared their information with us. We moved quickly but still found no witnesses. Convinced that the FBI scenario was accurate, I was back in the tavern the next day with a search warrant but all we got were some spent bullets in the wall. We were never able to find any witnesses and could never put a case together. Such was life in Charlestown.

***

Police-involved shootings were common. Too common, from my perspective. In one case officers shot and killed a man who, they reported, was threatening them with a rock. It's hard to believe a man with a rock can be life-threatening to two police officers armed with mace, nightsticks and guns.

In another case a group of detectives in the auto squad had been tailing a suspect in a stolen car and they finally decided to stop him on Haviland Street in the Back Bay. The suspect attempted to flee and the officers started shooting at the car. The driver, Elijah Pate, was killed. It was the officers' contention that Pate endangered their lives and tried to run them down in his attempt to escape. There were civilian witnesses who stated that Pate was out of the car and running when some of the shots hit him. Shooting at stolen cars is a bad idea. The investigation disclosed that Pate was first shot when in the car but then he continued to be shot at as he was running away. It's hard to stop once the shooting starts.

Police-involved shootings can be complicated and confused. Adrenaline can alter the senses. In Grove Hall, a robbery in a hallway spilled out on to the street and turned into a shootout between groups of bad guys. In the exchange one shooter ended up killing his friend who fell to the ground as the groups continued to trade gunshots.

An officer walking his beat nearby heard the shots and headed in, helped by citizens pointing the way. When he arrived both groups were there, guns still blazing. He ordered them to freeze but they were focused on their enemies and paid him no head. The officer fired towards one of the shooters and they now noticed him. Everyone ran off, leaving the already dead man on the ground .

214

The officer was very upset because he thought that he had killed the man on the ground.

***

Police suicides are an always-present problem and sometimes they come in clusters. Around this time three Boston officers died in the course of three days. Two of these were clear suicides and the other was probably an accident.

The first victim carried a personal automatic pistol in a shoulder holster. The model was known to be unreliable and it appeared that the officer wasn't aware of the gun's deficiencies. When he got into the front seat of his car the gun fell from his shoulder holster and discharged. The round hit him in the chest and killed him. This happened in Fields Corner, a busy area and there were plenty of witnesses.

The second officer was a detective who shot himself at home. He was an officer that I remembered as a young patrolman in Roxbury when I was the desk lieutenant.

The third officer was apparently having stress problems and was about to enter a stress relief program. He was a senior officer with over 30 years on the force.

***

Mayor Flynn and Commissioner Roache put their stamps on the department. Superintendent in Chief Jack Gifford was demoted to head of detectives while a number of patrol officers were promoted to deputy superintendent. It seemed easier to make deputy superintendent than to make sergeant in those days. Deputy and above are appointed positions, serving at the pleasure of the mayor. Some of those promotions were deserved but many seemed to me to be simply patronage. I guess the more things change the more they stay the same.

Soon we began to feel pressure from the new head of detectives. Each time the department makes changes in the hierarchy the new person wants to make an impression. Veteran officers understand but it is a nuisance.

An alert telephone repairman called us to report that when he was up in his cherry picker he saw a man carrying a form that appeared to be a human body out of a house. He then saw the man dig a shallow grave and throw the body into the hole. He continued to watch as the man filled the hole with dirt and left the area.

The police went to the area he described and started digging. They found the body of a 19-year-old woman from West Roxbury. She was still alive. The young woman was taken out of the hole and to the hospital where she died several hours later. The man who placed her in the hole was quickly located. He was arrested and charged with murder.

They were a couple. She was in love with him but he wasn't in love with her. He had borrowed several thousand dollars from her and bought a motorcycle. At some point her family wanted the money back and that led him to kill her. It was a beautiful bike.

The boyfriend was convicted of the murder. The family got the motorcycle

A body was hanging from a tree behind a block of stores on Blue Hill Ave. The victim had climbed up on the roof of the stores, made a jump and hung himself from a tree that grew alongside the rear of the store. The dead man was around 28 years old and stark naked. He had been dead for some time.

Hangings are almost always suicides but this one seemed suspicious. A seasoned homicide team responded to investigate.

The previous evening, at about 9:30, the man was on Devon Street. A woman from the neighborhood walked by and he grabbed her and put a knife to her throat. He forced her into his apartment.

The man raped and assaulted the young woman. She screamed and he nicked her throat with his knife to quiet her. It wasn't a fatal wound but she bled profusely. She continued to scream and neighbors became alarmed. They called out, demanding to know what was going on. The rapist became worried and still naked, opened his front door and attempted to reassure his neighbors that all was well. He then made the mistake of getting too far out of the front door. The girl pushed him out into the hallway and slammed the door shut locking him out, naked in the hallway. The rapist then went to the back door of the apartment. But his victim got there first and locked that door too.

She still feared that he might get back into the apartment so she ran out into the middle of Devon Street, naked, screaming and bleeding from the wounds on her neck. She spied a casual acquaintance and ran to him for help. The police responded and she provided a description of the rapist.

Meanwhile the rapist was still locked out, still naked. The fact that he was naked should have made him easy to find. It was now after midnight and getting pretty cool on a September night.

We could only surmise what went through the rapist's mind next. He likely realized he was going to get caught and decided to end his own life. He got hold of a sheet somehow, climbed up on a store roof, wrapped the sheet around his neck and then around a tree, swung himself off the roof and strangled to death. There was no serious damage to his body so he likely went off the roof easily. He had no previous criminal record but had committed a serious crime and paid for it with his life.

***

I was concerned about becoming insensitive. I went to the morgue for almost every major case. Bodies and traumatic damage no longer had an emotional impact on me. A four year old had been raped and then smothered to death. While I was going over the body of this little girl with the medical examiner I was shocked by my own indifference. I was interested only in obtaining evidence, teeth marks, semen, hairs, anything that could link the victim and suspect. I was not thinking of the little girl as a human being.

Not long after I was in the morgue watching as another medical examiner was taking apart the head of victim who had been beaten with a baseball bat. One of my colleagues from homicide was also present. It was his case. As we watched the doctor work I assumed that he felt the same way about the macabre nature of our work but I wasn't comfortable bringing the subject up. I suppose these feelings are common among those in our line of work.

In another instance, a police officer had been shot and his family had decided to donate his organs. I stood with the doctors in the emergency room. Two surgeons took out his heart as I watched. It amazed me to think that within hours that heart would be beating in someone else's chest. As usual in autopsies there was the normal banter among those present. The surgeons offered me a bypass if I could help them out with a speeding ticket in Connecticut. I told them that it was very difficult to fix tickets in Connecticut but if I could manage it, it would be worth at least a double bypass.

**

In 1986 I wrote an article that was published in the FBI National Academy magazine. It is a national publication with wide circulation among police officers. It had been at least ten years since an article was written and published by a Boston officer in that magazine. The article was about the value of entrance and apprehension teams. It's a model that has spread and become standard practice but it was a change from the ad-hoc approach that preceded it.

The commander of the Special Operations Unit, Marty Mulkern, developed the concept for these teams. It involved the use of five or six officers provided with bulletproof vests, heavy duty handheld shields, cutting tools, rams, heavy and light weapons - all designed to enabled the team to make a quick and overpowering entrance into any house, building, apartment or room and immobilize the occupants before they could act. The officers carry portable lights and plastic handcuffs and are well identified. The teams are well trained for entering barricaded drug houses and for the capture of armed and dangerous felons. They need at least an hour's notice, along with the specific location, the type of structure, the number and location of doors, a floor plan and a photo of the subject if possible. Once they are inside and have secured the scene, the team or teams await the arrival of the investigating officers. They take no part of any subsequent investigation.

These teams were a great concept in that they standardized entry operations. They spare untrained detectives from having to crash through doors and take unnecessary risks.

The Special Operations Unit, where the teams are assigned, even have an armored vehicle so officers can make their approach under fire. The idea was to avoid what had happened in Philadelphia in 1985 when an armed militant group called MOVE held off the police for several days. It was a tactical disaster. Philly PD finally used a helicopter to drop a bomb on the barricaded house, which not only didn't resolve the situation but it made it much worse. The house and most of the neighborhood burned down. People in the targeted house were killed including several children. It was a very bad day for the Philadelphia police.

***

The department had a spokesperson named Nancy. She and I sometimes clashed over what information should be released to the public. Nothing disturbed me more than hearing an account of a murder on television or the radio that closed stating that the police have no suspects. If I were a murderer I certainly would take comfort in hearing that. It's much better to say that the police are following active leads and hope to make an arrest soon. At a minimum it makes the criminal uneasy. The release of information is a tactical part of the investigation.

We also disagreed about the cause of death in sensitive cases. She wanted to paint the police department in the best light, which is her job, but I reminded her that the police do not determine the cause of death, the medical examiner does. A death on the Boston Common was typical of how we clashed. The mayor had just made a pitch about how safe the Boston Common was so admittedly it was rather awkward to report what appeared to be a murder right after that. Nancy solved this problem by declaring the death a suicide.

***

This was a case that Nancy wouldn't touch. Police were called to a School Street address in Jamaica Plain. Upon arrival they observed a car in a closed garage with two unconscious and naked bodies, male and female. There was evidence in the car that they were freebasing cocaine. The garage was full of gas fumes and the car had run out of gas. The two people were taken from the car. The female was about 24 years old and the male a bit older. The female was dead but the male had a pulse. He was revived and lived. It turned out that the dead girl was the male's daughter by a previous

219

marriage. Their terrible secret was now out in the open. He was alive but in the worst of all worlds. Everybody now knows that he had an incestuous relationship with his daughter. What a sad and tragic situation. A more just ending would have been him dying in the car.

**

At year's end there were 106 murders in the city for 1986. Our clearance rate of 58% was not great compared to the national rate, which was in the high sixties.

The next year started off with two murders and several suicides. One of the suicides involved a patient at Massachusetts General Hospital. A female patient got out on to a ledge on the fifteenth floor and was lying on it. When the police arrived they asked what she was doing and she replied, "Just getting some air."

She then sat up, leaned over, slipped off the ledge and fell to her death fifteen floors below. Not a word of this was in the paper or in any news outlet. Apparently Nancy's counterpart at the hospital was very good at their job.

**

I received an inquiry from the City of Boston Law Department relative to a man who was suing the city claiming that it was negligent in not discovering that he was innocent of murder. This in spite of the fact that he told us himself at the time that he did commit the murder.

The claimant, Steven Salas, had been at a party held in a commercial building near North Station. Also present were the brothers Michael and Thomas Dinovi. There was cocaine at the party and they all partook. Everyone had a gun. High on coke, Salas and the brothers started firing their guns at random targets in the building. No one was fighting. It was just dangerous horseplay. At one point the two brothers wandered off by themselves. A gunshot was heard. No one present was alarmed because there already had been plenty of shooting.

The brothers returned to the party. As they came back Steven Salas fired his gun over Michael's head. Michael fell to the floor. He was taken to MGH where he was pronounced dead of a bullet wound.

When the police arrived at the scene, Steven Salas gave his gun to the officers and told them that he shot Michael. He said the same thing to the homicide investigators. He was arrested and charged with murder. The guns belonging to the Dinovi brothers were also collected. The surviving brother, Thomas, was arrested and charged with violating gun laws and possession of cocaine.

Michael Dinovi's body was sent to the morgue. His clothes were removed and delivered to the Boston crime lab. A student intern logged them in and placed them in a storage area. The intern made a cursory examination of the clothes before putting them in the storage area. She noted that there was a bullet hole in the jacket and a spent bullet in the pocket of the jacket, though she did not call this to the attention of her superiors.

Steven Salas was indicted by the grand jury for the murder. It took two years before the case reached superior court for trial. The DA and the homicide investigators went down to the crime lab to inspect the clothes that Michael Dinovi was wearing when he was shot. They found the spent bullet in the jacket pocket along with a bullet hole in the jacket. This turned out to be the bullet that killed Michael Dinovi. It had not been fired by Steven Salas's gun but from his brother Thomas' gun.

It seems that when the two brothers left the immediate area of the party there was some horseplay and Thomas Dinovi shot his own brother. This was the single gunshot heard by others who were still at the party. Michael Dinovi had already been shot by his brother when they returned to the party. Steven Salas's bullet had missed Dinovi completely. It was a pure coincidence that Michael collapsed when Salas fired. When Steven Salas told the police that he had shot Michael Dinovi, Thomas Dinovi had remained silent.

What a mess. Thomas was found and pleaded guilty to shooting his own brother. It was a manslaughter case at best. The case against Steven Salas was dismissed, but he wanted to sue us. This case did not cover the police department with glory. It was a series of human errors that should not have happened. I never found out if Steven Salas received any money from the city but I doubt that he did.

***

I spoke to a group called Mothers of Murdered Children, a support group started in Charlestown several years ago. Two Charlestown mothers had invited me to come, both of whom had sons murdered.

At the meeting each person briefly described what happened to her son or daughter, how the police investigation went and if an arrest was made. It was very emotional. I was the only police officer present and I was the target of their dissatisfaction. It was the first time that a police officer had attended and they were expressing their frustration with some of the investigations, which, to that date, had not been fruitful. I didn't take the criticism personally. I told them about the effort the police make to investigate and solve murders, especially of children.

One man was especially critical. His son was killed near Dorchester High School. He and his wife had written many notes to the police commissioner complaining about the lack of progress in the investigation. I answered their queries each time. It had been a year and there were no arrests. We were not even close to a solution. The family, understandably, could not accept this. I asked the man to stop writing letters and come in and see me and we could go over the case file together. He never did. He did tell me that his wife had not left the house since the day her son was murdered.

After the meeting a couple of the mothers attached themselves to me as I was their only link into the investigations. Sadly, I rarely had good news for them. Almost 10 years later, the FBI was able to break into the Charlestown cabal and a lot of bad guys went to jail. For the most part, though, the murders in Charlestown went unsolved.

***

We were having a busy month. We were dealing with the aftermath of a multiple homicide in Dorchester. A young man entered his aunt's house near Savin Hill with an automatic rifle and started shooting everyone in the house. It seemed that he had disgraced himself in the community by stealing from his aunt. He decided to get even with the family for exposing him by killing them all. When he started shooting some of the family members ran out of the house and across the street. One was carrying a baby. She made it to a porch across the street. No matter. He shot and killed her. He also shot the baby but the baby survived. He was successful in killing five of his relatives including his aunt and uncle.

This man had fled Vietnam about two years earlier. His aunt and uncle took him into their house in Dorchester. He had difficulty adjusting to a new life in the United States and fell in with bad companions. A year went by and about $1,800 was found missing from the aunt's bank account. The bank researched and found that the young man had made an unauthorized withdrawal. His image was caught on the bank camera. There was no doubt who the thief was.

When his crime was discovered he left the house to live in New York City. He was there only a short time before he returned to Boston and asked to have a family conference. The killer berated them for ruining his good name in the Vietnamese community. Then he started his shooting rampage.

When the first officers arrived at the scene the man was still shooting from inside the house. They noted the dead woman and the injured baby on the porch of the house across the street. The entry team was summoned. The team created a diversion on one side of the house and crashed through a window on the other side. Inside they found the shooter slumped in a chair dead. He had shot himself in the head. There were bodies in different rooms all shot while trying to escape.

Two neighbors, Joseph and Donna Monroe happened to be on the scene immediately after the shooting started. They saw the bodies of the dead girl and the injured baby on the porch. They ran up to the porch, grabbed the baby and took her to safety. At the time, the scene was still active and they were in real danger of being shot. I made a proposal that they be awarded a good citizen's medal. Their actions were certainly heroic and the Police Commissioner decorated them a few months later.

Sergeant Doris and Detective Lundbohm were assigned to the case. There were a hundred details to attend to and an enormous amount of information to assimilate in a crime scene like this one. There were many officers involved, perhaps as many as 100 and all knew a little of what happened. Everybody had to make out reports. The priority was to collect all possible physical evidence quickly. It was a huge task but it got done.

***

It was common knowledge that the Boston Police Department had been corrupt in the 1950s, 1960s and into the 1970s. This changed when, in the 1970's, police commissioner Robert DiGrazia swept most of the crooks out and created a different, relatively honest, atmosphere. Of course you can never get them all so there was still corruption in the 1980s.

In 1987 six detectives were arrested on federal corruption charges. I knew some of the officers well and couldn't believe the charges. I also heard that two of the officers involved, a lieutenant and a sergeant, were cooperating witnesses. The lieutenant was a minor leaguer who I think got in over his head and made some mistakes. The sergeant had political connections and had been able to choose his assignments for years. They were both caught red handed and elected to wear wires and ensnare others who were marginally involved in order to save themselves.

Everyone I knew was searching their memories for instances when they had conversations with the two wired officers and what they had discussed. I remember that the lieutenant who was wired asked me about some bookies in South Boston around this time. I told him what I knew and that he might be able to catch a couple of them. I think that he actually arrested one of them. I don't know if he was wired when he spoke to me.

That same lieutenant asked another lieutenant, who was a friend of mine and who grew up in Charlestown, for the names of the major Charlestown bookies. He told him who they were and where they could be found. About a month later he asked my friend out to breakfast. During their conversation the wired lieutenant slipped my friend an envelope with $500 in it. He said that he had received $1,000 from the bookies and he felt it was only fair that my friend should get half as he gave him the information. My friend refused to take the money. He told the wired lieutenant that he gave him the information as police intelligence, not for a payoff. Some time later the FBI informed the police commissioner of this meeting and conversation. My friend's reputation was tarnished and his career aborted. He was guilty by association. These tactics were lazy and very close to entrapment.

***

It's sad to realize how empty some people's lives are. They're just dealt a bad hand in the lottery of life. A few days before Christmas I responded to a call at the Swiss Chalet, a motel on Morrissey Boulevard in Dorchester. A 60-year-old man was found hanging in the bath of one of the rooms. He had used the classic hotel hanging technique: one end of the rope was over the door and tied to the door handle, the other end was in a noose around the victim's neck. He had stood on a chair and jumped off.

We checked his suitcase and found nothing but some shabby clothes, a wallet with no money and a list of phone numbers. I called some of the numbers. One party answered and said that she knew the deceased and had lived with him for 16 years. In that period he had made her life a living nightmare. She described him as a drunk, a bad check passer, a loafer. The last time she talked with him she told him never to come near her again.

The deceased had no car. He had not paid for his room in three days and his rent was due. He had no income and no family. No one gave a damn whether he lived or died. He spent his last cash on a six pack of beer and drank four of them before he hung himself. His entire estate consisted of a half filled suitcase and two cans of Miller Lite.

***

Boston, like many other cities, had competing police organizations operating within the city limits. They all needed to justify their existence. Some had drug task forces independent of the city's main police's task force. There wasn't much cooperation between these agencies and the Boston Police. One of the bigger ones, the MDC (Metropolitan District Commission, responsible for parks, beaches and roadways) Police Department didn't know the city or the players well so bad things tended to happen when they went on a raid or made a bust in the city.

The MDC planned a drug operation in Hyde Park. They intended to buy $15,000 worth of coke from a couple of dealers. They were hoping to make a big drug bust. They did let us know about it but they left out the details. The members of our drug unit knew the drug dealers they were targeting. Our guys knew that the two alleged sellers were low-level guys who probably didn't have access to large amounts of drugs. They were probably conning the undercover MDC officers. This turned out to be true. There was never to be a sale. It

225

was the intention of the dealers to rip off the undercover officers' $15,000.

The day the bust was scheduled to go down, the undercover MDC officers went to a house in Hyde Park to make the deal. At the last minute the MDC asked the Boston Police to supply two detectives from the drug unit in order to give the appearance of a joint operation. The MDC officers flashed cash to the dealers and asked for the drugs. The dealers took out a shotgun and pointed it at the head of one of the undercover officers. Fortunately the officers were wearing wires so the MDC officers outside heard one of the undercover MDC officers say, "Why have you got that shotgun pointed at me?" At that point the MDC officers crashed into the house.

When the suspected dealer realized that the buyers were actually cops and that he was being set up he managed to grab one of the cop's guns and head for the door. When he got there he was met by two police officers, one from the MDC and one from the Boston Police. The fleeing drug dealer fired at the two police officers, hitting the MDC officer in the chest and the Boston officer in the arm. The officers returned fire and hit the dealer. He went a short distance and fell dead in the front yard. The MDC officer was alive a week later but having a tough time. He was 58, a little old to be involved in these operations, but a good detective. Luck was with him and he survived but I think his police career was over.

The detectives involved handled a bad situation well but the idea of conflicting jurisdictions is a recipe for trouble. The local police know their city and the players. The Boston Police drug unit served over 600 drug warrants in 1987 and no one was shot. The MDC served no more than four warrants and three people were shot.

A few years later the MDC was disbanded and their remaining members absorbed by the State Police.

***

Sometimes the job has unusual perks. I received a call from a casting office in New York City. Apparently Leonard Nimoy, of Star Trek fame, had seen me on television commenting on a homicide when he was visiting his native Cambridge a couple of weeks before. He thought I might be appropriate for a role in a movie he was making

226

called The Good Mother. They wanted me to come to New York for a screen test. I was game, so I accepted. The part that they had in mind for me was the lawyer who represented the mother at a custody hearing. I read the book that the movie was to be based on. It wasn't great but I got a good sense of the characters.

I went to New York and arrived at the hotel where the script was waiting for me. I read the script and did my best to memorize it. I did as I was told but the script was quite big and difficult to memorize.

The next morning I went to the studio where I met Nimoy and we had a short conversation, mostly about the police business. I sat down with a well-known actress who I recognized but whose name I didn't know. She and I read the script on camera. I was uncomfortable and my glasses kept slipping off my nose. She was acting the entire time. I discovered that it's not easy to act. In fact I found out that it was very hard. The reading took about thirty minutes and I returned to Boston.

I didn't get the part. But the process was great fun and I enjoyed doing it. There were many laughs later in the family circle. Jason Robards got the part I tried out for. Diane Keaton got the role of the good mother. My acting career was over.

***

A detective with the drug unit, Sherman Griffiths, was shot to death while serving a drug warrant on Bellevue Street in Dorchester. His drug team consisted of himself, Sergeant Amate and Detectives Luna and Schroeder. I was home when the shooting took place so my wife and I had some anxious moments after hearing preliminary reports since my son Richard was serving in the drug unit and working that night.

The drug team was on the second floor of a building on Bellevue Street and was about to take down the front door with a sledgehammer when the dealer inside fired through the door and hit Detective Griffiths in the head. The dealer then fled out a rear door and down the stairs and entered the first floor apartment. There were at least five people in that apartment, all junkies and drunks and even a small baby. The shooter passed the gun off to one of them.

The drug team made several basic mistakes in conducting the raid. First, never, ever, stand in front of a closed door when trying to get into an apartment or house. Second, never leave a rear door uncovered.

It was later determined who, in the first floor apartment, the gun was handed off to and the gun was recovered. The person who had the gun identified the man who gave it to him. The people on the first floor were tested for gun residue and the tests were negative including the person who had allegedly shot Griffiths.

In addition to all the other defects in this case the most serious difficulty turned out to be the credibility of the drug team.

In order to obtain the search warrant for this dwelling, a detective had used a phony informant on the sworn affidavit. After the raid went wrong he tried to bluff his way through. When the court ordered the team to produce the informant they came up with "X", "Y" and "John" and no further identification. Then the drug team made the situation worse when it suggested that the informant had been murdered. Lies upon lies. The case collapsed with terrible consequences for the officers.

The Boston Police took a lot of heat for this case as did the DA's office. Two of the detectives were tried in superior court and found guilty of perjury but were not given prison sentences. They were dismissed from the force.

In spite of all the faults, the DA felt that a case could still be won against the shooter because his fingerprints were found on the murder weapon. The case was moved out of Boston to Greenfield, in western Massachusetts because of all the publicity. It didn't matter in the end. The case was mortally damaged. It took the jury a very short time to return a verdict of not guilty. The killer of Detective Griffiths went free. It was not our finest hour. As a result of this case, the police department introduced a new set of strict rules for handling informants and implemented extensive training in drug operations.

***

By June of 1988 we had 50 homicides in the city. A recent victim was a 21-year-old kid named Tony. He was shot to death while moving his new Audi out of his driveway so that he could move his new Volvo in front of it. Two brand new cars for this young man. It turned out that he was a gang leader and a serious drug dealer.

A few weeks later Tony's mother came into homicide to reclaim her son's Audi, which we seized at the time of his murder. I didn't see any signs of grief. She complained about a small dent in the car and said the police made it. She seemed more concerned about getting possession of the car than she was about the progress of the investigation into the death of her son.

Louis McConkey, George Foley and Bruce Holloway worked on the case. After a lot of legwork and with the extensive street knowledge of the players involved they turned up a couple of witnesses who identified the shooter. He was arrested with the help of the police entry team.

***

In another case of lack of coordination in conflicting jurisdictions, the State Police initiated a chaotic incident in Boston. Unbeknownst to the Boston Police, they were conducting a drug investigation near Blue Hill Ave and American Legion Highway. An undercover trooper was going to buy drugs. A second trooper, also in plain clothes, was seated in an unmarked car nearby for backup. The backup trooper had her .357 Magnum in her handbag lying on the seat of the car. The car window was open.

Seeing a young woman seated in a car with her handbag next to her, a local robber made his approach. He punched the trooper, grabbed her handbag and took off. The trooper took off after him. She had a second gun in the car. She fired at the fleeing man but missed. The thief looked inside the handbag, found her .357 Magnum and shot back at her. By now the drug deal was long forgotten.

At some point the other trooper got into the chase. He caught the handbag thief but in doing so was shot four times. Incredibly, he still made the arrest. The handbag thief also was shot but his wounds were not life threatening. It was unclear just who shot him. It was fortunate that no one was killed.

A further investigation gave a clearer picture of what happened. The trooper who lost her gun caught up with the handbag thief, struggled with him and called for help. The other trooper responded and as he arrived, the handbag thief shot him with the stolen gun. He shot back, wounding the thief and possibly hitting his partner. No one really knows who shot whom as the bullet wounds were all through and through.

Both troopers performed courageously but, again, this could have been prevented if sufficient manpower and local knowledge were provided by the primary jurisdiction agency, in this case, the Boston Police.

***

A 20-year-old Boston man stole a Greyhound bus in Rhode Island and drove it to Boston. Two MDC officers spotted it downtown. The officers began following the bus around the city. Soon they were joined by nearby Boston officers. As the chase went on more and more officers joined in. The driver refused to stop, driving recklessly, including going down a one-way street in the wrong direction. Eventually he ended up on a dead end street and was forced to come to a stop, boxed in by cruisers behind him. He then backed up, hitting three police cars. Shots were fired at the bus but it kept moving backwards, plowing through the cruisers in reverse. Clear of the dead end street, the driver drove through Jamaica Plain with the police still in pursuit and still firing their guns. One Boston officer, intent on stopping the chaos, stood in the path of the bus and signalled the driver to halt. The bus continued towards the officer and he fired at the driver. The chase continued for a short distance until the bus knocked down a utility pole and careened into a house, coming to a stop.

The driver still didn't come out. The door was forced open and the driver found slumped behind the wheel, his clothes bloody from being hit by at least one bullet. He was taken to Boston City Hospital where he was pronounced dead. I was present at the autopsy. Many dozens of shots had been fired at the bus. The driver had been hit only once and there was no exit wound.

The bus was towed to the police garage. When examined, it was found to be full of bullet holes. There were an estimated 50 shots fired at the bus, five by the Boston Police and many more by MDC officers. Only six MDC officers admitted to firing their guns but there must have been many more that actually did. The newspapers were kind to the police but there was no question that this incident could have been handled better. Supervisors should have intervened and enforced tactical discipline to keep the chase from getting out of control.

We learned later that the young man was a relatively straight kid. He was a part-time employee of Greyhound and had fallen in love with the idea of being a Greyhound bus driver. No one knew why he snapped the way he did.

***

I received an unexpected call. The superintendent of the Criminal Investigations Bureau called and told me that I would be transferred out of Homicide. He said that the District Attorney called the commissioner and requested that I transfer out so that another Lieutenant, Ed McNeeley, could transfer in. I would be swapping places with McNeeley who was in District 1.

I had some misgivings about leaving homicide after so many years but I wasn't really unhappy about moving back to District 1.

The District Attorney was running for re-election the following year and, as is normal for politicians, he was wary of negative publicity. I was a little worried that I was being set up as a fall guy in several high publicity cases yet to go to trial. I need not have worried. It turned out that the motive behind the transfer was good old-fashioned politics. McNeely was a buddy of Assistant DA Frank O'Meara who headed the DA's homicide unit. He wanted to work in homicide and so, as I learned later, they engineered the change in a barroom.

I had two strong detective sergeants in District 1, Jim Barry on days and Walter Canney at night. The biggest problem I had right away was that Jim did all of the administrative work and I was left with little to do but basic supervision. I knew that this was how it was supposed to be but it still made me a little uneasy. My style was more hands on. But the station had a good computer system for tracking investigations and I concentrated on learning it.

I became more comfortable with the district as the days went on. It felt strange after four years away to get back into the station house routine dealing with the things that police officers encounter every day.

District 1 was a relatively quiet place compared to when I was there 15 years before. The Combat Zone was still there but activity was much reduced. People were still being robbed on Boston Common and in the Public Garden but nowhere near as often as in the past.

Return to District 1

Lieutenant Detective

I went out walking in the Combat Zone and Chinatown in plain clothes with the goal of familiarizing myself with the changing landscape. Since I had been a detective for many years I had that sense of invulnerability that police officers acquire when operating in their own area.

I came across two prostitutes robbing a motorist. I intervened, drove the girls off and sent the motorist on his way without getting myself into trouble. I was walking away from this scene when a good-sized young man confronted me and demanded money. I refused and identified myself as a police officer. He didn't believe me and started to get aggressive. After all, I was a 62-year-old grey-haired guy, alone in the Combat Zone. I had no radio. If the situation continued to deteriorate I would have had no option but to pull my gun. Fortunately my assailant became unsure of himself and backed off, giving me the opportunity walk away.

I returned to my unmarked police car and used the radio to request backup. A one-man unit responded and he and I toured the area looking for this guy. We found him and took him into custody. He was shocked but came along quietly.

At booking we discovered that he was wanted for armed robbery and had a violent record. I was lucky with the way things turned out. As one gets older it's important to know your limitations.

***

I received disturbing news from a deputy superintendent. Someone wanted to kill me. The information came from an undercover vice squad and seemed well founded. The person targeting me was from Winthrop. He was a junkie and a gun nut, not a good combination. I didn't recognize his name when I was told about the threat. It may have been that I arrested him many years ago. I started carrying my gun most of the time.

I looked at this guy's file but I still didn't recognize the name or his photo. Looking through his arrest record I noticed that another policeman, Gerald Daly, had arrested him. He probably had the wrong Daley. Gerald Daly retired from the Boston Police force years before. I decided to just let things play out and let this guy think that I was the one he was after.

***

I went into work one Saturday morning after receiving a telephone call that two young police officers had been beaten the night before. The two officers worked a first half then stayed in town and had a few drinks. Around 2:15 am they saw a girl being pushed around by three young men on State Street, near Quincy Market. The two officers identified themselves as police officers and told the young men who were abusing the girl to stop and go on their way. At that point the men turned on the two officers. One of the three went back to his car and came back with a baseball bat. The two officers took an awful beating. Just before they lost consciousness, one of them memorized the car license plate. The assailants fled and the officers were taken to the hospital. They had just been released and were waiting for me in my office when I arrived. They both looked terrible and I sent them to the ID section to have photos of their injuries taken.

The suspect's car was registered to a 21-year-old man from Newton. I drove the injured officers to his house and we found the car. I peered in and saw a baseball bat on the back seat. I had the car towed back to Boston and held it in the station house garage until I could get a warrant to search the car and seize the bat.

We learned that the car's owner was enrolled at Boston College and taking a class Monday morning, so I went to the school with the two injured officers. I interrupted the class and told the teacher that I would like to have a police officer look the class over and it would only take a few minutes. I brought one of the injured officers into the classroom and he immediately picked out Daniel Flynn as his assailant. Flynn was one of about forty students sitting at their desks, all close in age and dress. So it was a good identification.

Flynn was arrested and charged with assault and battery with a dangerous weapon, a bat. It's a 10-year felony.

At that point things got a little messy. The investigation disclosed that one of the two men with Flynn was a student at Massachusetts

Maritime Academy and had a brother who also happened to be a police officer in District 1. The other guy was thought to be a son-in-law of a detective in District 1. I was approached and asked to let things slide. There was no way I could waiver. I moved forward with the prosecution.

***

Not long after I left Homicide, turning over command to Ed McNeeley, the city was shaken by the Charles Stuart case.

Carol Stuart and her husband were driving home after attending a childbirth class at one of Boston's hospitals. They ended up pulling over in a high crime area where, as the husband reported, a black man attempted to rob them. In the course of the robbery this man shot and killed Carol and wounded Charles Stuart. Stuart was able to contact the police via a cell phone. It was a dramatic and well-publicized call for help.

Stuart described the assailant in some detail. The crime set off a massive and highly disruptive investigation in the nearby mostly African-American neighborhoods. Three weeks later homicide investigators, under intense pressure to solve the case, settled on a black man named Willie Bennet as the suspect. He was arrested and charged with the murder. A date was set to present the case to the grand jury. Bennet was not very savvy and may even have been manipulated by homicide detectives into making self-incriminating statements. He was on the fast track to a trial. It appeared that the case was solved. It was not.

Investigators had failed to focus on the husband as a suspect. It was a terrible error. They didn't validate his version of events. Because he was severely wounded they failed to think of him as a suspect. I heard that there were two homicide detectives who were suspicious of Charles Stuart but they were not on the inner team so their opinions were brushed aside.

Then the case broke in a completely unexpected direction. Charles Stuart was released from the hospital, having recuperated. When crossing the Mystic River Bridge he leaped into the river and killed himself. His story had begun to unravel. There was no robbery. There was no black assailant. He had killed his wife and shot himself. He had an accomplice, his brother, who was actually at the scene and took the gun used in the shootings, disposing it in the Pines River in Revere. Apparently Charles Stuart was interested in another woman.

It was not a good day for the homicide unit. I don't know if I would have made the same mistakes but I like to think that I wouldn't have. McNelley and the DA took lots of heat. We all knew that heads would roll and they did. One homicide detective was suspended for a year. McNeeley was transferred out.

**

Police need the public's support when we use deadly force. Society places a great deal of trust in the officers in allowing them to employ deadly force when necessary. To earn the public's support we need to scrutinize each incident where deadly force is used and follow the facts where they lead, even if they lead to an uncomfortable conclusion.

When I was in District 1, there was a State Police-led drug investigation on Hanover Street in the North End. As is often the case, the State Police failed to notify the local police of this activity. I was in charge of the detectives and had no knowledge of their activities until after the fact.

The plan was to have an informant buy $8,000 worth of cocaine. Troopers followed their informant into the North End. The informant stopped his car on Hanover Street and two low-level minor league drug dealers got in the car. State police officers in plainclothes were a short distance behind the vehicle. They had instructed their informant to tap the brake pedal lightly if he was in trouble. Not the best signal for obvious reasons.

A few minutes later the informant inadvertently hit his brakes and the troopers thought their guy was in trouble. One trooper approached the car, thought that he saw a flash of metal and fired his gun, hitting and killing the man sitting in the passenger seat. The individual shot was 19. Before he died he was heard to say, "Why did you shoot me?"

No drugs or guns were found in the car. The only thing that could have caused the flash of metal was a cigarette lighter. It seemed that every high-ranking officer in the State Police responded to the scene, along with an assistant DA. Representatives of the Attorney General's office were on the scene too. There was an argument over who was going to investigate this case. The State Police took over the investigation

There was a two-day delay before the car was searched. There was no inquest. Months later the DA quietly ruled the shooting justified. The newspapers paid little attention. The Boston Police played no role in the investigation.

***

I came into the possession of a hand. A detective in my office, assigned to the Robbery Task Force, was cleaning out the desk of a fellow officer who had just been killed in a plane crash. He found the hand all on its own in a desk drawer and delivered it to me with no documentation. I sent it to the medical examiner.

***

Two detectives from the town of Malden came to the station and told me they had an informant who was going to take part in an armed robbery of a money courier at a Boston hotel. The informant was slated to be one of three participants in the robbery. His motive for telling the police was unclear. Maybe he really did not want to rob anybody but was afraid of not participating and was looking for a way out. Or he may have fancied himself as an undercover cop.

The informant came to the detectives' office with the two Malden officers and sketched out the robbery. The plan was to rob a female courier who would be taking money and receipts from the hotel to a bank nearby. The informant would be driving the car. A second robber would enter the bank lobby and spray paint the security cameras while a third man, who would have a gun, would force the courier to give up the cash. Our informant told us that the robbers had inside information about the security company guarding the bank so we kept our plans confined to a very small circle. We told the informant that we would allow him to escape if possible and if that did not work we would provide cover for him. We agreed not to disclose that he was working for us.

I considered letting the courier do her normal thing without telling her of the expected robbery but we talked it over and agreed to tell

237

her and let her decide if she wanted to be involved. Fortunately she was a courageous woman so she agreed to the plan. The security company was informed and agreed as well. We told the courier to simply follow her usual routine and we would be there to back her up and help her as needed.

I formulated a plan to thwart the robbery using 17 detectives. I tried to think of every possible contingency. A few detectives posed as utility workers and were stationed in or near Edison trucks. The Edison people supplied us with helmets and other equipment.

The day of the holdup arrived. The holdup team arrived on schedule. One man entered the bank lobby, sprayed the cameras and then re-joined the other two. The three of them stood on the street waiting for the courier to appear, about 40 yards from where I was standing with two detectives.

I received a call on my walkie-talkie that the security people changed their mind at the last second and didn't allow their courier to go out with the money. We had no choice but to move against the three would-be holdup men. I approached them with two detectives. Another detective who was behind us pulled his gun a bit prematurely and started yelling at the suspects. We were lucky. They didn't run. We arrested them and recovered the gun and spray paint.

The downside of the operation was that instead of an attempted armed robbery charge, we could only charge the would-be robbers with conspiracy to rob and unlawful possession of a firearm.

Nevertheless it went down well for us. Nobody got hurt and the robbery was prevented. We were able to dismiss the case against our informant without giving him up. Police officers like these operations. It is the image of the job portrayed on television. Once in a while, it actually does happen that way.

District 5

Captain

The marks for the captain's test were released. I had done well. The police commissioner announced that there would be promotions within the next 30 days. This meant a lot to me. I had waited many years for the promotion process to move forward.

I was promoted to captain along with 24 others. On the day I was promoted I looked at my recruit class photo from 1951. Out of the 100 officers in my class only three were still working as police officers. John and Richard were promoted to sergeant at the same ceremony and there was a nice article and photo in the newspaper focusing on the family angle.

But retirement was looming. I suffered the usual fate of those coming to the end of their career in the police department. I was transferred to the West Roxbury station and given minimal duties. When I reported there the deputy in charge, Gerry McHale and the captain, Bill Parlon, could not have treated me more kindly. I had no real responsibilities and that was fine. In retrospect it was a perfect place for someone in my position. It helped me make the transition from full-time police officer to full-time retiree.

If someone had told me earlier in my career that I wouldn't mind being out of the loop I would have said they were crazy. But I've always felt that no one should continue to work as a police officer beyond 65. Even officers in command or administrative positions should leave the police force by then. It's the nature of the job. As you get older you become cautious and reluctant to take chances. It's hard to be effective if you're always playing it safe.

Good police officers have a hard time walking by an incident without getting involved. If they see something wrong they simply have to take action. Other officers seem never to see anything wrong and, hence, avoid controversy. They took the police job but never really engaged with the public or confronted criminals. They pick up their pay checks but don't feel the call of duty.

One day a captain called a young patrolman into his office. Maybe he saw the patrolman as something of a troublemaker. The captain posed a question. "If no one was watching, couldn't you just walk by a sticky situation without getting involved? No one would know," the captain added anxiously.

"I would know," the officer responded.

ACKNOWLEDGMENTS

I would like to thank my wife Eleanor for the love, support and infinite patience she provided over the years. I miss her.

I would also like to thank my family, the children and grandchildren, who helped with their suggestions for modifications that ultimately made this a better book. I would also like to acknowledge the valuable contribution of Any Lawler, who edited the first draft.

Over the years I worked with many good police officers. They provided depth to my story and camaraderie in my professional life.

From the early days there was Tom Ryan, Bob Tierney, Ed Tobin, Bob Kelley, Ted Madden, John Vance, Mark Madden, Jack Gallagher, George Slattery, Jack Sullivan, Paul Donelan, Bob Harvey and Eddie McManus. A great bunch.

When I served in Vice and Narcotics, Joe Smith and Jake Bird were the members of my team. Both were outstanding detectives.

I also worked with some great detectives in Homicide, among them John Harrington, Jack Spencer, Bill Smith, George Whitely, Bob Hudson and Frank Mulvey. Later, as a supervisor in Homicide, I was supported by a hardworking and talented group of investigators including John Doris, Charlie Horsley, Brendan Bradley, Marie Donahue and Jim Curran. I should also acknowledge my mentors, Lieutenant James McDonald and Lieutenant Jack Barry.

I would be remiss if I did not mention a colleague and a kindred spirit, Captain John Ciccolo. We were friendly competitors and shared many of the same career goals. He never failed to offer support to me when I needed it and I always appreciated that.

- John J Daley, Captain (Ret.) Boston Police Department

Made in the USA
Lexington, KY
31 August 2014